P9-CAO-022

Daily Devotions

Dr. Jack Van Impe

*Biblical inspiration for
every day of the year
with Dr. Jack and Rexella.*

JACK VAN IMPE MINISTRIES

Box J, Royal Oak, Michigan 48068

Box 1717, Postal Station A
Windsor, Ontario N9A 6Y1

ISBN 0-934803-59-5 (PB)
ISBN 0-934803-58-7 (HB)

All Scripture quotations are from the King James Version of the Bible.

Copyright © 1986 by Jack Van Impe Ministries
Reprinted, January 1987

CONTENTS

We are clean
through the Word

Christians are completely cleansed by the blood of Christ at salvation. The experience of the new birth changes one from head to toe. However there are times that the believer may soil his feet as he walks through this world. Jesus said in John 13:10: *He that is washed needeth not save to wash his feet.*

The disciples wore open sandals and the feet were always in contact with the earth. They did not need a complete bath after every walk, but needed only to rewash the feet. In our daily walk through a sin-sick world, we too need to have our feet washed and re-washed. This comes through a daily cleansing of the Word of God. Jesus said, *You are clean through the Word* (John 15:3).

Yes, one is sanctified and cleansed *with the washing of water by the word* (Ephesians 5:26). The more one bathes himself in the Word of God, the less need there is for a re-washing of the feet. The psalmist, in chapter 119 verses 9 and 11, declares: *Wherewithal shall a young man cleanse his way? by taking heed thereto according to thy word.* Again: *Thy word have I hid in mine heart, that I might not sin against thee.*

Jack and Rexella Van Impe

January

THIS MONTH'S STUDY

Time and Eternity

Days 1,2,6,8,9,10,12, and 29 contain quotes from "Knight's Master Book of Illustrations" by Walter B. Knight, pub. Wm. B. Eerdmans Publishing Company, Grand Rapids, Michigan, used by permission. Day 14 from "Isaiah" by Alfred Martin, pub. Moody Press, Chicago, Illinois. Day 15 from "Israel's Final Holocaust" by Jack Van Impe and Roger F. Campbell, pub. Thomas Nelson Publishers, Nashville, Tenn. Day 18 from "Daniel the Prophet" by H.A. Ironside, pub. Loizeaux Brothers, Neptune, N.J. Day 19 from "Paths to Power" by A.W. Tozer, pub. Christian Publications, Harrisburg, Pa. Day 22 from "Romans in the Greek New Testament" by Kenneth Wuest, pub. Wm. B. Eerdmans Publishing Company, Grand Rapids, Michigan. Day 23 from "Pepper 'N Salt" by Vance Havner, pub. Fleming Revell Company. Old Tappan, N.J. Day 16 from "The Pursuit of God" by A.W. Tozer, pub. Christian Publications, Harrisburg, Pa. Days 13,28, and 31 from "Let's Communicate" by Roger Campbell, pub. Christian Literature Crusade, Fort Washington, Pa.

THE EVERLASTING ARMS

MEMORY VERSE: *The eternal God is thy refuge, and underneath are the everlasting arms: and he shall thrust out the enemy from before thee; and shall say, Destroy them* (Deuteronomy 33:27).

When did God have His beginning?

Who was before Him?

These common questions have but one answer: God is eternal. He has always existed. Note this revelation to Isaiah: *Ye are my witnesses, saith the LORD, and my servant whom I have chosen; that ye may know and believe me, and understand that I am he: before me there was no God formed, neither shall there be after me. I, even I, am the LORD; and beside me there is no saviour* (Isaiah 43:10,11).

Go back in time as far as you like and God is there: *In the beginning God created the heaven and the earth* (Genesis 1:1).

Man is tied to time. We reckon time in segments because our lives are limited to approximately threescore years and ten (see Psalm 90:10). All plans for the future must be conditioned on whether or not we will be alive.

God has no such limitation. He will always exist. His promises are forever because He will endure forever. Because He lives, we can lean on the everlasting arms and be "safe and secure from all alarms."

F. B. Meyer explained: "The Oriental shepherd was always ahead of his sheep. He was in front. Any attempt upon them had to take him into account. Now God is in front. He is in the tomorrows. It is tomorrow that fills men with dread. But God is there already, and all tomorrows of our life have to pass before Him before they can get to us."

As Fanny Crosby said, we are "safe in the arms of Jesus," the everlasting arms.

PEOPLE OF DESTINY

MEMORY VERSE: *And who knoweth whether thou art come to the kingdom for such a time as this?* (Esther 4:14).

God has a perfect plan for every life. Each Christian has the opportunity to become God's person for the hour. Standing at the portal of this new year, we will do well to learn from people of destiny of the past. George Burger has written:

"I will, like Paul, forget those things which are behind and press forward; like David, lift up mine eyes unto the hills from whence cometh my help; like Abraham, trust implicitly in my God; like Enoch, walk in daily fellowship with my Heavenly Father; like Jehoshaphat, prepare my heart to seek God; like Moses, choose rather to suffer than to enjoy the pleasures of sin for a season; like Daniel, commune with my God at all times; like Job, be patient under all circumstances; like Caleb and Joshua, refuse to be discouraged because of superior numbers; like Joseph, turn my back on all seductive advances; like Gideon, advance even though my friends be few; like Aaron and Hur, uphold the hands of my spiritual leaders; like Isaiah, consecrate myself to do God's work; like Stephen, manifest a forgiving spirit toward all who seek my hurt; like Timothy, study the Word of God; like the heavenly host, proclaim the message of peace on earth good will toward men; and like my Lord himself, overcome all earthly allurements by refusing to succumb to their enticements.

"Realizing that I cannot hope to achieve these objectives by my own strength, I will rely on Christ for *I can do all things through Christ which strengtheneth me*" (Philippians 4:13).

Esther risked her life to save her people. And God honored her faith and courage. She was ready and willing to do God's will whatever the cost. Are you?

TIME TO FORSAKE SIN

MEMORY VERSE: *For this shall every one that is godly pray unto thee in a time when thou mayest be found: surely in the floods of great waters they shall not come nigh unto him* (Psalm 32:6).

Sin brings sorrow.

You cannot sin and win.

David here describes the agony of sin's consequences. Before confessing his sins to the Lord he was miserable; he felt old; his life was like a barren desert. Afterward, he feels the release of full forgiveness.

Matthew Henry has written: "And what tongue can tell the happiness of that hour, when the soul, oppressed by sin, is enabled freely to pour forth its sorrows before God, and to take hold of his covenanted mercy in Christ Jesus! Those, that would speed in prayer, must seek the Lord, when, by His providence, He calls them to seek Him, and, by His Spirit, stirs them up to seek Him. In a time of finding, when the heart is softened with grief, and burdened with guilt; when all human refuge fails; when no rest can be found to the troubled mind, then it is that God applies the healing balm by His Spirit."

Today is the day to end backsliding; to forsake sin.

All the misery of man proceeds from sin. Still, knowing the grief of transgressing, man coddles temptation until he falls prey to it.

How foolish!

This moment belongs to the heart that acknowledges its sin and comes humbly to the Saviour...claiming His forgiveness...walking a new way.

Sin is the enemy of happiness, the friend of failure.

Forsake the way of sin...while there is time.

HARD TIMES

MEMORY VERSE: *They shall not be ashamed in the evil time: and in the days of famine they shall be satisfied* (Psalm 37:19).

Difficult days come to both the righteous and the wicked. Though Christians will escape the Tribulation period, they have tribulation during their sojourn on this planet. Jesus said: *In the world ye shall have tribulation* (John 16:33).

Trouble is never pleasant but it may build faith. Peter speaks of the "trial of your faith." And C. H. Spurgeon wrote: "Time and trouble try the truth. Whether a man is really good or not is discovered by his perseverance in a good way. It is easy to run well just for a spurt, but to keep up the pace for years is the difficulty."

Christians experiencing hard times are assured of triumph. God directs the steps of His people. George Muller, the man of prayer and faith had made a note in his Bible beside Psalm 37:23: *The steps of a good man are ordered by the LORD...* Muller had written: "Yes, and the stops too!" He guides when we are marching and guards when it is necessary to stop and rest because of some affliction.

And then there is this thrilling promise: *Though he fall, he shall not be utterly cast down...* (Psalm 37:24). The child of God may be down but he is never out. The Lord upholds him with His hand.

Time flows continually. This year may hold some difficult days. If so, remember that our Lord is with us in the good times and the bad: *When thou passest through the waters, I will be with thee; and through the rivers, they shall not overflow thee: when thou walkest through the fire, thou shalt not be burned; neither shall the flame kindle upon thee* (Isaiah 43:2).

Hard times ahead? Perhaps. But the righteous will never be forsaken. Our times are in His hands. What a safe place!

THE TIME OF TROUBLE

MEMORY VERSE: *Blessed is he that considereth the poor: the LORD will deliver him in time of trouble* (Psalm 41:1).

Life is like an echo: what we send out comes back to us. Too often we think of this truth as only applying in times of loss. We are quick to quote the law of sowing and reaping when one is reaping sorrow, forgetting that the primary message of that law is a guarantee that those who do good will receive blessings: *Let him that is taught in the word communicate unto him that teacheth in all good things. Be not deceived; God is not mocked: for whatsoever a man soweth, that shall he also reap* (Galatians 6:6,7).

The psalmist promises help in the time of trouble for persons who consider the poor. The word "poor" here literally means "dangling." The reference then not only includes those who are struggling financially but who are slipping in other areas of life as well. This is a call to respond to the needs of the discouraged, the poverty stricken, the sick, and those who are the victims of any other condition that has them sidelined.

How many dangling people do you know?

While salvation cannot be earned through social concern or acts of charity, God has called His people to good works: *For we are his workmanship, created in Christ Jesus unto good works, which God hath before ordained that we should walk in them* (Ephesians 2:10). And these good works carry the promise of blessings returned: *Cast thy bread upon the waters: for thou shalt find it after many days* (Ecclesiastes 11:1).

One way then to prepare for troubled times is to give unselfishly to those in need.

Give to the dangling ones.

TREMBLING HANDS

MEMORY VERSE: *What time I am afraid, I will trust in thee* (Psalm 56:3).

How many hours of this year do you expect to spend in fear?

Trembling times come to all. Blessed is the person who understands that God loves him and is able to deliver him from danger. He can transform fear into faith.

Dr. James McConkey, in his book on prayer, says that one summer when he was ill he spent the season on the shores of the Great Lakes. Sailing was the only recreation he could find and one day while he was sailing in the middle of a bay, the wind suddenly died out completely. McConkey's boat was absolutely still. There seemed not a breath of air moving. The hot rays of the August sun beat down mercilessly upon his weak body. He had come out with a stiff breeze, and naturally he now began to pray for a breeze to take him home.

For an hour Dr. McConkey prayed, but no breeze came. Then he saw a boat coming toward him. An old fisherman, realizing McConkey was helpless without any wind, was on his way out to row the sailboat to harbor.

Dr. McConkey says he learned an important lesson through that fearful experience. He had been praying for a breeze but his real need had been for deliverance from the situation. While God denied the words of his petition, He provided for his need.

We cannot remove the trembling times from this coming year. But we can follow the good advice given by David. When fear's paralysis grips us, we can look to Jesus and exchange fear for faith. Danger means it is time to trust in Him. Time segments that would be lost to fear can become moments of victory. When afraid, trust in Him.

AN ACCEPTABLE TIME

MEMORY VERSE: *But as for me, my prayer is unto thee, O LORD, in an acceptable time: O God, in the multitude of thy mercy hear me, in the truth of thy salvation* (Psalm 69:13).

Experiencing trouble, the psalmist fills his mouth with expressions of deep feeling: a flood is overwhelming his soul, he is sinking in deep mire, he is crossing a body of water and it is about to cover him, he is tired of crying, his throat is dry, he has difficulty seeing.

Much of David's misery had to do with others. His enemies hated him and they had no reason to be his enemies. Even members of his family had turned on him. People gathered in groups to drink and ridicule him. Some considered him a religious fanatic.

In his sorrow, the psalmist turns to the Lord for help and expresses confidence that the Lord will hear him in an acceptable time. But what is an acceptable time? To whom is this time acceptable?

David is simply expressing the wonderful truth that we can all call upon the Lord when we are having trouble. Some shrink from praying when in difficulties, thinking they will be accused of only coming to God in times of great need. Christians need to remember that they are invited to come to Christ with their burdens at precisely the time of need: *Let us therefore come boldly unto the throne of grace, that we may obtain mercy, and find grace to help in time of need* (Hebrews 4:16).

Come then when you feel overwhelmed with problems.

Come when the lump in your throat won't go away.

Come when others have turned against you.

Come when people gather in little groups to talk about you.

Come NOW...it's an acceptable time.

A SHORT TIME

MEMORY VERSE: *Remember how short my time is: whereof hast thou made all men in vain?* (Psalm 89:47).

Impatience in prayer is all too common. The outstanding characteristics of the great New England preacher Phillips Brooks were poise and imperturbability. His close friends, however, knew that, at times, he suffered moments of frustration and irritability. One day a friend saw him pacing the floor like a caged lion. "What is the trouble, Dr. Brooks?" asked the friend. "The trouble is that I'm in a hurry, but God isn't!" Brooks replied.

The psalmist is so impatient in praying here that he fears he may die before God answers: *Remember how short my time is.*

But God is always on time.

The deadline you are facing may be moving up fast but there is time enough for God to do what He wants done. Beyond that, one is left with what man wants done. And that may not be important at all.

Andrew Murray wrote: "Be assured that if God waits longer than you could wish, it is only to make the blessing doubly precious. God waited four thousand years, till the fullness of time, ere He sent His Son. Our times are in His hands; He will avenge His elect speedily: He will make haste for our help, and not delay one hour too long."

A. J. Gordon said: "The promises of God are certain, but they do not all mature in ninety days."

F. B. Meyer warned: "The Bible seldom speaks, and certainly never its deepest, sweetest words, to those who always read in a hurry." And so it is with prayer. Let us take time to pray. And let us take time in prayer, lingering long enough to speak and to listen. Let us then allow time for God to answer at the precise moment that fits into His perfect will. The time may seem short...but He has time.

A LIFETIME

MEMORY VERSE: *The days of our years are threescore years and ten; and if by reason of strength they may be fourscore years, yet is their strength labour and sorrow; for it is soon cut off, and we fly away* (Psalm 90:10).

Life is short at its longest.

In later years, one looks back over decades as if they were but passing moments. The march toward the end of life begins at birth. Phillip Bailey said, "We should count time by heartbeats."

A lady who had lived all her life in the country took her first train ride to a town fifty miles from her home. She had planned this adventure for a long time and had looked forward to it with great pleasure.

On boarding the train, she hunted for the best seat, cared for her small parcels, and adjusted the blinds on the windows just right so that she could see everything along the way. When she was comfortably settled she thought over all she had done when leaving her home and began to worry about one thing and another that she might have left undone. She was so taken with her concerns about home that almost before she knew it the conductor was calling the name of her station and the long awaited trip was over. When she arose to leave the train, she was heard to say: "Oh, my, if I had only known that we would be here so soon I wouldn't have wasted my time in fussing."

Too much lifetime is wasted fussing.

Paul advised us to forget the things that are behind (see Philippians 3:13). Jesus taught us to stop being anxious about tomorrow (see Matthew 6:34). In forgetting the regrets of yesterday and laying aside the anxieties of tomorrow, we are left with today. And that is all we really ever have in which to live and serve the Lord.

Give Him your best today.

WISE USE OF TIME

MEMORY VERSE: *So teach us to number our days, that we may apply our hearts unto wisdom* (Psalm 90:12).

Phillips Brooks wrote: "A friend says to me, 'I have not time or room in my life for Christianity. If it were not so full! You don't know how hard I work from morning till night. When have I time, where have I room for Christianity in such a life as mine?' It is as if the engine had said it had no room for the steam. It is as if the tree said it had no room for the sap. It is as if the ocean said it had no room for the tide. It is as if the man had said he had no room for his soul. It is as if the life had said it had no time to live. It is not something added to life; it is life. A man is not living without it. And for a man to say, 'I am so full in life that I have no room for life,' you see immediately to what absurdity it reduces itself."

The first wise use of time is that moment of coming in faith to Christ that brings new birth. Jesus said: *Verily, verily, I say unto thee, Except a man be born again, he cannot see the kingdom of God* (John 3:3). From that point on, wisdom dictates using time to lay treasures in heaven through service for Christ.

It is *wise* to take time to pray.

It is *wise* to take time to read the Bible.

It is *wise* to take time to tell others of Jesus.

It is *wise* to take time to help those who are in need.

It is *wise* to take time to bear the burdens of those who are troubled.

It is *wise* to value spiritual things above material things.

It is *wise* to act in faith.

In view of the brevity of life, we must learn to number our days and apply our hearts to wisdom. Any other course results in a wasted life.

A TIME FOR EVERYTHING

MEMORY VERSE: *To every thing there is a season, and a time to every purpose under the heaven* (Ecclesiastes 3:1).

The Christian life is intended to hold great variety. From the beginning, God offered man a life free from boredom and full of blessings.

Our first parents were told they could eat of every tree of the garden except one. Sadly, they focused on that one restriction. How much better to major on all the good God has given.

Solomon observed that God has established a perfect order in His creation without sacrificing variety. Some narrow their interests to one field. They have no real concern about any area of life except the one in which they make their living. Their conversation is monopolized by that one subject. Communication with others is lost because the impression is given that no other field of labor or interest is important other than their own.

It is time for the one-track person to broaden his horizons.

All horizons must, of course, be subject to God's Word and His will. Compromise in the name of outreach is hypocrisy.

You have time to do all that you ought to do.

You have time to do all that God wants you to do.

God will enable you to do all that He wants you to do.

He will give grace to endure anything you encounter in doing His will.

God's plan for your life is an orderly plan. Often it is a plan that calls for important moves at crucial times with each step moving you on to greater usefulness.

In that wonderful adventure called God's will for your life, what time is it? *He hath made every thing beautiful in his time* (Ecclesiastes 3:11).

THE TIME OF YOUR LIFE

MEMORY VERSE: *Remember now thy Creator in the days of thy youth, while the evil days come not, nor the years draw nigh, when thou shalt say, I have no pleasure in them* (Ecclesiastes 12:1).

A Sunday school teacher became deeply concerned for the conversion of a teenage girl in her class. Lovingly and earnestly she spoke to the girl about salvation. The girl listened respectfully but decided against Christ, saying that in later years she would give consideration to her relationship with the Lord. The teacher went away with a heavy heart.

On her way home, the teacher came up with a plan to impress upon the girl the unfairness of her decision. Stopping at a florist's shop she bought a dozen roses. She then kept the roses in the florist's box for several days, after which she sent them to the girl.

Upon receiving the box, the girl was elated but when she opened the gift she was disgusted. "Some joke," she said.

Shortly thereafter, the teacher called on the class member again and explained that she had sent the wilted flowers. "When you chose not to give Christ your youthful years, you decided to present to Him later a life faded and withered like those roses," she said.

The girl understood and responded: "I see it. It will not be that way. I will give myself to Christ right now and live for His glory."

Youth is a wonderful time. Often young people resent being told that they are living through the time of their lives, but it is true. What older person would not give all for the opportunity of living through his teens again?

Those who surrender to Christ in youth discover life's secret early and are equipped to build a life that endures...even into old age.

THE EVERLASTING GOD

MEMORY VERSE: *Hast thou not known? hast thou not heard, that the everlasting God, the LORD, the Creator of the ends of the earth, fainteth not, neither is weary? there is no searching of his understanding* (Isaiah 40:28).

Isaiah's task was difficult: to minister to a depressed people. He had to convince them that the everlasting God cared about them.

Were they about to give up? God never faints.

Were they tired in battle? God never gets weary.

Were they at wit's end? God's understanding is unsearchable.

Were they weak? God imparts His strength to those who trust Him.

Where they depending on their own strength? They would surely fail.

And God has not changed. The everlasting One still takes care of His own. Wava Campbell has expressed this in her poem:

SOLACE
God weighs your grief and heartache;
He has an accurate scale;
He knows about your burdens
To every last detail.
God measures all your trials:
A perfect rule has He;
He knows about your problems
Whatever they may be.
So come and lay your weary heart
Upon the Holy One,
And He will give you perfect rest
Through Jesus Christ His Son.

...Wava Campbell

HE INHABITS ETERNITY

MEMORY VERSE: *For thus saith the high and lofty One that inhabiteth eternity, whose name is Holy, I dwell in the high and holy place, with him also that is of a contrite and humble spirit, to revive the spirit of the humble, and to revive the heart of the contrite ones* (Isaiah 57:15).

Eternity escapes our power of reason. Because we are creatures of time, everything seems to need a beginning and an ending. Our great God is eternal...Isaiah says He inhabits eternity. We live in the twentieth century. Someday a gravestone may mark a birth date and a date of death for most of us. God needs no such memorial. He has always existed...He will always exist...And He is alive...forevermore.

The miracle of this great truth is that He cares about us. In his book *Isaiah*, Alfred Martin says, "Earthly sovereigns are thought of as dwelling with the exalted and proud ones; the great Sovereign of all dwells with the humble believer. This is a consolation and an encouragement to the trusting heart. There is a danger, however, that the believer will fasten his thoughts on himself rather than upon God; then he loses his humility. A real glimpse of God, such as Isaïah has described from his own experience in chapter 6 will provoke contrition and humility."

Now consider this shocker: The Eternal One offers eternal life on the basis of faith alone. The One who originated all the complex formulas of physics that students ponder and scientists use to reach the far areas of space has made eternal life available on such a simple basis that children understand and accept it: the basis of faith...trust in the Lord Jesus Christ. *And this is the record, that God hath given to us eternal life, and this life is in his Son* (1 John 5:11).

Trust in Christ today and receive ETERNAL life.

January 15   Jeremiah 30:1-11

THE TIME OF JACOB'S TROUBLE

MEMORY VERSE: *Alas! for that day is great, so that none is like it, it is even the time of Jacob's trouble; but he shall be saved out of it* (Jeremiah 30:7).

For nearly two thousand years, Christians have been living in a parenthesis, a prophetic interval, a time "in between."

During this prophetic interval, sometimes known as the Church Age, both Jews and Gentiles who are born again through faith in Christ become part of the body of Christ or the bride of Christ. The signal that the "in between" time has ended will be the removal of the Church (the bride of Christ) from the earth. This great event is described in a number of Bible portions. One of the clearest is 1 Thessalonians 4:13-18.

The event that ends the Church Age and ushers in the seventieth week of Daniel's prophecy is the return of Christ for His Church. This coming of Christ in the air is known as the Rapture of the Church; it involves the resurrection of the Christian dead as well as the exit from earth of all believers living at that time.

With the removal of the Church, earth plunges into its most awful hour. Of this time Jesus said, *For then shall be great tribulation, such as was not since the beginning of the world to this time, no, nor ever shall be* (Matthew 24:21). He was speaking of the seven year period known as the Tribulation, or the Time of Jacob's Trouble.

There are difficult days ahead for Israel and for the world. This unprecedented period of Tribulation is not to be confused with daily tribulations which all of God's people pass through. And those who receive Christ before He comes will escape the coming Tribulation...the Time of Jacob's Trouble.

Are you ready for the Lord's return?

...From *Israel's Final Holocaust*.

TIME TO STAND

MEMORY VERSE: *But if not, be it known unto thee, O king, that we will not serve thy gods, nor worship the golden image which thou hast set up* (Daniel 3:18).

Man's vanity has often carried him to unbelievable ends. Consider Alexander the Great, the Caesars, Napoleon, or Hitler. History has a number of examples of leaders demanding worship. In the coming Tribulation period, the final world dictator will insist on being worshipped.

King Nebuchadnezzar of Babylon also let pride become his undoing. Constructing a great image in the plain of Dura he demanded that at a certain signal all in his kingdom fall down and worship it. Three in the crowd wouldn't cooperate, Shadrach, Meshach, and Abednego, Hebrews who had been brought to Babylon in the captivity of their people. As a result of their defiance of the king's order, these three were thrown into a burning fiery furnace. God wonderfully protected them there. As the song written about their experience says: "They wouldn't bend; they wouldn't bow; they wouldn't burn."

When the king looked into the furnace he saw four men walking in the flames. His reaction is worth remembering. He said: *Lo, I see four men loose, walking in the midst of the fire, and they have no hurt; and the form of the fourth is like the Son of God* (Daniel 3:25). God had not forsaken His own in their time of trial. They stood for Him and He delivered them.

They were so committed to the Lord that they were determined to be true even if no deliverance came.

Those three men must have been conspicuous when all the company on the plain of Dura bowed and left them standing. But they are the only ones of that crowd that we know by name today. God honored them for standing. And He will honor those who stand for Him today.

TIME TO PRAY

MEMORY VERSE: *Now when Daniel knew that the writing was signed, he went into his house; and his windows being open in his chamber toward Jerusalem, he kneeled upon his knees three times a day, and prayed, and gave thanks before his God, as he did aforetime* (Daniel 6:10).

When trouble came, Daniel was prayed up.

This faithful prophet was in the habit of prayer.

The fact that Daniel had a regular time for prayer reveals that he counted prayer worthy of his time. He did not consider time spent in prayer wasted. If we were to total the hours most Christians spend in prayer the sum would be woefully small.

Why?

Because too many discount the importance of prayer.

Some claim to be doers while allowing others to do the praying. The truth is that most successful Christian doers are mighty in prayer. That is the reason they accomplish so much.

Since prayer is conversation with God, our Father must be grieved that we do not spend more time praying. Would not an earthly parent's heart be broken if his children considered all other activities more important than conversing with him? How shall we answer for our lack of prayer when we appear at the Judgment Seat of Christ? (See 2 Corinthians 5:10.)

Daniel's faithful praying saved his life. God answered his prayers and the lions were unable to harm him. Even King Darius was moved by the miracle and sent a proclamation throughout the kingdom telling of Daniel's deliverance by the Lord.

A lion's den may await.

Take time to pray.

THE TIME OF THE END

MEMORY VERSE: *But thou, O Daniel, shut up the words, and seal the book, even to the time of the end: many shall run to and fro, and knowledge shall be increased* (Daniel 12:4).

Time is winding down. No one knows the day nor the hour of the Lord's coming, but many sense that something is in the wind and students of Bible prophecy are aware of the many signs of our day that point to the return of our Saviour.

Writing on our text, Dr. H. A. Ironside commented: "Daniel was told to shut up the words and seal the book, even to the Time of the End. This is in marked contrast with the message of the angel to the Apostle John at the close of the Book of Revelation. *And he saith unto me, Seal not the sayings of the prophecy of this book: for the time is at hand* (Revelation 22:10). The present age or church period is looked at as being but a moment, so to speak, in the ways of God. Messiah having come and been rejected by Israel, the next thing in prophetic order is the Time of the End. If this dispensation is made a little longer, it is but an evidence of God's long-suffering to sinners, being not willing that any should perish; but that all should turn to Him and live.

"John says that all Christians who really believe in the return of the Lord take steps to get their lives in order. That is, they do more than sit around and speculate over the identity of the Antichrist. They forsake sin and seek the will of God in every area of life. Here are John's words: *Beloved, now are we the sons of God, and it doth not yet appear what we shall be: but we know that, when he shall appear, we shall be like him; for we shall see him as he is. And every man that hath this hope in him purifieth himself, even as he is pure* (1 John 3:2,3). Expect His return every day."

TIME TO SEEK THE LORD

MEMORY VERSE: *Sow to yourselves in righteousness, reap in mercy; break up your fallow ground: for it is time to seek the LORD, till he come and rain righteousness upon you* (Hosea 10:12).

Hosea is calling for revival among his people. He reminds them that it is time to seek the Lord. In order to do so, he says, they must break up their fallow ground.

A fallow field is one that has been neglected, one that has not felt the plow for a long period of time. A. W. Tozer has written: "The fallow field is smug, contented, protected from the shock of the plow and the agitation of the harrow. Such a field, as it lies year after year, becomes a familiar landmark to the crow and blue jay. Had it intelligence, it might take a lot of satisfaction in its reputation; it has stability; nature has adopted it; it can be counted upon to remain always the same while the fields around it change from brown to green and back to brown again. Safe and undisturbed, it sprawls lazily in the sunshine, the picture of sleepy discontentment. But it is paying a terrible price for its tranquility: Never does it see the miracle of growth: never does it feel the motions of mounting life nor see the wonders of bursting seed nor the beauty of ripening grain. Fruit it can never know because it is afraid of the plow and the harrow."

What a picture of most present day Christianity! Especially in America! Too many Christians have settled down to an easy life that is undisturbed by the plow of God's Word. Instead of allowing the Bible to do its work of correction, many have settled for nothing more than a kindly respect for the Scriptures. After preaching time comes discussion time...not revival time. And the world is unmoved by such cold and formalistic Christianity...if indeed it can be called that.

Has your life become fallow? It's time to seek the Lord.

WHAT TIME IS IT?

MEMORY VERSE: *But of that day and hour knoweth no man, no, not the angels of heaven, but my Father only* (Matthew 24:36).

Somewhere in time there is a sacred date known only to the Lord, the date of Christ's return for His Bride...the Church. No one on earth can tell the day or pinpoint the hour of this long promised event. We know only that it is sure to come and that wise ones get ready for it.

In his book, *Pepper 'N Salt*, Dr. Vance Havner tells of a wild duck that came down on migration into a barnyard and liked it so well that he stayed there. In the fall his former companions passed overhead and his first impulse was to rise and join them, but he had fed so well that he could rise no higher than the eaves of the barn. As time passed, the day finally came when his old fellow travelers could pass overhead without his even hearing their call. Many Christians have become content in this world and scarcely hear the call of God concerning the needs in their lives. Preaching doesn't touch them. They have settled down in the barnyard and have forgotten they belong to the Lord.

On that special day to come, they will hear the call of the Lord and will rise to meet Him. All who have been born again will be taken in the Rapture of the Church...but many will be ashamed. The weight of worldly trinkets had overloaded them. John warned: *And now, little children, abide in him; that, when he shall appear, we may have confidence, and not be ashamed before him at his coming* (1 John 2:28).

The coming of Christ is imminent...an event to be expected at all times. He will return right on time. PERHAPS TODAY!

Remember who you are.

The time of His coming draws nigh.

Get out of the barnyard.

HIS TIME

MEMORY VERSE: *And he said, Go into the city to such a man, and say unto him, The Master saith, My time is at hand; I will keep the passover at thy house with my disciples* (Matthew 26:18).

When Jesus said, "My time is at hand," He was speaking of His death on the cross that would soon take place. Have you forgotten all He did for you at that time? Wava Campbell has written:

> Could my soul forget its Saviour:
> He who saved me by His grace,
> He who set His love upon me
> When unlovely was my case?
> Raging storms and dashing waters
> Must His gentle voice obey;
> Could the fallen soul He lifted,
> In rebellion turn away?
> Even oxen know their master
> And they yield to his control;
> Could the soul Christ gave direction
> Turn and seek a lesser goal?
> Could my soul forget its Saviour?
> Jesus, never let it be;
> Take my heart and let it ever
> Be securely bound to Thee.
> Ties to earth still fight to linger;
> Help me break them ere they start,
> That You may have full possession,
> Lord, forever of my heart.

...Wava Campbell

HIS ETERNAL POWER

MEMORY VERSE: *For the invisible things of him from the creation of the world are clearly seen, being understood by the things that are made, even his eternal power and God-head; so that they are without excuse* (Romans 1:20).

Looking up into a star-filled sky or beholding the swirling clouds of an approaching storm, one feels like bursting into a chorus of "How Great Thou Art"! Creation gives evidence of the existence of the eternal Creator. That is Paul's message in our text.

Commenting on this portion of Scripture Dr. Kenneth Wuest wrote: "The things which are invisible of God, namely, His eternal power and Godhead, are clearly seen. What a paradox, invisible things which are visible. This state of things has been true since the creation of the universe. The eternal power and Godhead of the Creator have been since that time and are now understood by the things that have been made, namely the material creation. Man, reasoning upon the basis of the law of cause and effect, which law requires an adequate cause for every effect, is forced to the conclusion that such a tremendous effect as the universe, demands a Being of eternal power and of divine attributes. That Being must be the Deity who should be worshipped."

The psalmist sets forth the same arguments: *The heavens declare the glory of God; and the firmament sheweth his handywork. Day unto day uttereth speech, and night unto night sheweth knowledge. There is no speech nor language, where their voice is not heard* (Psalm 19:1-3).

One look at the sky, the sea, a mountain range, or a beautiful sunset should be enough to convince anyone that God exists. His eternal power declares His existence. But that is not all: He loves us. And the cross is proof of His love. Understanding His eternal power and love ought to take us to the heights and keep us there.

January 23   Romans 13:7-14

HIGH TIME

MEMORY VERSE: *And that, knowing the time, that now it is high time to awake out of sleep: for now is our salvation nearer than when we believed* (Romans 13:11).

We live in a strategic period of history. This is not time for lazy, lethargic Christianity. There is too much at stake, too much to do.

Vance Havner hit the target when he wrote: "We have too many casual Christians who dabble in everything but are not committed to anything. They have a nodding acquaintance with a score of subjects but are sold on nothing." Evaluating the conditions in many churches he said, "Most church members live so far below the standard, you'd have to backslide to be in fellowship. We are so *subnormal* that if we were to become normal, people would think we were abnormal!"

And all this when closing time seems to be upon us!

The prospect of the Lord's soon return ought to awaken us to the need of total involvement in taking the gospel to the world. D. L. Moody said, "I have felt like working three times as hard since I came to understand that my Lord is coming again." How has that truth affected your life?

In what areas of Christian responsibility are you lethargic? What would a genuine awakening do to your lifestyle? Which of your present activities would cease? How would your involvement in your church change? What would happen to your giving?

Time is counting down.

Days of opportunity are slipping away.

Christ is coming.

It is high time to awake out of sleep.

ETERNAL THINGS

MEMORY VERSE: *While we look not at the things which are seen, but at the things which are not seen: for the things which are seen are temporal; but the things which are not seen are eternal* (2 Corinthians 4:18).

Most spend their time working and scheming to get visible assets; money, property, stocks, bonds, etc. Yet all these things are temporal...tied to time. And because they are temporal their value is fleeting.

Some material possessions are fleeting in value because our time on earth is limited. No matter how enduring the possession, the lifetime of the possessor determines the life of its usefulness to that person. Homes and automobiles are of no value to those who have passed from this life. The other dimension to the brevity of use of earth's trinkets is the fact that someday they will all be destroyed. In view of this truth, Peter wrote: *Seeing then that all these things shall be dissolved, what manner of persons ought ye to be in all holy conversation and godliness* (2 Peter 3:11).

But some things have lasting value.

Jesus said: *Lay not up for yourselves treasures upon earth, where moth and rust doth corrupt, and where thieves break through and steal: But lay up for yourselves treasures in heaven, where neither moth nor rust doth corrupt, and where thieves do not break through nor steal* (Matthew 6:19-20).

Faithful service for Christ may not bring earthly acclaim or material rewards, but treasures in heaven await the Christian who gives of himself in labor for his Lord. Suffering here may be difficult but it cannot be compared with the blessings awaiting those who stand true to the Saviour: *For our light affliction, which is but for a moment, worketh for us a far more exceeding and eternal weight of glory* (2 Corinthians 4:17).

January 25   Ephesians 5:8-17

REDEEMING THE TIME

MEMORY VERSE: *Redeeming the time, because the days are evil* (Ephesians 5:16).

Matthew Henry says: "Time is a talent given us by God, and it is misspent and lost when not employed according to His design. If we have lost our time heretofore, we must double our diligence for the future. Of that time which thousands on a dying bed would gladly redeem at the price of the whole world, how little do men think, and to what trifles they daily sacrifice it!"

H.C.G. Moule points out that Paul is calling for us to buy up every opportunity, and adds: "Do this, remembering that you will need do it if you are to be really serviceable to Him; it will not do to let things drift, as if circumstances would take care of themselves." He explains that world conditions demand diligence in seizing opportunities to serve the Lord. In his words: "...the 'days' of your human life in a sinful world do not lend themselves to holy uses where the man who lives them does not watch for opportunities."

Actually, the thought here is that of a businessman buying up valuable articles. And time is one of life's greatest values.

Emerson said, "One of the illusions of life is that the present hour is not the critical, decisive hour. Write it on your heart that every day is the best day of the year. He only is rich who owns the day, and no one owns the day who allows it to be invaded with worry, fret, and anxiety."

THIS is the day to serve the Lord. It may be the only day any one of us will ever own. What would you do if you knew this would be your final opportunity? What service for your Lord have you longed to do but have not found the time nor the courage?

Do it today.

January 26   1 Timothy 1:12-20

THE KING ETERNAL

MEMORY VERSE: *Now unto the King eternal, immortal, invisible, the only wise God, be honour and glory for ever and ever. Amen* (1 Timothy 1:17).

God is unchanging...eternal.
And He is in charge of all things.

This compound truth caused Paul to burst forth in a doxology...a song of praise. In the most difficult of circumstances Paul found reasons to rejoice because he knew that the Eternal God was working out all things well.

Since our Lord is the King eternal, He deserves first place in our lives. However, those who give Him the preeminence often find that it proves costly. A. W. Tozer explains: "The moment we make up our minds that we are going on with this determination to exalt God over all, we step out of the world's parade. We shall find ourselves out of adjustment to the ways of the world, and increasingly so as we make progress in the holy way."

He continues: "Our break with the world will be the direct outcome of our changed relation to God. For the world of fallen men does not honor God. Millions call themselves by His Name, it is true, and pay some token respect to Him, but a simple test will show how little He is really honored among them. Let the average man be put to the proof on the question of who is above, and his true position will be exposed. Let him be forced into making a choice between God and money, between God and men, between God and personal ambition, God and self, God and human love, and God will take second place every time."

But you do not have to be average. Determine by God's grace to break out of the mold; to give the King eternal first place in your heart. The rewards will begin today and continue for ever and ever.

END-TIME RELIGION

MEMORY VERSE: *Preach the word; be instant in season, out of season; reprove, rebuke, exhort with all longsuffering and doctrine* (2 Timothy 4:2).

Some blame church conditions on the times and long for the good old days, but even in Timothy's time compromise and coldness were becoming epidemic. Paul gave young Timothy good advice for dealing with these problems. He was to preach the Word at every opportunity, applying it in reproof, rebuke, and with exhortation. He was to preach from a heart of love for his hearers, being longsuffering toward them. His sermons were to be filled with the great doctrines of the faith. He was to be true to his calling even though it should bring criticism and persecution. He must do the work of an evangelist, winning souls in both his pulpit and private ministry.

When pastors preach the Word and members apply the Word, putting away foolish divisions and following their pastor in soulwinning and missionary outreach, churches will flourish. Paul's formula doesn't fail. Even today. The power of the gospel is unchanged.

There is a danger in blaming the ills of a church on the times. While present conditions may not be conducive to revival, that does not mean that revival cannot come. Whenever Christians get thoroughly right with God, blessings are sure to result. Revival can come in our day to Christians in America and to any local church. The Bible method of opposing evil and conquering for Christ has not changed. And a genuine revival is our nation's greatest need.

If my people, which are called by my name, shall humble themselves, and pray, and seek my face, and turn from their wicked ways; then will I hear from heaven, and will forgive their sin, and will heal their land (2 Chronicles 7:14).

DEPARTING TIME

MEMORY VERSE: *For I am now ready to be offered, and the time of my departure is at hand* (2 Timothy 4:6).

Christians go to heaven when they die. Death is departing time. Paul wasn't looking forward to centuries in a grave awaiting the Resurrection. He had already expressed his assurance of arriving in heaven immediately following death: *We are confident, I say, and willing rather to be absent from the body, and to be present with the Lord* (2 Corinthians 5:8); *For me to live is Christ, and to die is gain...For I am in a strait betwixt two, having a desire to depart, and to be with Christ; which is far better* (Philippians 1:21,23).

As time counts down for the child of God, he is simply approaching his departure date when he will embark for heaven. In her poem, "A Christian Death," Wava Campbell has written:

> Rejoice with me, my friends, I say rejoice!
> I see my Master's face, I hear His voice.
> It calls me from my misery and pain
> To heaven's gate; how glorious is my gain.
> I ran the race of life with all my might;
> I turned not to the left, nor to the right.
> And now I have arrived, I am set free;
> Rejoice with me, my friends, rejoice with me!

Nearing his departure date, Paul looked back over life and felt good about his investment of the years. What words of satisfaction and triumph: *I have fought a good fight, I have finished my course, I have kept the faith* (2 Timothy 4:7). Having spent his days serving Christ, he could look in both directions at departure time and have confidence.

Are you ready for departing time?

THE TIME OF NEED

MEMORY VERSE: *Let us therefore come boldly unto the throne of grace, that we may obtain mercy, and find grace to help in the time of need* (Hebrews 4:16).

Throughout our threescore and ten there are crisis times. Trouble may approach from a number of directions: health, finances, family, storms, earthquakes, national crises, death. In these times of anxiety, it is good to know that we can come to the throne of grace to obtain help for each occasion.

And God knows what we need.

When Adoniram Judson was dying, news came to him that some Jews in Turkey had been converted through reading the account of his suffering in Burma. "This awes me," said Judson to his wife. "This is good news. When I was a young man, I prayed for the Lord to send me to the Jews in Jerusalem as a missionary. But He sent me to Burma to preach and to suffer the tortures of imprisonment. Now, because of my sufferings, God has brought some Jews in Turkey to repentance."

In our deepest sorrows, God understands. Walter Brown Knight shares this helpful thought: "Sometimes when our souls are overwhelmed by sorrow, our prayers lie so deep in our innermost being that we are powerless to articulate them in words. How comforting it is to know that we do not need words to pray prevailingly." Paul agrees: *Likewise the Spirit also helpeth our infirmities: for we know not what we should pray for as we ought: but the Spirit* [himself] *maketh intercession for us with groanings which cannot be uttered. And he that searcheth the hearts knoweth what is the mind of the Spirit, because he maketh intercession for the saints according to the will of God* (Romans 8:26,27).

Troubled?

Tell it to Jesus. He's listening in your time of need.

ETERNAL SALVATION

MEMORY VERSE: *And being made perfect, he became the author of eternal salvation unto all them that obey him* (Hebrews 5:9).

Salvation is eternal.

At the moment of new birth one receives eternal life: *Verily, verily I say unto you, He that heareth my word, and believeth on him that sent me, hath everlasting life, and shall not come into condemnation; but is passed from death unto life* (John 5:24); *And this is the record, that God hath given to us eternal life, and this life is in his Son. He that hath the Son hath life; and he that hath not the Son of God hath not life. These things have I written unto you that believe on the name of the Son of God; that ye may know that ye have eternal life, and that ye may believe on the name of the Son of God* (1 John 5:11-13).

Since eternal life begins at salvation, simple logic demands that it never be terminated. If eternal life could be lost it would not have been eternal when received. And as we have seen, the Bible says that upon receiving Christ we have eternal life as a present possession.

Each Person of the Trinity guarantees the security of the believer: *My sheep hear my voice, and I know them, and they follow me: And I give unto them eternal life; and they shall never perish, neither shall any man pluck them out of my hand. My Father, which gave them me, is greater than all; and no man is able to pluck them out of my Father's hand. I and my Father are one* (John 10:27-30); *And grieve not the holy Spirit of God, whereby ye are sealed unto the day of redemption* (Ephesians 4:30).

The old hymn says it well:

"More secure is no one ever

Than the loved ones of the Saviour."

Through faith in Christ you have ETERNAL life.

THE TIME IS AT HAND

MEMORY VERSE: *Blessed is he that readeth, and they that hear the words of this prophecy, and keep those things which are written therein: for the time is at hand* (Revelation 1:3).

Israel is a nation.

Russia has a form of government built on atheism.

The Common Market moves toward a United States of Europe.

What does it all mean?

To most students of the Bible it means that we are living in the last days.

The weight of evidence for the truth of Bible prophecy is now so strong that any informed person would have to close his eyes to escape seeing its fulfillment.

Christ is coming!

He will come in fulfillment of His promise to the disciples: *I will come again, and receive you unto myself* (John 14:3).

He will come as promised by the two angels who appeared at His ascension. These heavenly messengers announced, *This same Jesus, who is taken up from you into heaven, shall so come in like manner as ye have seen him go into heaven* (Acts 1:11).

He will come as described by Paul, the apostle: *For the Lord himself shall descend from heaven with a shout, with the voice of the archangel, and with the trump of God: and the dead in Christ shall rise first: Then we which are alive and remain shall be caught up together with them in the clouds to meet the Lord in the air: and so shall we ever be with the Lord* (1 Thessalonians 4:16,17).

Yes, Jesus will return.

Even so, come, Lord Jesus (Revelation 22:20).

February

THIS MONTH'S STUDY

Acts in Action

Days 1 and 16 contain quotes or information from "Lectures on Acts," by H. A. Ironside, published by Loizeaux Brothers, Neptune, N.J.; Days 2,4,8,12,21,24, and 25 from the "Three Thousand Illustrations for Christian Service," "Knight's Master Book of Illustrations," and "Knight's Treasury of Illustrations" all by Walter B. Knight, published by Wm. B. Eerdmans Publishing Company, Grand Rapids, Michigan. Used by permission. Days 13, 15, and 17 from "Let's Communicate" by Roger F. Campbell, published by Christian Literature Crusade, Fort Washington, Pa.; Day 26 from "Man: The Dwelling Place of God" by A. W. Tozer, published by Christian Publications, Inc., Harrisburg, Pa.

WHAT TIME IS IT?

MEMORY VERSE: *And he said unto them, It is not for you to know the times or the seasons, which the Father hath put in his own power* (Acts 1:7).

The question asked by the disciples just before the ascension of Jesus was to be expected: *Lord, wilt thou at this time restore again the kingdom to Israel?* They were familiar with the many prophecies concerning the kingdom and they longed for their fulfillment.

"It is not for you to know...." the Lord replied.

And still no one knows.

Writing on this text, Dr. H. A. Ironside said, "Men persist in endeavoring to ferret out that which is the Father's own secret, and so they attempt by various ways to find out when the King will come...Some day He will make everything plain. When God's time comes prophecy will be fulfilled to the letter."

While the disciples were not told the date of the setting up of the kingdom, they were told what to do at that moment and in the immediate future. They were to wait for the promise of the Father and when that was fulfilled they were to witness at home and to the entire world.

We do not know when Jesus will return but we do know that we are to be busy taking His Word to the world. The disciples were to wait and then witness because the coming of the Holy Spirit would make their witnessing effective. On the Day of Pentecost the Holy Spirit came, enabling the disciples to be powerful witnesses. But no more waiting is required. Since Pentecost, all believers are baptized by the Holy Spirit into Christ's Body the moment they are born again through faith in Christ. When the King returns...witnessing opportunities will be over.

It's time to witness for Christ today.

What are you waiting for?

FELLOWSHIP

MEMORY VERSE: *And they continued steadfastly in the apostles' doctrine and fellowship, and in breaking of bread, and in prayers* (Acts 2:42).

Millions have joined in singing the great song of fellowship, "Blest Be the Tie That Binds," written by John Fawcett, an English Baptist minister. The song was written to commemorate an experience in Fawcett's life.

In 1772, after only a few years in pastoral work, John Fawcett was called to a large and influential church in London. His farewell sermon had been preached in his country church in Yorkshire and the wagons loaded with his furniture and books stood ready for departure to the new home and work.

Fawcett's congregation was brokenhearted.

Men, women, and children gathered about him and his family with sad and tearful faces.

Finally, overwhelmed with the sorrow of those they were leaving, Dr. Fawcett and his wife sat down on one of the packing cases and gave way to tears.

"Oh, John!" lamented Fawcett's wife, "I cannot bear this! I know not how to go!"

"Nor I, either," returned her husband. "And we will not go. The wagons shall be unloaded, and everything put in its old place."

The congregation was filled with joy and their continued fellowship was the basis for the song by John Fawcett that has blessed so many for so long.

The Early Church was strong in fellowship.

The church that is strong in fellowship is strong in its witness in the community.

What are you doing to deepen fellowship in your church?

SUCH AS I HAVE

MEMORY VERSE: *Then Peter said, Silver and gold have I none; but such as I have give I thee: In the name of Jesus Christ of Nazareth rise up and walk* (Acts 3:6).

Luke, the physician, wrote the Book of Acts. It is properly called The Acts of the Apostles. And it is a book of action; the story of the Early Church on the move.

The first Christians had little of this world's goods. They had no expensive church buildings, none of the things that make a church appear successful in our day.

People are easily awed by trappings that are designed to impress, but spiritual power is far more important. The church at Laodicea, described in the Book of Revelation, looked prosperous but was poor in the areas that really mattered: *Because thou sayest, I am rich, and increased with goods, and have need of nothing; and knowest not that thou art wretched, and miserable, and poor, and blind, and naked...* (Revelation 3:17).

As Dr. Luke recorded the experience of Peter and John in their encounter with the lame man, he must have felt the pain and frustration of this one who had been afflicted for so long. Luke knew the limitation of man in helping some who are helpless.

"Silver and gold have I none," said Peter. And the poor man's heart must have drooped. But then the blessing came...he was healed of his affliction.

Peter had neither silver nor gold and therefore was not accountable to give what he did not have. But what he did have was exactly what the blind man needed.

Let us give "such as we have" that others may be blessed.

WITH JESUS

MEMORY VERSE: *Now when they saw the boldness of Peter and John, and perceived that they were unlearned and ignorant men, they marvelled; and they took knowledge of them that they had been with Jesus* (Acts 4:13).

An examining committee, composed of ministers, had met to look into the qualifications of Billy Sunday to be ordained as a gospel minister. Among other questions fired at the world-famous former baseball player was a request that he identify a well-known church father, describing some of his writings.

Billy was stumped.

After fumbling around for a moment, he said, "I never heard of him! He was never on my team!"

For a time, indecision characterized the distinguished preachers. Finally one of them moved that Billy Sunday be recommended for ordination, adding that Billy had already won more souls for Christ than all his examiners.

Billy had been with Jesus.

The boldness and success of the disciples bothered the theologians who opposed them. The Sadducees rejected any teaching about resurrection and were therefore completely at odds with Peter and John, the spokesmen for the disciples.

These servants of Christ were not awed by their learned opponents. They spoke with power and had more understanding than the religious leaders who had spent their lives debating theological questions.

Why?

Because they had been with Jesus.

Many lessons are best learned at the feet of Jesus.

Want to be effective for Christ?

Take time to be with Jesus.

THE COST

MEMORY VERSE: *Then Peter and the other apostles answered and said, We ought to obey God rather than men* (Acts 5:29).

There has always been a cost involved in total surrender to Christ. Early Christians risked their lives for the sake of the gospel. Threatened with imprisonment and the loss of life they deemed it more important to obey God than men.

Every century has seen its martyrs; the twentieth more than any other. But martyrdom may not always mean death. Sometimes it is more difficult to live for Christ than to die for Him. We are called to be living martyrs: *I beseech you therefore, brethren, by the mercies of God, that ye present your bodies a living sacrifice, holy, acceptable unto God, which is your reasonable service. And be not conformed to this world: but be ye transformed by the renewing of your mind, that ye may prove what is that good, and acceptable, and perfect, will of God* (Romans 12:1,2).

Paul warned: *Yea, and all that will live godly in Christ Jesus shall suffer persecution* (2 Timothy 3:12). And that inspired axiom has not changed to this day.

The apostles were placed in prison for their preaching but God delivered them. Of this, Matthew Henry says: "There is no prison so dark, so strong, but God can visit His people in it, and, if He pleases, fetch them out. Recoveries from sickness, releases out of trouble, are granted, not that we may enjoy the comforts of life, but that God may be honoured with the services of our life."

What is the cost of a Christ-centered life?

Obedience...pleasing God rather than men.

Whose servant will you be today?

CHURCH ON THE MOVE

MEMORY VERSE: *And the word of God increased; and the number of the disciples multiplied in Jerusalem greatly; and a great company of the priests were obedient to the faith* (Acts 6:7).

Leaders in the Early Church were men of limitation. They simply could not care for all the needs of all the people all the time. When others in the church began to shoulder responsibility, the church began to move. And that is the Bible plan.

Little is accomplished when all the work of a church is left to the pastor. Regardless of his dedication, drive and discipline, he is but one person and will find himself frustrated in trying to meet the needs of so many.

When a congregation is on the move, its members care for one another and for others. They are not content with spectator Christianity nor even with fulfilling their obligations to serve on boards and committees. Their interest is in personally ministering to people. To them it is not enough to listen to sermons and analyze them. They are, themselves, "sermons in shoes."

Generally great ministers are produced by great churches. Asked once for the secret of his ministerial success, John Wesley answered: "It is the people. From one Sunday to the next they are continually at it."

Christianity began with a tiny minority. Those fiery believers soon multiplied into thousands and gained the reputation of turning the world upside down (see Acts 17:6). But the task was not accomplished by the leaders alone.

Ask your pastor about opportunities to serve. Your desire to help will be a blessing to his heart.

And the activity in the Lord's work will be good for yours.

THE STANDING SAVIOUR

MEMORY VERSE: *And said, Behold, I see the heavens opened, and the Son of man standing on the right hand of God* (Acts 7:56).

Stephen was a first. He was one of the first deacons. He was the first person other than an apostle to be given power to perform miracles. And he was the first Christian martyr.

Having been faithful in serving tables, Stephen was given a wider ministry: *And Stephen, full of faith and power, did great wonders and miracles among the people* (Acts 6:8). But his increased outreach brought increased opposition. When the religious leaders heard this dynamic deacon they gathered a mob to stone him.

Before the stones started flying, Stephen was given a glimpse into heaven where he saw the Lord Jesus standing on the right hand of God.

Standing?

Yes, standing.

Doesn't the Bible say that Jesus sat down at the right hand of God following His sacrifice on the cross?

Yes, but this was a special occasion. One of His servants was in serious trouble. So the Saviour was standing. He would personally welcome him into His presence in a few minutes. So He stood. He cares.

Note also that His title, "The Son of Man," is used here. As the Son of Man, He can identify with the needs of all men—all people...their burdens, their sorrows, their fatigue, their persecutions.

Stephen was prepared for martyrdom before it took place. He was given a special blessing for a special occasion. When the stones came crushing in upon Stephen, he was able to pray for those who were attacking him unjustly. He had been given dying grace by his living Saviour.

Christians do not face trouble alone.

Their loving Saviour understands.

Jesus always rises to the occasion.

PERSECUTION

MEMORY VERSE: *Therefore they that were scattered abroad went every where preaching the word* (Acts 8:4).

Some of the greatest advances for Christ have been made during times of persecution. In the first century as persecution increased, believers were forced to leave their homes and flee to other areas. As they went they preached God's Word and their number increased. The pressure brought on these early Christians simply enlarged their ever widening circle of witness.

Others have also given their best when persecuted.

One day John Wesley preached to a great throng in an outdoor meeting. He pleaded with his hearers to flee from the wrath to come. Later Wesley said, "Many of the people acted like beasts and did their best to disturb the meeting. They tried to drive a herd of cows into the crowd, but without success. Then they began to throw stones—showers of them. One of them struck me between the eyes. I wiped away the blood, and went right on, declaring that God has given to them that believe, not *the spirit of fear, but of power, and of love, and of a sound mind* (2 Timothy 1:7). I saw what a blessing it is when it is given us, even in the lowest degree, to suffer for His name's sake!"

We know little of suffering for Christ in this good land. The heritage given America by those who laid the foundation of our government has kept our nation a place of religious freedom. Still some persecution comes to dedicated Christians by people who do not like to see a strong witness for Christ.

If persecution comes your way today...use the opportunity to tell others of Jesus. His rewards will be greater than any suffering we may endure (see Romans 8:18).

SURRENDER

MEMORY VERSE: *And he trembling and astonished said, Lord, what wilt thou have me to do? And the Lord said unto him, Arise, and go into the city, and it shall be told thee what thou must do* (Acts 9:6).

When Stephen died the Church suffered a great loss, but God cares for His work and raises up others to replace those who are promoted to heaven. The work of Christ is never dependent on the survival of one person.

Often the Lord calls the most unlikely into His service. Saul had stood guard over the coats of those who stoned Stephen. Who would have suspected that he would soon be converted to Stephen's Saviour?

Saul's conversion teaches us that the most difficult cases are not hopeless. It is unlikely that any of those early Christians expected Saul to be saved...certainly not to become the greatest missionary ever. If the believers in Damascus knew that Saul was headed their way they may have prayed for deliverance from his persecution but probably few would have dared believe he would be born again enroute to their city.

The secret of Saul's usefulness as a Christian may be found in his initial reaction to his encounter with Christ. His response: *Lord, what will thou have me to do?* indicates immediate and total surrender. He gave his life to the Saviour with no strings attached. From that point on, his desire would be to know the will of God and do it.

Every useful servant of Christ has come to the point of unconditional surrender. D. L. Moody determined to be a man who was completely yielded to the will of God and the world still reaps the benefits.

Will you surrender to the Saviour?

Unconditionally?

REMISSION OF SINS

MEMORY VERSE: *To him give all the prophets witness, that through his name whosoever believeth in him shall receive remission of sins* (Acts 10:43).

Can any man forgive sins?

Some think so and they confess their sins to men.

Usually this conviction is based on John 20:23: *Whose soever sins ye remit, they are remitted unto them; and whose soever sins ye retain, they are retained.* This promise given to the disciples by Jesus is thought to have passed the authority to remit (forgive) sins down through the centuries causing it to belong to certain men today.

But was Jesus giving His disciples the authority to forgive sins and thus become His agents on earth to hear confessions?

Not at all.

Our text is proof of the proper interpretation of the message of Christ to His disciples concerning the remission of sins. When Peter ministered to Cornelius and his household he explained that remission of sins comes through faith in Christ.

Now we know the answer.

The disciples were given the gospel message and the authority to guarantee the remission of sins to all who acted upon it, receiving the Lord Jesus Christ as personal Saviour. And that is still true today.

Cornelius had been a devout and respected man but without Christ he was lost. His sins were still charged against him. Judgment awaited him. He had no hope. Thankfully, he responded to the gospel and was born again. The moment he trusted in Christ as his Saviour the record was made clean; his sins were remitted.

Come to Christ just as you are. Receive Him as your personal Saviour and your sins will be forgiven...all of them.

CHRISTIANS

MEMORY VERSE: *And when he had found him, he brought him unto Antioch. And it came to pass, that a whole year they assembled themselves with the church, and taught much people. And the disciples were called Christians first in Antioch* (Acts 11:26).

Jerusalem had been the first center of Christianity. When persecution drove believers in all directions they carried the good news of Christ's death and resurrection with them. The gospel took root in Antioch with many turning to the Lord, and word of the work there spread throughout the area. When people get on fire for Christ, the news gets out. Let any church have genuine revival and interest will grow to the point that visitors will come from great distances. That happened in Antioch and when the word reached Jerusalem they sent Barnabas to investigate.

Barnabas was impressed with the happenings in Antioch. We are told that he saw the grace of God. That is, he observed the work of God in the lives of the converts in Antioch and the evidence of Holy Spirit conviction in the hearts of those who had not yet believed.

Convinced that the church at Antioch had a great future, Barnabas went to seek for Saul (later called Paul) so that he could teach these new converts the basics of their new life in Christ. Saul accepted the invitation and for a year he and Barnabas met with the believers in Antioch, teaching them God's Word and encouraging them in the faith.

What a great year it was!

The community recognized these believers as people whose lives were centered in Christ and they began to call them "Christians." The name has stayed with us through all these centuries.

Do others think of you as a Christian? Do you walk worthy of the name?

February 12   Acts 12:1-17

A PRAYING CHURCH

MEMORY VERSE: *Peter therefore was kept in prison: but prayer was made without ceasing of the church unto God for him* (Acts 12:5).

When Peter was cast into prison, the Church did not demonstrate publicly to secure his freedom but they demonstrated their confidence in the power of prayer by unitedly calling upon God for his release. The Early Church was convinced that spiritual weapons were more powerful than any known to man: *For though we walk in the flesh, we do not war after the flesh: (For the weapons of our warfare are not carnal, but mighty through God to the pulling down of strong holds;) Casting down imaginations, and every high thing that exalteth itself against the knowledge of God, and bringing into captivity every thought to the obedience of Christ* (2 Corinthians 10:3-5).

Prayer is the answer in every crisis.

Abraham Lincoln, whose birthday we celebrate today, had learned that important lesson. When the fate of the nation was hanging in the balance during the Civil War and the battle of Gettysburg was in the making, Lincoln was calm and assured. His serenity was reassuring but mystifying to his generals and they inquired: "How can you be so self-possessed in this hour of the nation's mortal peril and darkness?" Lincoln replied, "I spent last night in prayer before the Lord. He has given to me the assurance that our nation will be preserved!"

God answered the prayers of the Church made on Peter's behalf. An angel entered the prison and delivered him safely past the guards and to freedom. His chains were broken by the power of prayer.

Prayer still breaks chains and sets captives free.

Pray for those in bondage to self and sin. And expect their release.

FREE FROM THE LAW

MEMORY VERSE: *And by him all that believe are justified from all things, from which ye could not be justified by the law of Moses* (Acts 13:39).

Christians are free from the Law since all its demands were fulfilled by the death of Christ on the cross: *For Christ is the end of the law for righteousness to every one that believeth* (Romans 10:4).

We live by a higher standard than the Law: *But the fruit of the Spirit is love, joy, peace, longsuffering, gentleness, goodness, faith, meekness, temperance: against such there is no law* (Galatians 5:22,23).

Wava Campbell's poem "Liberty!" makes this truth personal.

LIBERTY!
My soul look upward, sons of men;
Oh bind me not with chords again
Of laws, and rules, and other cord
That comes from you, and not the Lord.
'Tis but the outward things you see;
God sees the very heart of me.
Did not my Master come to save
From laws, and rules, and doctrines grave?
Oh bind me not! Christ set me free!
That I might ever only be
His loving slave.

...Wava Campbell

The church at Galatia had fallen into the error of believing that one keeps his salvation by adherence to the Law. Paul called the church back to the life of faith with this unmistakable declaration: *I do not frustrate the grace of God: for if righteousness come by the law, then Christ is dead in vain* (Galatians 2:21).

May the fruit of the Spirit be evident in each of our lives today.

SPEAKING BOLDLY

MEMORY VERSE: *Long time therefore abode they speaking boldly in the Lord, which gave testimony unto the word of his grace, and granted signs and wonders to be done by their hands* (Acts 14:3).

Upon arriving in Iconium, the apostles enjoyed great success: many believed. Perhaps the reason for this is found in Acts 13:52: *And the disciples were filled with joy, and with the Holy Ghost.* Matthew Henry says: "The apostles spake so plainly, with such evidence and proof of the Spirit, and with such power; so warmly, and with such concern for the souls of men; that those who heard them could not but say God was with them of a truth."

Notice that the first preaching of the gospel in Iconium was done in the synagogue. This was nearly always the case in any city where the apostles started a ministry. It is important to remember that this preaching in the synagogue did not constitute a church service as we know it today. The Early Church met on the first day of the week for fellowship, preaching, the breaking of bread, and prayer. They went to the synagogues to preach to those who had come there as loyal Jews and who needed to hear the gospel. These meetings in the synagogues were preaching missions...evangelistic efforts...sometimes debates. They took place on the Sabbath Day. When a church was established from the converts won at the synagogue the believers met on the first day of the week (see Acts 20:7).

The people of Iconium were soon divided over the gospel. Opposition organized and it became dangerous to speak for Christ. Nevertheless, the apostles spoke boldly and God honored their faith. Fear and faith are opposites.

Speak boldly for Christ today.

SAVED BY GRACE

MEMORY VERSE: *But we believe that through the grace of the Lord Jesus Christ we shall be saved, even as they* (Acts 15:11).

Several young ladies were talking. "Don't use that word 'saved' when you talk to me," one said. It is strange that such a good word has come into disrepute.

If a man is drowning, he is glad to be saved. If a building is burning, the whole community rejoices over those who are saved. Why then this change of attitude about being saved from sin?

Perhaps it is because sin is not considered that serious. Yet the Bible indicts all men as sinners and pronounces death as a result. *For all have sinned, and come short of the glory of God* (Romans 3:23). *For the wages of sin is death; but the gift of God is eternal life through Jesus Christ our Lord* (Romans 6:23).

Another reason men dislike the word "saved" may be its inference that the sinner must be rescued from above. Our pride in accomplishment has invaded the spiritual realm. We like to think that we have become refined enough to have gained some favor with God. Surely our honesty, compassion, and reputation must carry some weight in heaven. But they don't.

Apart from God's grace (unmerited favor), there is not an ounce of hope for the best of us. *For by grace are ye saved through faith; and that not of yourselves: it is the gift of God: Not of works, lest any man should boast* (Ephesians 2:8,9).

The temptation to regress into law keeping has been a problem to the Church from the earliest time. That was the reason for the calling of the council of apostles and elders at Jerusalem. Some today are still trying to sidestep God's grace and earn their way to heaven.

We're saved by grace. Spread the good news.

DUNGEON DOXOLOGY

MEMORY VERSE: *And at midnight Paul and Silas prayed, and sang praises unto God: and the prisoners heard them* (Acts 16:25).

When Paul wrote to the church at Rome he told them he had learned to glory in tribulations. His experience in the Philippian jail is proof of the truth of his statement. With their feet fast in stocks and their backs bruised and bleeding, Paul and Silas sang praises at midnight...perhaps the night's most depressing hour.

Dr. H. A. Ironside says, "Those dear men, afflicted, miserable, unable to sleep, could not move without anguish; yet as they lay in that dungeon their hearts went out to God, presenting their case before Him, and assured He heard, they lifted up their hearts in glad thanksgiving for His grace."

H. B. Gibbud was feeling depressed and gloomy one morning and was interrupted by a knock on his study door. On opening the door he saw a scrubwoman who said, "Brother Gibbus, I am Sophie, the woman God called to scrub and preach."

"Oh, yes," Gibbud responded, "I have heard of you."

"Brudder," Sophie said, "the Lord has sent me to preach to you. This is my text—'Glory in Tribulations.' Now, Brudder, G-L-O-R-Y don't spell GROWL."

Gibbud's face lit up. He said it was the beginning of a new and glad day of victory for him.

What is it that has you depressed?

What trouble has you defeated?

The world is watching to see how you react to pressures and problems.

Will you fill today's dungeon with sighs or songs?

Prayer and praise can break depression's chains and set you free.

SEARCHING THE SCRIPTURES

MEMORY VERSE: *These were more noble than those in Thessalonica, in that they received the word with all readiness of mind, and searched the scriptures daily, whether those things were so* (Acts 17:11).

Paul commended the Bereans because they searched the Scriptures daily. The Bible deserves our daily attention because it is the verbally inspired Word of God.

Some doubt this foundational fact; yet without a dependable Bible, Christianity would crumble. Thankfully, there is ample evidence of inspiration.

The unity and harmony of this divine library is miraculous. Taking over 1,600 years in the writing, it stands without flaw or contradiction. It dwarfs all other literature, and withstands the test of the ages.

Fulfilled prophecy is another strong witness. Facts about nations, empires, and moral and social conditions were foretold centuries before their occurrence. Details about the incarnation of Christ were given with pinpoint accuracy.

The Bible also contains statements of scientific truth. Revelations concerning the suspension of the earth in space (see Job 26:7) and the roundness of the earth (see Isaiah 40:22) are just a few of its teachings that awaited acceptance while men struggled with now-discarded theories about our world.

Perhaps most convincing is the Saviour's guarantee of the authority of the Scriptures. Jesus picked the most difficult portions of the Old Testament and associated himself with them. Creation, the flood, the destruction of Sodom, and the experience of Jonah, are all declared true by Jesus Christ.

Search the Scriptures every day.

HOLD NOT THY PEACE

MEMORY VERSE: *Then spake the Lord to Paul in the night by a vision, Be not afraid, but speak, and hold not thy peace* (Acts 18:9)

When Paul entered Corinth, there was not a Christian in the city. Moreover it was a city of sin...desperately wicked. The reputation of Corinth was so bad that an immoral woman in another city was referred to as a "Corinthian." An especially wicked man might be known as one who "corinthianizes."

While Paul was in Corinth, he made tents to earn a living and reasoned in the synagogue every sabbath. His witness among the Jews raised such opposition that he turned to the Gentiles.

A major victory came when the chief ruler of the synagogue was won to Christ and soon many Jews and Gentiles had been converted. As a result, Corinth witnessed its first baptismal service. This public expression of faith must have stirred up the enemies of the gospel for immediately after the baptismal service Paul was encouraged by the Lord to continue his ministry there without fear.

Now note this interesting statement made to Paul by the Lord: *I have much people in this city* (Acts 18:10). Had you or I been looking over the crowds in Corinth we would have seen them as wicked and unlovely, perhaps unreachable. But the Lord saw them as they would be after Paul presented the gospel to them. Among the thousands were many who would believe and become new creatures in Christ; old habits of life would drop away, and they would become radiant Christians. Paul must not hold his peace for he would be God's instrument in reaching them.

How do you see the people of your community?
How does God see them?
Perhaps you are His instrument to reach them.
Hold not thy peace.

MISSING THE MESSAGE

MEMORY VERSE: *Then said Paul, John verily baptized with the baptism of repentance, saying unto the people, that they should believe on him which should come after him, that is, on Christ Jesus* (Acts 19:4).

On the Day of Pentecost, all believers were baptized by the Holy Spirit. Now, however, upon arriving in Ephesus, Paul meets certain disciples of John the Baptist who know nothing about the Holy Spirit. Their knowledge is limited to repentance and baptism.

Did John not speak of the Holy Spirit? He certainly did: *I indeed have baptized you with water: but he shall baptize you with the Holy Ghost* (Mark 1:8).

Did John not speak of Christ as the One who should die for sinners and in whom faith was required for salvation? Yes he did: *The next day John seeth Jesus coming unto him, and saith, Behold the Lamb of God, which taketh away the sin of the world* (John 1:29).

How then did these disciples miss the message? Why had they not placed saving faith in Christ? Why were they ignorant of the coming of the Holy Spirit?

Like many today, they had gone through all the outward motions as was expected of them...even to being baptized, but they had not really been listening. Somehow they had been swept along with others who had been responding to John's preaching and were never born again.

When Paul understood their plight, he explained the gospel to them, telling them they had missed the heart of John's message...that salvation came through faith in Christ. They saw their need, received Christ, and were baptized as believers. What a great day it was for these men who now had listening and believing hearts.

We must move past form to faith.

May God give us listening hearts.

WHICH DAY?

MEMORY VERSE: *And upon the first day of the week, when the disciples came together to break bread, Paul preached unto them, ready to depart on the morrow; and continued his speech until midnight (Acts 20:7).*

Most Christians worship on Sunday. Some look upon this practice as sin. Charges are often hurled at earnest believers, labeling them as "sun worshippers" or even the recipients of the "mark of the beast." Some who worship on Sunday are insecure as to the proper day and are easy prey for sabbath-keeping groups whose Saturday worship may be but a tiny part of a whole system of legalism.

The honest Bible student must face the fact that Saturday is the Sabbath. But sabbath-keeping was part of the Law that was nailed to the cross: *Blotting out the handwriting of ordinances that was against us, which was contrary to us, and took it out of the way, nailing it to his cross; And having spoiled principalities and powers, he made a shew of them openly, triumphing over them in it. Let no man therefore judge you in meat, or in drink, or in respect of any holy day, or of the new moon, or of the sabbath days: which are a shadow of things to come; but the body is of Christ (Colossians 2:14-17).*

The first day of the week then became the day or worship for the New Testament Church. NO WONDER! This was the day of our Lord's resurrection (see John 20:1) signaling complete victory.

Perhaps the spiritual meaning of the first day of the week is the most important reason for observing it as the day of worship. The Sabbath pictures the Law perfectly. Under law, one worked and then rested. The first day of the week pictures grace. Under grace, we enter into our rest in Christ and then we work to serve Him.

• For a more thorough study, order our tract *Help Concerning the Sabbath.*

February 21 — Acts 21:1-15

READY

MEMORY VERSE: *Then Paul answered, What mean ye to weep and to break mine heart? For I am ready not to be bound only, but also to die at Jerusalem for the name of the Lord Jesus* (Acts 21:13).

Baron von Wely renounced his title and wealth and went as a missionary to Dutch Guiana. There he rendered sacrificial and loving service to God. In speaking of his forsaking all to follow Christ, he said, "The title 'wellborn' means nothing to me since I have been born again in Christ. The title 'lord' means nothing to me since I desire only to be the servant of the Lord Jesus. What is it to me to be called 'Your Grace' when I have need of God's grace? Away with these empty vanities! I will stay at the feet of Jesus, learn of Him, and have no hindrance in serving Him aright."

Evangelist J. Wilbur Chapman asked General Booth, founder of the Salvation Army, what had been the secret of his success. Booth hesitated for a second and tears came into his eyes and began to run down his cheeks, and then he said: "I will tell you the secret. God has had all there was of me to have. There have been men with greater opportunities; but from the day I got the poor of London on my heart, and a vision of what Jesus Christ could do, I made up my mind that God would have all there was of William Booth. And if there is anything of power in the Salvation Army today, it is because God has had all the adoration of my heart, and the power of my will, and all the influence of my life."

Paul had surrendered all to his Saviour. Nothing could deter him from the path of duty in serving his Lord. He was always ready to endure suffering for the cause of the gospel. Neither bonds nor the ultimate sacrifice could keep him from responding to God's call.

Are you ready to do God's will today?

HURTING JESUS

MEMORY VERSE: *And I answered, Who art thou, Lord? And he said unto me, I am Jesus of Nazareth, whom thou persecutest* (Acts 22:8).

Paul must have told his conversion story many times. Five of these occasions are recorded for us in the Bible. He never tired of calling to mind what had happened to him on the road to Damascus. Here he is giving his testimony to a great company of people gathered in the court of the Temple in Jerusalem as he defends himself against accusations being made about him.

Most are familiar with the ingredients in Paul's conversion: there was the light from heaven and the voice of Jesus questioning him about his persecutions and then, of course, his response. Imagine how surprised the persecutor of Christians must have been when he discovered he had been persecuting Jesus...that is what the voice said, "I am Jesus of Nazareth, whom thou persecutest."

But how could that be?

Paul had never personally hurt Jesus...only those who professed to know Him as Saviour.

Now an important truth surfaces: Jesus feels all the hurts of His people. To persecute a Christian is to persecute Jesus.

Have you wondered just how close Jesus is? Consider this revelation given to Saul (Paul) on the road to Damascus. He not only knows every wound you experience but He feels it as well...even the one you are grieving over today.

Is your heart heavy? He feels the ache...the lump in your throat. You do not carry your burdens alone. And you do not need to seek revenge. Those who have injured you have inflicted pain on Jesus and they must face Him one day in judgment.

Be kind to Christians. Don't be guilty of hurting Jesus.

WITNESSING IN ROME

MEMORY VERSE: *And the night following the Lord stood by him, and said, Be of good cheer, Paul: for as thou has testified of me in Jerusalem, so must thou bear witness also at Rome* (Acts 23:11).

Paul was in serious trouble.

His enemies were so angry that there was danger of a breakthrough of the mob and the loss of life. The chief captain feared that Paul would be pulled to pieces (vs. 10).

But the Lord stood by him.

We often need someone to stand by us. Christians can be sure that their Lord is there in every crisis: *When thou passest through the waters, I will be with thee; and through the rivers, they shall not overflow thee: when thou walkest through the fire, thou shalt not be burned; neither shall the flame kindle upon thee* (Isaiah 43:2).

The Lord encouraged Paul.

"Be of good cheer," He said. How often those good words were spoken by Jesus! Perhaps you need them at this very moment. Try this wonderful promise: *These things I have spoken unto you, that in me ye might have peace. In the world ye shall have tribulation: but be of good cheer; I have overcome the world* (John 16:33).

The Lord commissioned Paul.

There was a mission to carry out at Rome and Paul had been chosen for the job. Imagine the challenge of Rome...capital of the empire. And Paul was being sent there to serve...to witness.

Has God used you in your "Jerusalem"? Have you taught a class? Led a prayer group? Spoken to a neighbor about Christ? Then God may have a greater and more important task for you.

Be of good cheer...life's greatest challenge is just ahead.

A CONVENIENT SEASON

MEMORY VERSE: *And as he reasoned of righteousness, temperance, and judgment to come, Felix trembled, and answered, Go thy way for this time; when I have a convenient season, I will call for thee* (Acts 24:25).

The submarine SQUALAS and its crew lay helpless at the bottom of the Atlantic Ocean, two hundred forty feet below the surface. The crew sent up smoke flares, hoping that their location would become known. The submarine SCULPIN did locate them. A ten-ton diving bell was lowered several times, bringing to safety the thirty-three surviving members of the crew of the ill-fated SQUALAS. Not one of the thirty-three men said to their rescuers, "I will think it over," or "I will wait for a more convenient season," or "I am in good condition as I am," or "There is too much to give up," or "I don't understand the workings of that diving bell," or "I'll think about it until tomorrow"! All instantly and gratefully accepted the means of escape from death.

Felix came under great conviction of sin as he listened to Paul but he was not willing to get right with God. He trembled over his sins but would not trust in Christ to be saved from them. Not wanting to close the door completely, he simply put off his decision until a convenient season. But the road to hell is paved with good intentions and two years later Felix was still lost.

Some hope to be like the dying thief who was saved in his final hour but it must be remembered that there were two thieves and only one turned to the Saviour in time.

What is your relationship to God?

What are you going to do about it?

When?

INCREDIBLE

MEMORY VERSE: *Why should it be thought a thing incredible with you, that God should raise the dead?* (Acts 26:8).

Christianity is distinguished from the religions of the world by the resurrection of Jesus Christ. He said that His resurrection would be the sign of His deity: *Jesus answered and said unto them, Destroy this temple, and in three days I will raise it up* (John 2:19). To the carnal mind, resurrection is incredible. But Christ arose and we can rest full faith on this certainty.

One of the many interesting incidents to come out of the annals of old England is that of the conversion of two great men who were skeptics. One was the eminent Gilbert West. The other was Lord Littleton, famous English jurist and a light in the literary world. They were agreed that Christianity should be destroyed, but they further agreed that in order to destroy it two things were necessary. They must disprove the resurrection of Jesus and explain the conversion of Saul in a way that met the demands of skepticism. There was a task for each of these master minds, and each accepted his task.

West assumed the task of getting rid of the resurrection and Littleton would dispose of the Scripture that had its setting on the Damascus road (the conversion of Saul). They took ample time, a year or more, and then came together to compare notes.

When they met, both were Christians, each confessing to his conversion as a result of his own research. The resurrection fact withstood the test of unfriendly, but honest investigation, as did Saul's conversion. Both facts still stand.

Christ is alive.

And here you are worrying.

That's incredible!

NOT DISOBEDIENT

MEMORY VERSE: *Whereupon, O king Agrippa, I was not disobedient unto the heavenly vision* (Acts 26:19).

In relating his testimony to King Agrippa, Paul reveals some details that are not given in previous accounts of his conversion, particularly concerning his call to the ministry. While he was still blind and trembling, the former persecutor was commissioned to be a minister and a witness who would turn people from darkness to light and from the power of Satan unto God.

What an honor to be called to serve the Lord!

A. W. Tozer has written: "To be called to follow Christ is a high honor; higher indeed than any honor men can bestow upon each other.

"Were all the nations of the earth to unite in one great federation and call a man to head that federation, that man would be honored above any other man that ever lived. Yet the humblest man who heeds the call to follow Christ has an honor far above such a man; for the nations of the earth can bestow only such honor as they possess, while the honor of Christ is supreme over all. God has given Him a name that is above every name."

He continues: "One thing is certain; the call of Christ is always a promotion. Were Christ to call a king from his throne to preach the gospel to some tribe of aborigines, that king would be elevated above anything he had known before. Any movement toward Christ is ascent, and any direction away from Him is down."

Paul responded to the call of God and we still reap the benefits of his obedience.

When God calls...obey.

Remember...every call of Christ is a promotion.

ALMOST

MEMORY VERSE: *Then Agrippa said unto Paul, Almost thou persuadest me to be a Christian* (Acts 26:28).

Paul was in bonds.
King Agrippa was in bondage.
Paul was a prisoner of Rome.
King Agrippa was a prisoner of sin.
Paul was innocent before the earthly judge.
King Agrippa was guilty before the Judge of all the earth.
Paul was certain about salvation.
King Agrippa came close but retreated into unbelief.
Paul offered the king eternal life.
King Agrippa declined.
Paul left his meeting with King Agrippa unharmed.
King Agrippa left his meeting with Paul unhelped.
All the world is divided as were Paul and King Agrippa that day. Some are sure of heaven and are building their lives around eternal things...laying up treasures in heaven where they shall go when their journey is over. Others are so taken with the passing honors and treasures of this world that they are blind to the issues of life that really matter.
Paul or King Agrippa...which are you?
Are you almost a Christian?
Almost being a Christian is like almost being alive.
Come to Christ and receive Him by faith.
Be an altogether Christian.
It's the only way to get life all together.

ONLY THE SHIP

MEMORY VERSE: *And now I exhort you to be of good cheer; for there shall be no loss of any man's life among you, but of the ship* (Acts 27:22).

Life is all that counts.

Never mourn over the loss of money. Who can tell what good things God will do in your life because you have less. When D. L. Moody's father died, a creditor came and took the wood that had been cut for the winter. Think of entering a cold New England winter without fuel and heavy of heart because of grief. The situation sounds almost unbearable. Yet God must have done a deep work in young Moody. See what he became in later years.

Never mourn the loss of a house. It is but brick, mortar, and wood. Jesus had no permanent dwelling and said that He was more homeless than the foxes and the birds. Do you have less than He?

Never mourn the loss of an automobile. It is but metal, plastic, and rubber. Did your loved one survive the accident? That is all that matters. The car can be replaced. Don't be guilty of being upset over bent fenders and broken glass. Waste no tears over stained upholstery. Thank the Lord for survivors.

Paul encouraged his captors who were caught in a storm at sea by telling them that all of them would live through the ordeal. "Be of good cheer," he exhorted them. And why not? They would only lose the ship.

Have you been distraught over the loss of some earthly possession? Or even the fear of such loss?

Rearrange your priorities. Look around you and see those living loved ones. Lift your heart in praise to God that you have only lost the ship.

PAUL'S HOUSE IN ROME

MEMORY VERSE: *And Paul dwelt two whole years in his own hired house, and received all that came in unto him* (Acts 28:30).

The journey to Rome had been long and dangerous. Paul's life had seemed to be in jeopardy many times. Still, he knew that he would arrive safely there because that was the promise of God: *And the night following the Lord stood by him, and said, Be of good cheer, Paul: for as thou hast testified of me in Jerusalem, so must thou bear witness also at Rome* (Acts 23:11). That revelation was Paul's guarantee of a safe arrival in Rome regardless of the threats along the way.

Conditions in Rome were not nearly as bad for Paul as he might have anticipated. He had known that he would bear witness for Christ there as had been promised, but he may have envisioned this witnessing being carried on in a prison cell. Instead, he was provided with a house, hired for him as his residence for two years. We often expect less than God gives. He is better than our faith and that is fortunate for all of us.

Paul's house became a center for preaching and witnessing. We don't know all the details but we do know that he was not forbidden from preaching the kingdom of God and teaching concerning the Lord Jesus Christ. And knowing what we do of Paul, it is certain that he made the most of his opportunities. Citizens of Rome who passed Paul's home may have said, "Oh, that is Paul's house. It is always packed with people who want to hear about his conversion and they are never disappointed. He is continually teaching his visitors about the Lord Jesus Christ."

The action at the end of the Book of Acts is in Paul's house.

What's happening in your house that glorifies God?

Why not dedicate your house to Him today?

March

THIS MONTH'S STUDY

The Death and Resurrection of Christ

Days 7,9,14,15,17,26,27 contain quotes or information from "Three Thousand Illustrations for Christian Service," "Knight's Master Book of Illustrations," and "Knight's Treasury of Illustrations" all by Walter B. Knight, published by Wm. B. Eerdmans Publishing Company, Grand Rapids, Michigan. Used by permission. Day 5 is from "Let's Communicate" by Roger Campbell, published by Christian Literature Crusade, Fort Washington, Pennsylvania.

THE COMING CRUCIFIXION

MEMORY VERSE: *Ye know that after two days is the feast of the passover, and the Son of man is betrayed to be crucified* (Matthew 26:2).

The crucifixion of Christ should not have taken His disciples by surprise. He had revealed His coming death and resurrection to them on numerous occasions. Still, when that hour arrived, they had difficulty accepting it.

We are not unlike them.

We have been promised persecution if we live for Christ (see John 15:20), yet we are shocked when others reject our Christian witness.

We have been told there are trials to endure in the Christian life (see 1 Peter 4:12), yet we become depressed when trouble comes to us.

We have been warned that chastisement follows disobedience (see Hebrews 12:6), yet we wander and then groan: "Why did this happen to me?"

When Jesus arrived in Jerusalem, the storms were already gathering. The religious leaders had their wicked plot in motion. His pure life had rebuked their hypocrisy and they would put up with it no more. He claimed to be the Son of God and they were enraged by the authority with which He spoke. They had tried to embarrass Him with difficult questions but He had confounded them with His answers. His miracles seemed unanswerable and they suspected He was performing them in the power of the devil. Enough. They would destroy Him.

To spring their hellish trap, the Saviour's enemies needed someone on the inside—and Judas would volunteer. But this was no surprise to Jesus. Every step He had taken had been toward the cross (see John 6:64).

And still men wonder if He loves them!

WELL DONE

MEMORY VERSE: *When Jesus understood it, he said unto them, Why trouble ye the woman? for she hath wrought a good work upon me* (Matthew 26:10).

Oliver Wendell Holmes said, "The human race is divided into two classes—those who go ahead and do something and those who sit still and inquire, 'Why wasn't it done the other way?'"

Mary of Bethany had undoubtedly wanted to do something for Jesus ever since the raising of her brother Lazarus. He had intervened in her hour of grief and despair. She had sat at His feet and learned valuable spiritual lessons. Finally, she settled on a way to show her dedication and appreciation for all He had done for her. She would use her alabaster box of precious ointment to refresh Him after one of His journeys.

Reaction to Mary's sacrifice was probably predictable. Regardless of what you do for Christ, some will complain! And how righteous they may sound! "This ointment might have been sold for much and given to the poor," said those who watched and criticized. They sounded pious. But Jesus knew their hearts and rebuked them.

Have others been critical of you after some act of sacrificial service? Don't let it get you down. It is easier to grumble than to give. It is easier to be part of the faction than to get into the action.

Never mind. Jesus understands. His "well done" is all that matters. He will care for the critics and will reward those who serve Him with their best (see Luke 14:14).

March 3   Matthew 26:14-16

WHAT'S YOUR PRICE

MEMORY VERSE: *And said unto them, What will ye give me, and I will deliver him unto you? And they covenanted with him for thirty pieces of silver* (Matthew 26:15).

The betrayal of Jesus was foretold in the Old Testament: *Yea, mine own familiar friend, in whom I trusted, which did eat of my bread, hath lifted up his heel against me* (Psalm 41:9).

Even the price of betrayal was prophesied: *And I said unto them, If ye think good, give me my price; and if not, forbear. So they weighed for my price thirty pieces of silver* (Zechariah 11:12).

It is revolting to think of Judas selling the Lord. Dr. Harry Rimmer wrote of him: "Judas. A name that has become a byword in all civilized nations. A man who has become an object of abhorrence. The outstanding example of greed, the climax of treachery; and the apogee of all that is despicable." It is hard to imagine putting a price on loyalty to Jesus.

But some still have their price!

Some are loyal to Jesus unless it costs too much. The price may be reckoned to money, popularity, prestige, or pleasure. At what point does your dedication die? How much temptation is required to topple you? What's your price?

Christ deserves our loyalty and dedication at all costs. He paid the supreme price to redeem us. Loyalty to Him should be priceless.

Let it be known! YOU'RE NOT FOR SALE!

THE LAST PASSOVER

MEMORY VERSE: *And the disciples did as Jesus had appointed them; and they made ready the passover* (Matthew 26:19).

The Children of Israel had been observing the passover since the day of their deliverance from slavery in Egypt. The record of the first passover is given in Exodus 12. Through the centuries, the choicest lambs had been brought for sacrifice at passover, symbolizing God's salvation for His people at that time and looking forward to the coming of the Saviour.

Jesus met with His disciples to eat the passover meal. It was to be the last passover. In his book, "The King of the Jews," Dr. John R. Rice wrote: "There would have been no reason for a passover lamb and the feast of unleavened bread except to picture the coming crucifixion of Jesus Christ. Therefore His disciples should have expected His Crucifixion, which had been so clearly foretold before, to occur at the time of the passover—in fact, at the very hour when the passover lamb was being slain, on the day of the preparation (John 19:14,31).

John the Baptist had announced, *Behold the Lamb of God, which taketh away the sin of the world* (John 1:29). Now the Lamb of whom all the Old Testament sacrifices had spoken, had come to the last passover. Not one more animal sacrifice would be required. His sacrifice would be sufficient for the sins of all: *All we like sheep have gone astray; we have turned every one to his own way; and the LORD hath laid on him the iniquity of us all* (Isaiah 53:6).

Christ is enough!

COMMUNION

MEMORY VERSE: *For this is my blood of the new testament, which is shed for many for the remission of sins* (Matthew 26:28).

Following the last passover, Jesus instituted the first Communion service. It is important to remember that salvation is not gained through taking Communion. This Christian experience is the celebration of sins forgiven through the death of Christ on the cross.

The Communion service looks both backward and forward. In sharing Communion, we look back to the cross and forward to His return: *For as often as ye eat this bread, and drink this cup, ye do shew the Lord's death till he come* (1 Corinthians 11:26).

At the Lord's table, we rejoice in the great love of God that caused Him to send His Son to die for us. We anticipate meeting our Saviour. We feel the warmth of Christian fellowship, and thank God for the tie that binds our hearts in Christian love.

Still there is a solemn note here. We are to judge ourselves (see 1 Corinthians 11:31). A stern warning accompanies the instructions for Communion: *Wherefore whosoever shall eat this bread, and drink this cup of the Lord, unworthily, shall be guilty of the body and blood of the Lord* (1 Corinthians 11:27).

Frightening? Yes, if we must become worthy through our own good works. Thankfully, that is not the case. We become worthy through Christ: *If we confess our sins, he is faithful and just to forgive us our sins, and to cleanse us from all unrighteousness* (1 John 1:9).

Communion speaks of our daily walk with Jesus made possible through His shed blood.

THE PROMISE

MEMORY VERSE: *But after I am risen again, I will go before you into Galilee* (Matthew 26:32).

The days approaching the cross were dark for the disciples. Their faith seemed ready to falter. The reason? They somehow kept missing the promise of the Resurrection.

From the beginning of His ministry, the Saviour emphasized His coming victory over death. His critics asked Him for a sign of His authority. He answered, *Destroy this temple, and in three days I will raise it up* (John 2:19). It was not until after the Resurrection that His disciples remembered that wonderful promise: *When therefore he was risen from the dead, his disciples remembered that he had said this unto them; and they believed the scripture, and the word which Jesus had said* (verse 22).

Strange—His enemies kept track of every declaration of His deity and called for a guard at the tomb to prevent His resurrection. His disciples did not remember the promise until after it was fulfilled.

How like those disciples we often are! Neglecting the Book of God's promises—the Bible—we fret and stew over a thousand things. We pray but doubt—commit burdens to the Lord and take them back again—tremble over trifles. Then, when God has been faithful in carrying us through, we remember that He has promised to do so. We have escaped our expected tragedy through the goodness of God, but what mileage we have placed on our bodies and minds because we have neglected His promises. And all for no reason.

It's a good day to stand on the promises of God!

THY WILL BE DONE

MEMORY VERSE: *He went away again the second time, and prayed, saying, O my Father, if this cup may not pass away from me, except I drink it, thy will be done* (Matthew 26:42).

The four most difficult words to say are these: "THY WILL BE DONE." They are a declaration of complete submission to the will of another. Our stubborn will does not surrender easily.

Perhaps the reason we have so much trouble giving in to God's will is our fear that He will give us some task that we will not enjoy or that He will send us to some place that is not pleasant. We forget that God always gives His best to those who leave the choice with Him.

Dr. James M. Gray wrote: "I once saw a painting of a large boat laden with cattle that were being ferried across an angry, swollen river in time of storm. The artist had so cleverly pictured the dark, threatening clouds and the play of the treacherous, jagged lightening I instantly concluded that the freight of the poor dumb cattle was marked for destruction. But the title of the painting was simply 'Changing Pasture.' Many times we imagine that God's plans mean disaster and affliction, but He is only 'changing pastures' for our good and the good of others."

Hudson Taylor shared some lessons He had learned about submitting to God's will. He said, "I am no longer anxious about anything, as I realize the Lord is able to carry out His will, and His will is mine. It makes no matter where He places me, or how. That is rather for Him to consider than for me; for in the easiest positions He must give me His grace, and in the most difficult, His grace is sufficient."

Here then is a safe prayer: "THY WILL BE DONE."

TEN THOUSAND ANGELS

MEMORY VERSE: *Thinkest thou that I cannot now pray to my Father, and he shall presently give me more than twelve legions of angels?* (Matthew 26:53).

Treachery reached its height in the betrayal of Jesus by Judas. One cannot help but wonder what went through the traitor's mind. Having seen the miracle power of Christ, he must have feared divine judgment for his act. Perhaps that is the reason for the great multitude of people accompanying him, armed with swords and clubs. Common sense should have told him, however, that Christ could only be taken by His enemies if He allowed it. Judas had been present at the feeding of the five thousand, the stilling of the angry sea, and the raising of Lazarus. Did he now imagine that the combined might of this mob could compare with the power of the wind or the steel hand of death?

In that awful hour, Peter made an attempt to rescue Christ through human effort. He drew a sword and cut off the ear of the high priest's servant. Later, speaking in the power of the Holy Spirit, Peter would capture the ears of the multitude gathered for Pentecost, but this was not Peter's day for conquest. Jesus intervened and healed the earless servant. Then He allowed a glimpse of His awesome resources by telling His disciples and the others that twelve legions of angels were at His disposal. Nevertheless, He had not come to destroy men but to save them. To fulfill the Scriptures, He went with His accusers. His destination was the cross.

The Saviour's power was held in abeyance so that we might be saved. He gives His power to those who trust Him so they can be victorious in daily life.

THE SILENT SAVIOUR

MEMORY VERSE: *But Jesus held his peace. And the high priest answered and said unto him, I adjure thee by the living God, that thou tell us whether thou be the Christ, the Son of God* (Matthew 26:63).

Isaiah had prophesied the silence of Jesus before His accusers: *He was oppressed, and he was afflicted, yet he opened not his mouth: he is brought as a lamb to the slaughter, and as a sheep before her shearers is dumb, so he openeth not his mouth* (Isaiah 53:7).

It is never easy to be silent when we are right or feel that our rights are being ignored. But that day the innocent Saviour stood accused before the high priest and did not defend himself.

What an example!

Here was living proof of His ability to live the Sermon on the Mount: *Ye have heard that it hath been said, Thou shalt love thy neighbour, and hate thine enemy. But I say unto you, Love your enemies, bless them that curse you, do good to them that hate you, and pray for them which despitefully use you, and persecute you* (Matthew 5:43,44).

Jesus had not come to defend himself. He had come to die. False accusations would be heaped against Him. Perjurers would provoke a verdict of guilty against the only man on earth ever to be completely righteous. He who held His Father's name in highest reverence would be declared guilty of blasphemy by the high priest. And who can understand divine restraint in view of Matthew 26:67: *Then did they spit in his face, and buffeted him; and others smote him with the palms of their hands.*

Still, He held His peace.

And at trifles, we are offended.

DENYING CHRIST

MEMORY VERSE: *And Peter remembered the word of Jesus, which said unto him, Before the cock crow, thou shalt deny me thrice. And he went out, and wept bitterly* (Matthew 26:75).

At the beginning of the Reformation, Martin of Basle came to a knowledge of the truth. Afraid to make a public confession of Christ, he wrote a leaf of parchment: "O most merciful Christ, I know that I can be saved only by the merit of Thy blood. Holy Jesus, I acknowledge Thy sufferings for me. I love Thee! I love Thee!" Then he removed a stone from the wall of his chamber and hid the message there. It was not discovered for more than a hundred years.

About the same time, Martin Luther found the truth as it is in Christ. He said: "My Lord has confessed me before men; I will not shrink from confessing Him before kings." The world knows what followed.

Sitting in the outer court during the accusation of Jesus, Peter played the coward. He was afraid to own his Lord publicly. What began as simple cowardice ended with cursing and swearing. Backsliding is subtle. One seldom intends to go as far in sin as he ultimately finds himself.

After Peter's third denial, the cock crowed as had been prophesied by Jesus. That bird's clock was synchronized with heaven. Upon hearing him, Peter went out and wept bitterly. Denying Christ had gained him nothing and had robbed him of personal victory.

Jesus said, *Whosoever therefore shall confess me before men, him will I confess also before my Father which is in heaven* (Matthew 10:32).

Think about it!

PILATE BEFORE CHRIST

MEMORY VERSE: *And when they had bound him, they led him away, and delivered him to Pontius Pilate the governor* (Matthew 27:2).

The world speaks of Christ standing before Pilate for judgment. There is a sense in which that was true. But in a greater dimension, Pilate stood before Christ. Rank must be considered. On that day, the earthly judge stood before the Judge of all the earth.

Pilate was uncomfortable. There was something different about this prisoner. He marveled at the calm Christ. Somehow, he must have sensed that his prisoner was in charge of the situation. Pilate was on trial.

On a future day, we shall all stand before Christ. Christians will appear before Him at the Judgment Seat of Christ: *For we must all appear before the judgment seat of Christ; that every one may receive the things done in his body, according to that he hath done, whether it be good or bad* (2 Corinthians 5:10). Lost people will stand before Him at the Judgment of the Great White Throne: *And I saw a great white throne, and him that sat on it, from whose face the earth and the heaven fled away; and there was found no place for them* (Revelation 20:11).

But we must face the fact that we are standing before Him now! Decisions determine destiny. Christians who long to receive rewards on that great day, must serve now. Lost people who intend to be saved before it is too late should be saved now (see 2 Corinthians 6:2).

What is your answer to the call of Christ TODAY?

Your verdict today will determine His verdict in judgment.

PILATE'S QUESTION

MEMORY VERSE: *Pilate saith unto them, What shall I do then with Jesus which is called Christ? They all say unto him, Let him be crucified* (Matthew 27:22).

Proud Pilate asked a question that has echoed through the centuries. It reveals the agony of indecision on life's greatest question.

It is a personal question. "What shall I do with Jesus, who is called Christ?" Though he would have liked to avoid answering or delegating the decision to another, he was the only one who could make that life or death decision. There were many pressures upon Pilate that day. The crowd had rejected his offer to free Jesus and had chosen Barabbas. His wife had sent word about a strange dream that had her upset. The noisy crowd continued their chant and he wanted to please them. He would have to decide.

It is a question that demands action. "What shall I do with Jesus, who is called Christ? Pilate tried to escape making a decision by publicly washing his hands of the entire situation. But he could not get away with neutrality. He must decide.

It is a question about Jesus. What shall I do with Jesus, who is called Christ?" Pilate had made some important decisions in his life but they were all dwarfed by this one. This question was about the Saviour. It was not about religious ceremonies or laws, but about a person. That Person was Jesus.

We are faced with a decision such as Pilate had to make, a decision about Jesus.

What will you do then with Jesus, who is called Christ?

March 13 — Matthew 27:27-32

THE CROWN OF THORNS

MEMORY VERSE: *And when they had platted a crown of thorns, they put it upon his head, and a reed in his right hand: and they bowed the knee before him, and mocked him, saying, Hail, King of the Jews!* (Matthew 27:29).

Angels must have marveled at the cruelty of man when the Son of God was prepared for crucifixion. The One whom heaven praised was rejected, humiliated, and mocked by Pilate's soldiers. As a part of their mockery, they placed a crown of thorns upon His head.

Though the wicked soldiers did not realize it, their hand-made ugly crown was symbolic. Christ was made a curse for us in order to redeem us. Notice the place of thorns in the curse brought by sin: *And unto Adam he said, Because thou hast hearkened unto the voice of thy wife, and hast eaten of the tree, of which I commanded thee, saying, Thou shalt not eat of it: cursed is the ground for thy sake; in sorrow shalt thou eat of it all the days of thy life; Thorns also and thistles shall it bring forth to thee; and thou shalt eat the herb of the field* (Genesis 3:17,18).

Nature has suffered because of the sins of man. Christ died to pay for our sins. When He returns to reign, the earth will know release. All creation awaits that day: *For we know that the whole creation groaneth and travaileth in pain together until now. And not only they, but ourselves also, which have the firstfruits of the Spirit, even we ourselves groan within ourselves, waiting for the adoption, to wit, the redemption of our body* (Romans 8:22,23).

The work of Christ on the cross was a complete work.

And we are complete in Him!

SPECTATORS

MEMORY VERSE: *And sitting down they watched him there* (Matthew 27:36).

Rembrandt, the famous artist, painted a picture of the Crucifixion. Vividly he portrayed Christ suffering in nameless agony on the cruel cross. He depicted the various attitudes of those about the cross toward the Saviour by their facial expressions. Apart from the Saviour's death, the most significant thing about the painting is the artist's portrayal of himself, standing in the shadows on the edge of the onlookers. This was Rembrandt's way of saying, "I was there too! I helped crucify Jesus!"

One of the most moving accounts of the Crucifixion I have read came from the pen of a man who wrote later that he longed to know for sure about how to reach heaven. He knew all the details of the Saviour's death, but evidently did not know the Saviour. I wrote to him, explaining the way of salvation. How sad to be but a spectator at the cross.

Paul wrote to Timothy and explained that the last days would be characterized by perilous times. He added that in those final hours people would be *ever learning, and never able to come to the knowledge of the truth* (2 Timothy 3:7). In other words, information would be easily available, but application would be scarce. It is not enough to know the truth. We must act on it.

Do you know all about Jesus but still not know Him? Are you but a spectator to salvation? Some who can recite many Bible verses have never received the Saviour. Have you? If not, take Him as your own right now. Today is the day of salvation.

THE CROWDS AT THE CROSS

MEMORY VERSE: *And they that passed by reviled him, wagging their heads* (Matthew 27:39).

When George Nixon Briggs was governor of Massachusetts, three of his friends visited the Holy Land. While there, they climbed Golgotha's slope and cut from the summit a small stick to be used as a cane. On their return home, they presented it to the governor, saying, "We wanted you to know that when we stood on Calvary we thought of you." Accepting the gift with all due courtesy and gratitude, the governor tenderly added: "But I am still more thankful, gentlemen, that there was Another who thought of me there."

All types of people were represented in the crowds at the cross. There were the reckless ones who gambled for the garments of Jesus. They mocked and spat upon Him, rejecting His love and sacrifice. The doubters were there, starting their taunts with their characteristic "if." Those who were familiar with Jesus but faithless were there. They remembered His promise of resurrection but thought its fulfillment impossible. The religious ones were there, talking about salvation but rejecting the Saviour: *He saved others; himself he cannot save* (Matthew 27:42). The "seeing is believing" crowd was there. They promised to believe if He would come down from the cross.

Jesus died for all. His salvation is offered to all, regardless of previous failure or background. He changes doubters and down-and-outers: *And such were some of you: but ye are washed, but ye are sanctified, but ye are justified in the name of the Lord Jesus, and by the Spirit of our God* (1 Corinthians 6:11).

FATHER, FORGIVE THEM

MEMORY VERSE: *Then said Jesus, Father, forgive them; for they know not what they do. And they parted his raiment, and cast lots* (Luke 23:34).

There were seven statements made by Jesus from the cross. The first was His word of forgiveness. It demonstrates His position as the mediator between God and men: *For there is one God, and one mediator between God and men, the man Christ Jesus* (1 Timothy 2:5).

The Saviour's prayer for forgiveness must have shocked His crucifiers. They were professional executioners and were accustomed to the anger and venom of their objects of execution. Here was One who prayed for them and asked forgiveness for their act of ignorance.

The prayer must have aggravated the religious leaders who had called for His death. They were so self-righteous that they thought their awful deed was justified. Besides, the forgiving heart of Jesus bothered them. He had continually promised forgiveness to those whom they thought were beyond help. "This man receiveth sinners," they had said of Him. Thankfully, their observation was correct.

Forgiveness. What a good word! It places the past behind us forever. It assures a future to those who do not deserve another day.

Forgiveness flows from God to man because of the sacrifice of Jesus on the cross. A Christian is one who has been forgiven—and one who is forgiving: *And be ye kind one to another, tenderhearted, forgiving one another, even as God for Christ's sake hath forgiven you* (Ephesians 4:32).

In the light of what Jesus said from the cross, what are you going to do about forgiving others?

TODAY, IN PARADISE

MEMORY VERSE: *And Jesus said unto him, Verily I say unto thee, To day shalt thou be with me in paradise* (Luke 23:43).

There were three crosses on Calvary's hill. Jesus died on the center cross with a thief on either side. Two who died that day were completely guilty. One was completely innocent. Two died there paying their debts to society. One died paying our debt of sin.

The second statement of Christ from the cross was to a dying thief who trusted in Him as his Lord and Saviour. And what great faith the dying criminal demonstrated. He believed while surrounded by a crowd of doubters. He saw Jesus in His most difficult hour and owned Him as his King. He accepted the promise of the Resurrection. He looked at a cross and saw a kingdom.

The dying thief's faith was rewarded. Jesus said, "Today, thou shalt be with me in paradise." What great heart questions are answered in this single statement of Jesus! Can one be saved in his dying hour? Can one be saved after a lifetime of wickedness? Can one be saved without baptism or communion? Can one be sure of heaven after death? To the one who believes Christ's word to the thief, these are questions no more.

Copernicus was a great mathematician. His studies and calculations revolutionized the thinking of mankind about the universe. At death's door, he saw himself not as a great scholar but only as a sinner in need of the Saviour. He chose the following words for his tombstone: "I do not seek a kindness equal to that given to Paul. Nor do I ask the grace granted to Peter. But that forgiveness which Thou didst grant to the robber—that, I earnestly crave!"

Jesus saves thieves, scholars, and other sinners. Trust Him today.

BEHOLD THY SON

MEMORY VERSE: *When Jesus therefore saw his mother, and the disciple standing by, whom he loved, he saith unto his mother, Woman, behold thy son! (John 19:26).*

The first word of Christ from the cross was an expression of forgiveness, the second an expression of assurance, and the third an expression of affection. G. Campbell Morgan said that the first word shows His pity for men, the second His power toward those who believe in Him, and the third His provision for those on whom His love is set.

This word reminds us of Jesus and the family. In His dying hour, He spoke of motherhood and sonship. The family was instituted by God and confirmed by Christ. In the Incarnation, Jesus chose to accept the discipline of a home. He insisted on the sanctity of the home and had time for children.

This word reminds us of Jesus and the faithful few. Only a few were there. The others had forsaken Him and fled. How few were the faithful—but how faithful were the few! They stood at the cross. It was not an easy place to stand. People are willing to rally to many banners, but those who stand at the cross must prepare to be in the minority.

This word reminds us of the faithfulness of Jesus to His own. Jesus cared for Mary's needs. He cared for her emotional needs by sending her away before the darkness. He cared for her spiritual needs by dying for her. He cared for her temporal needs by charging John to treat her as his mother.

Isn't it good to belong to Him?

FORSAKEN

MEMORY VERSE: *And about the ninth hour Jesus cried with a loud voice, saying, Eli, Eli, lama sabachthani? that is to say, My God, my God, why hast thou forsaken me?* (Matthew 27:46).

Martin Luther once set time aside to study Christ's fourth word from the cross. After long concentration, he pushed himself back from his desk and exclaimed: "God forsaken of God! Who can understand that?"

But there are some truths here that we can understand.

This word from the cross is the word of identification. It is spoken from the darkness that had descended over Calvary at that time. Here Jesus identifies with the sinner's darkness. Darkness speaks of sin: *The night is far spent, the day is at hand: let us therefore cast off the works of darkness, and let us put on the armour of light* (Romans 13:12). Jesus, the light of the world, suffered in darkness to deliver us from darkness.

Jesus also identified with the sinner's uncertainty. "Why?" He cried. And this is the One who always spoke with authority. A lost person lives in uncertainty. He asks: "Why am I here? What is life all about? Where are we headed?" Jesus identified with the sinner's uncertainty so that we might be certain forever: *These things have I written unto you that believe on the name of the Son of God; that ye may know that ye have eternal life* (1 John 5:13).

Finally, Jesus identified with the sinner's separation from God. He took the sinner's place and was forsaken that we might never be forsaken: *For he hath made him to be sin for us, who knew no sin; that we might be made the righteousness of God in him* (2 Corinthians 5:21).

I THIRST

MEMORY VERSE: *After this, Jesus knowing that all things were now accomplished, that the scripture might be fulfilled, saith, I thirst* (John 19:28).

The fifth word from the cross reveals the humanity of Jesus Christ. He was the Son of God and the Son of Man. In His humanity He felt what we feel. Though God never becomes weary, as the Son of Man, Christ experienced fatigue. He became hungry. His heart was broken at a grave. On the cross, He became thirsty. The Book of Hebrews says it well: *Seeing then that we have a great high priest, that is passed into the heavens, Jesus the Son of God, let us hold fast our profession. For we have not an high priest which cannot be touched with the feeling of our infirmities; but was in all points tempted like as we are, yet without sin. Let us therefore come boldly unto the throne of grace, that we may obtain mercy, and find grace to help in time of need* (Hebrews 4:14-16).

Another reason for the Saviour's cry, "I thirst," was so that the Scripture might be fulfilled. At least 333 Old Testament prophecies converge in the Person of Christ. The Word of God is so important to Jesus that He uttered every word necessary to fulfill it. Writing of the coming death of Christ, the psalmist had said, *They gave me also gall for my meat; and in my thirst they gave me vinegar to drink* (Psalm 69:21). Let unbelievers deny it and sinners defy it, but the Bible stands. Jesus fulfilled every word that had to do with Him and with salvation.

The One who thirsted on the cross provides living water to satisfy thirsty souls. Come to Him and drink!

IT IS FINISHED

MEMORY VERSE: *When Jesus therefore had received the vinegar, he said, It is finished: and he bowed his head, and gave up the ghost* (John 19:30).

Many leave this world with their tasks unfinished. The pen drops from the writer's hand before the manuscript is completed. The painter's brush falls before the painting is done. The composer's symphony lacks its final notes because he has answered the call of death. The work of the sculptor stands forever veiled. But Christ is the great Finisher. On the cross, He finished the work of redemption.

At the beginning of the Bible, creation is finished: *Thus the heavens and the earth were finished, and all the host of them* (Genesis 2:1). At the end of the Bible, perfection is finished: *And he said unto me, It is done. I am Alpha and Omega, the beginning and the end. I will give unto him that is athirst of the fountain of the water of life freely* (Revelation 21:6). Between these two great divine accomplishments stands the completed work of redemption that Christ announced in His sixth word from the cross.

The Mighty Finisher had completed all the requirements of the Law. He had completed all the types set forth in the Old Testament sacrifices. He had completed all the suffering required to pay for our sins. The debt was paid.

"It is finished" was a message of conquest. This was not a sign of defeat but a cry of victory. Enough of this beat-down, depressed, and defeated Christianity. In Christ we are victors! Hallelujah!

March 22   Luke 23:44-49

INTO THY HANDS

MEMORY VERSE: *And when Jesus had cried with a loud voice, he said, Father, into thy hands I commend my spirit: and having said thus, he gave up the ghost* (Luke 23:46).

The seventh word from the cross demonstrates that Jesus was in complete control throughout His Crucifixion. He had been the target of assassins throughout His life. Herod had tried to kill him when he was a child. Satan had tried to lure Him into suicide. A group from the synagogue in Nazareth tried to cast Him headlong from the brow of a hill. At the feast of the dedication in Jerusalem, a crowd took up stones to stone Him. None of these attempts were successful because the hour for which He was born had not arrived.

Jesus had come as the Good Shepherd to give His life for the sheep. Attempts at taking His life by His enemies were futile because He had come to lay it down. He explained: *As the Father knoweth me, even so know I the Father: and I lay down my life for the sheep. And other sheep I have, which are not of this fold: them also I must bring, and they shall hear my voice; and there shall be one fold, and one shepherd. Therefore doth my Father love me, because I lay down my life, that I might take it again. No man taketh it from me, but I lay it down of myself. I have power to lay it down, and I have power to take it again. This commandment have I received of my Father* (John 10:15-18).

How encouraging the words, "Father, into Thy hands I commend My spirit," must have been to the dying thief who had just owned Christ as Lord. He knew then that he had trusted the Victorious One. And so have we!

THE RENT VEIL

MEMORY VERSE: *And, behold, the veil of the temple was rent in twain from the top to the bottom; and the earth did quake, and the rocks rent* (Matthew 27:51).

The death of Christ ended the dispensation of the Law. To make this clear, the veil of the Temple was miraculously torn from the top to the bottom at the moment of His death. What does that mean to you and me?

It means that the priesthood as described in the Old Testament is finished. Christ is our high priest: *But Christ being come an high priest of good things to come, by a greater and more perfect tabernacle, not made with hands, that is to say, not of this building; Neither by the blood of goats and calves, but by his own blood he entered in once into the holy place, having obtained eternal redemption for us* (Hebrews 9:11,12).

It means that the sabbaths, feasts, and ceremonies of the Law have been fulfilled and are not to be observed today. *Blotting out the handwriting of ordinances that was against us, which was contrary to us, and took it out of the way, nailing it to his cross; And having spoiled principalities and powers, he made a shew of them openly, triumphing over them in it. Let no man therefore judge you in meat, or in drink, or in respect of an holyday, or of the new moon, or of the sabbath days: Which are a shadow of things to come; but the body is of Christ* (Colossians 2:14-17).

It means that all can be saved, regardless of race or position. Salvation is entirely by grace through faith (see Ephesians 2:8,9). So do not wait any longer. Come to the Saviour today!

FAITHFUL WOMEN

MEMORY VERSE: *There were also women looking on afar off; among whom was Mary Magdalene, and Mary the mother of James the less and of Joses, and Salome* (Mark 15:40).

Women were last at the cross and first at the tomb. They were also among the faithful who gathered after the ascension to await the coming of the Holy Spirit: *These all continued with one accord in prayer and supplication, with the women, and Mary the mother of Jesus, and with his brethren* (Acts 1:14). Through the centuries, women have been faithful in prayer and witnessing. Only eternity will reveal their vital role in bringing people to Christ.

The man is fortunate who has a Christian wife who upholds him in prayer and encourages him in daily life. The pastor is fortunate who has a corp of faithful women who pray for his ministry. The church is blessed that has a good number of women who reach out to boys and girls and adults with hearts of compassion and interest.

Women have often been first on the mission field. At a large gathering of Christians a few years ago, the names of modern day martyrs in missionary service were placed at various points around the auditorium. There were more women named as martyrs than men.

And who can tell the impact of women in their work as mothers. Spurgeon wrote: "I cannot tell you how much I owe to the solemn words of my good mother." Susannah Wesley was the mother of nineteen children, among whom were John and Charles Wesley. Near her grave stands a marble monument, fourteen feet high. Time may finally destroy that marble memorial but the influence of this devout mother will stand forever. *Favour is deceitful, and beauty is vain: but a woman that feareth the LORD, she shall be praised* (Proverbs 31:30).

SECRET SAINTS

MEMORY VERSE: *And after this Joseph of Arimathaea, being a disciple of Jesus, but secretly for fear of the Jews, besought Pilate that he might take away the body of Jesus: and Pilate gave him leave. He came therefore, and took the body of Jesus* (John 19:38).

Many surprises are due us in heaven. Most would have judged Joseph of Arimathaea as lost. They would in turn have judged Judas to be saved. Salvation is an act of the heart. Some timid souls who never walk forward in public invitations will walk the golden streets of heaven.

While it is possible to be very quiet about our relationship with Christ, it is highly improper. Jesus has identified with us publicly and we ought to do the same for Him. Of all the disciples, only Joseph is spoken of as being a secret disciple, though Nicodemus, who first came to Jesus by night, was evidently also quiet about his faith in Christ.

It is at the cross that we gain courage to confess Christ openly. Nicodemus and Joseph, who had been silent saints before Calvary, could not continue that way after witnessing the death of Christ on the cross. They now confront the very person who ordered the Crucifixion and ask for the body of Jesus, identifying with Him whatever the cost.

Have you been ashamed of Jesus? See Him bearing your shame.

Have you trusted Him secretly? See Him dying for you publicly.

Have you feared the cost of a public testimony? Consider the cost of Calvary's cross.

The world is in darkness. It's time to shine!

GREAT GUARANTEES

MEMORY VERSE: *But now is Christ risen from the dead, and become the firstfruits of them that slept* (1 Corinthians 15:20).

In the Resurrection, God has given us three great guarantees.

The Resurrection guarantees the Saviour. When the critics of Christ called for some proof of His deity, He told them there would be but one sign given: THE RESURRECTION. *Destroy this temple,* He said, *and in three days I will raise it up* (John 2:19). After the Resurrection, the disciples remembered that statement and its fulfillment fired their faith and sent them out to carry His message to the world.

The Resurrection guarantees salvation. Many years ago, two English lawyers, skeptics, set out to destroy Christianity. Their names were Gilbert West and Lord Littleton. They agreed that two Christian teachings must be disproved if they were to succeed: the resurrection of Christ and the conversion of Paul. West assumed the task of getting rid of the Resurrection and Littleton tackled the conversion of Paul. Their plan was for each to research his subject for one year. At the end of that time, they would come together and prepare to present their findings to the world. *When they met, one year later, both were Christians, each confessing to his conversion as a result of his own research!*

The resurrection of Christ guarantees our similar resurrection. On that first Easter, Mary wept because the tomb was empty, but that very fact signaled the emptying of the graves of all believers at the return of Christ. And that's what Easter is all about!

THE CONQUERED GRAVE

MEMORY VERSE: *But thanks be to God, which giveth us the victory through our Lord Jesus Christ* (1 Corinthians 15:57).

One hundred years ago, a very wealthy woman who had been opposed to the doctrine of the Resurrection died. Before her death she gave orders that her grave should be covered with a slab of granite; that around it should be placed square blocks of stone, and that the corners should be fastened to each other and to the granite slab by heavy iron clamps. Upon the covering, this inscription was to be placed: "THIS BURIAL PLACE PURCHASED TO ALL ETERNITY MUST NEVER BE OPENED."

The doubting lady had gone to great trouble to secure herself against an event in which she professed not to believe.

However, time mocked her.

Not long after her death, a tiny birch tree seed sprouted and the root found its way between the side stone and the upper slab and grew there. Slowly, but steadily, it forced its way until the iron clamps were torn apart. Finally the granite lid was raised and made to rest upon the trunk of the large and flourishing birch tree.

Nearly two thousand years ago, another grave was sealed. The authority of the Roman Empire was enlisted to see that it should never be opened. It was the grave of Jesus.

Three days later, the stone that had been placed at the entrance of the tomb was rolled away. Christ arose! Death could not hold Him: *Whom God hath raised up, having loosed the pains of death: because it was not possible that he should be holden of it* (Acts 2:24).

What good news to tell to doubting people!

AND PETER

MEMORY VERSE: *But go your way, tell his disciples and Peter that he goeth before you into Galilee: there shall ye see him, as he said unto you* (Mark 16:7).

Peter had not intended to become a backslider. Boldly he had proclaimed his loyalty, even being willing to stand alone. But there is a difference between determination and daily living. Dedication is only tested in the fire of experience. It is one thing to talk about ability to overcome temptation and quite another to prove it when doing battle with the tempter.

After his three denials of Christ, Peter went out and wept bitterly. The gospels are silent about his actions during the Crucifixion and some have thought he fled the scene, but in his first epistle he states that he was a witness of the sufferings of Christ (see 1 Peter 5:1). What a sad picture he presents as he watches the Lord's sufferings through his tears!

Interestingly, in the instruction given to the women who came to the tomb after the Resurrection, Peter is the only disciple that is named. The message of the Resurrection must go to brokenhearted Peter. By that time, he may have doubted that he could be considered one of the disciples, so the Lord made sure that he knew that he was invited to the coming meeting with them. Though he had failed, His Lord loved him.

You may live with doubts and regrets. Perhaps you had great hopes of serving Christ but temptation came and you yielded. Now you think the Lord is through with you. Remember Peter. Like the denying disciple, you are the special object of God's love!

DOUBTING THOMAS

MEMORY VERSE: *And Thomas answered and said unto him, My Lord and my God* (John 20:28).

"Doubting Thomas," we call him. And with reason. He simply would not believe that Jesus had risen from the dead. There was no mistaking his opinion of the first Resurrection report: *Except I shall see in his hands the print of the nails, and put my finger into the print of the nails, and thrust my hand into his side, I will not believe* (John 20:25).

We aren't told why Thomas missed the first meeting with the disciples after the Resurrection when Jesus appeared. Perhaps he had a good excuse for not attending the gathering called by the risen Christ. One thing is sure: MISSING THAT MEETING MADE HIM A DOUBTER AND ESTABLISHED HIS REPUTATION THROUGH THE CENTURIES. He would always be known as "Doubting Thomas."

There is, however, another side to the story. Thomas had left all to follow Christ. He went with the Lord through some pretty difficult days. To the best of our knowledge, he experienced approximately one week of doubt in his entire Christian experience. There may have been more doubting days than that for Thomas but we have no scriptural authority for saying so.

At the second appearance of Christ to the disciples, Thomas was present. When confronted with his faithless statement, he surrendered completely and cried, "My Lord and my God." From that time on it seems sure that Thomas was an outstanding Christian and that he died as a martyr in India where, because of preaching the gospel, he was thrust through with a spear. We label Thomas because of one weak week.

Sadly, we often treat other Christians the same way!

March 30   Luke 24:13-32

BURNING HEARTS

MEMORY VERSE: *And they said one to another, Did not our heart burn within us, while he talked with us by the way, and while he opened to us the scriptures?* (Luke 24:32).

Two discouraged disciples were retreating—going home. They had trusted that Christ was the One who would redeem Israel, but the Crucifixion had brought them to despair.

Emmaus was their destination and somewhere along that road the Saviour came and walked with them. Miraculously, the eyes of the Emmaus disciples were held by God so that they were unable to recognize Jesus. As might be expected, He asked them why they were sad. After they had told Him all about their burden, He opened the Scriptures to them and taught them about himself. What a Bible lesson that must have been! Remembering those moments, they said later that their hearts had burned within them as they listened to Him.

Burning hearts are needed today.

Who has not witnessed the fire of new converts or of those newly committed to the Saviour? Their love for Christ and others has sometimes ignited entire congregations that had become cool and complacent. With warmth and zeal, those newly born have often led mature but mechanical members of the body of Christ back to the experience of fervent love and power.

Dwight L. Moody prayed, "Lord, make me not only warm, but red hot!"

David Dawson wrote: "Fire warms! And who of us does not like to feel the warm glow among God's people?"

Ask God to give you a burning heart. You may set your church afire. And every community needs to witness that blessed glow!

GO!

MEMORY VERSE: *Go ye therefore, and teach all nations, baptizing them in the name of the Father, and of the Son, and of the Holy Ghost* (Matthew 28:19).

Last words are important. However, the last words of Jesus came not from dying lips. He had risen from the grave and His final words to His disciples were spoken just before His ascension to heaven. Those words make up the Great Commission. They are words that call upon all Christians to go with the gospel message.

It has been said that 95 percent of Christians do not win souls to Christ. Hopefully those sad statistics are wrong, but it is sure that few are really involved in obeying the Lord's call to go.

What happens when Christians do not go? Friends, neighbors, and family members are deprived of the message of salvation. Churches stand still. The joy of leading others to the Saviour is missed. Eternal rewards are forfeited.

Most do not lead others to Christ because they do not go. God has given a wonderful promise to those who go: *He that goeth forth and weepeth, bearing precious seed, shall doubtless come again with rejoicing, bringing his sheaves with him* (Psalm 126:6).

Some do not go because they are afraid. They fear what others will say. They fear the response they will receive. But Christ has promised His power to those who go.

It is not easy to go with the gospel. A thousand other activities will vie for your time. The love of ease will fight your determination to obey our Lord's commission. Nevertheless, in going there is great blessing.

Go with the gospel!

April

THIS MONTH'S STUDY

Concentrating On 1 Corinthians

Days 1 and 26 contain quotes or information from "Studies in First Corinthians" by M. R. DeHaan, pub. Zondervan Publishing House, Grand rapids, Michigan; Days 2,7,9,15,18,19, 24,28, and 30 from "Three Thousand Illustrations for Christian Service," "Knight's Master Book of Illustrations," and "Knight's Treasury of Illustrations," all by Walter B. Knight, pub. by Wm. B. Eerdmans Publishing Company, Grand Rapids, Michigan, Used by permission. Days 8,21,22, and 25 from "Let's Communicate," by Roger F. Campbell, pub. by Christian Literature Crusade, Fort Washington, Pa.; Day 23 from "Weight! A Better Way to Lose," by Roger F. Campbell, pub. by Victor Books, Wheaton, Illinois.

April 1   1 Corinthians 1:1-17

GOD IS FAITHFUL

MEMORY VERSE: *God is faithful, by whom ye were called unto the fellowship of his Son Jesus Christ our Lord* (1 Corinthians 1:9).

The church at Corinth had many problems. It was torn by strife and divisions and its members were spiritual babies...immature. Dr. M. R. DeHann wrote: "The Corinthian church was a carnal church. Many of its members were but recently converted from paganism and found it difficult to separate themselves from their old life. As a result the epistle is largely corrective and exhortatory, rather than doctrinal. Paul severely condemns their carnal practices and childish sectarianism."

DeHaan continues: "The Corinthians were far from blameless in their walk and in their conduct. They were carnal, wicked, worldly, and contentious; but, says Paul, 'God is faithful,' in spite of your unfaithfulness. He that hath begun a good work in you will not admit defeat, but will finish it in the end. It will never be said of God that He saved a man, and then couldn't keep him. Ah, no! He will keep on dealing with him and if need be, rebuke that soul, pleading, admonishing, chastening, and even removing by death if necessary, but at the end He will present him blameless in the day of Jesus Christ." (See Hebrews 12:5-11.)

Evidence of the carnality in Corinth is found in their following of men rather than Christ. Many are like them, driving hundreds of miles to hear some favorite preacher when they cannot even be counted on to be regular in the Sunday evening service in their home church. The answer to their problem could be found in recognizing that God is faithful. Ultimately all men fail or disappoint. Jesus never fails and there is no disappointment in Him.

All others fail.

He is faithful.

FOOLISHNESS

MEMORY VERSE: *For the preaching of the cross is to them that perish foolishness; but unto us which are saved it is the power of God* (1 Corinthians 1:18).

In the second century, Justin Martyr wrote: "Many spirits are abroad in the world, and the credentials they display are splendid gifts of mind, learning, and of talent. Christian, look carefully. Ask for the print of the nails."

The conflicts in the church at Corinth were beyond the reach of tact or psychology, the message of the cross was the only answer. Lost people need to hear this message to be saved and Christians never outgrow their need of the preaching of the cross for daily growth.

The cross is the cure for divisions. Churches that are torn by gossip and backbiting need to be reminded of the Lord's sacrifice on the cross. Those who nurse hurt feelings need to stand at the cross and see their Saviour enduring the shame and pain of that awful hour. Who has the right to be offended in the light of His sufferings there?

Have you been wronged? Consider the cross.

Do you wonder about full forgiveness? Consider the cross.

Do you doubt God's love? Consider the cross.

The message of the cross is not popular today. Many prefer religion that is not so stern...so demanding. The preaching of the cross reveals all people as sinners and Christ as the only Saviour. Man's sinful nature and his pride object to that kind of teaching. Beautiful sanctuaries are fine but the cross seems out of date...foolishness.

But the way of the cross leads home...there is no other way but this.

Let this old and true message change your life. And God's way will not seem foolish anymore.

April 3 1 Corinthians 2:1-8

THE LORD OF GLORY

MEMORY VERSE: *Which none of the princes of this world knew: for had they known it, they would not have crucified the Lord of glory* (1 Corinthians 2:8).

Angels must have marveled at the cruelty of man when the Lord of glory was prepared for crucifixion. The One whom heaven praised was rejected, humiliated, and mocked by Pilate's soldiers and the heartless crowd. As a part of their mockery, they placed a crown of thorns upon His head.

Though His crucifiers did not realize it, their hand-made ugly crown was symbolic. Christ was made a curse for us in order to redeem us. Notice the place of thorns in the curse brought by sin: *And unto Adam he said, Because thou hast hearkened unto the voice of thy wife, and hast eaten of the tree, of which I commanded thee, saying, Thou shalt not eat of it: cursed is the ground for thy sake; in sorrow shalt thou eat of it all the days of thy life; Thorns also and thistles shall it bring forth to thee; and thou shalt eat the herb of the field* (Genesis 3:17,18).

Paul knew that the confusion and carnality in the church at Corinth could only be conquered by exposure to the message of the cross. These backslidden believers needed a glimpse of Calvary; a new appreciation of all that took place on that rugged hill. And the problems in churches today require the same remedy.

Some know all about the cross but have never made the message personal. One of the most moving accounts of the Crucifixion I have read came from the pen of a man who wrote later that he longed to know for sure about how to reach heaven. He knew all the details of the Saviour's death but did not know the Lord of glory.

Make the Lord of glory the Lord of your life today.

THE MIND OF CHRIST

MEMORY VERSE: *For who hath known the mind of the Lord, that he may instruct him? But we have the mind of Christ* (1 Corinthians 2:16).

What does Paul mean by the mind of Christ?

What is the attitude of one who has the mind of Christ?

In his letter to the Philippians, Paul says this is demonstrated through humility: *Let this mind be in you, which was also in Christ Jesus: Who, being in the form of God, thought it not robbery to be equal with God: But made himself of no reputation, and took upon him the form of a servant, and was made in the likeness of men: And being found in fashion as a man, he humbled himself, and became obedient unto death, even the death of the cross* (Philippians 2:5-8).

An example of the humility of Christ is given in His silence before His accusers: *He was oppressed, and he was afflicted, yet he opened not his mouth: he is brought as a lamb to the slaughter, and as a sheep before her shearers is dumb, so he openeth not his mouth* (Isaiah 53:7).

That day the innocent Saviour stood accused before the high priest and did not defend himself.

Jesus had not come to defend himself. He had come to die. False accusations would be heaped against Him. Perjurers would provoke a verdict of guilty against the only man on earth ever to be completely righteous. He who held His Father's name in highest reverence would be declared guilty of blasphemy by the high priest. And who can understand the divine restraint illustrated in Matthew 26:67: *Then did they spit in his face, and buffeted him; and others smote him with the palms of their hands.* Still He held His peace.

Troubled? Struggling? Remember, we have the mind of Christ.

ARE YE NOT CARNAL?

MEMORY VERSE: *For while one saith, I am of Paul; and another, I am of Apollos; are ye not carnal?* (1 Corinthians 3:4).

To be carnal is to be given to fleshly appetites. Often we think of this as having to do with certain activities that we have labeled "worldly." The problem actually goes much deeper.

In this text, Paul cites as evidence of carnality the divisions in the church caused by looking to men instead of Christ. In the first chapter he had rebuked them for this sin as follows: *Is Christ divided? was Paul crucified for you? or were ye baptized in the name of Paul?* (1 Corinthians 1:13).

Looking to the crucified One cures carnality. Think of all His suffering there for you and me. In focusing on the death of Christ, we cringe at the pain inflicted by the nails and the thorns. The physical agony of crucifixion is almost indescribable. But as unbearable as the physical pain of the cross must have been, the Saviour's travail of soul was greater. Having never sinned, He took the sins of the world upon Him: *For he hath made him to be sin for us, who knew no sin; that we might be made the righteousness of God in him* (2 Corinthians 5:21). In the light of His suffering and death for us, we ought to put away fleshly goals and live for Him. Christ must be the center of our thoughts and our affections.

When believers look to the One who died for them, they cease the worship of men. Those who now drive hundreds of miles to hear some favorite preacher but cannot make it to the evening service in their home church, have a change of heart.

Looking to Jesus makes us spiritual.

THE FOUNDATION

MEMORY VERSE: *For other foundation can no man lay than that is laid, which is Jesus Christ* (1 Corinthians 3:11).

The foundation of the Christian faith is the gospel. And the gospel is this: *Christ died for our sins according the scriptures; And that he was buried, and that he rose again the third day according to the scriptures* (1 Corinthians 15:3,4).

Apart from the Resurrection...there is no gospel.

Here is the fact that separates Christianity from the religions of the world: CHRIST IS RISEN!

C. H. Spurgeon wrote: "The fact of the Resurrection is the key-stone of Christianity. Disprove the resurrection of our Lord, and our holy faith would be a mere fable; there would be nothing for faith to rest upon if He who died upon the tree did not rise again from the tomb; then 'your faith is vain;' said the apostle, 'ye are yet in your sins,' while 'they also which are fallen asleep in Christ are perished.' All the great doctrines of our divine religion fall asunder like the stones of an arch when the keystone is dislodged, in a common ruin they are all overthrown, for all our hope hinges upon that great fact. If Jesus rose, then is this gospel what it professes to be; if He rose not from the dead, then is it all deceit and delusion. But brethren, that Jesus rose from the dead is a fact better established than almost any other in history.

"My dear hearers, are you resting your everlasting hopes upon the resurrection of Jesus Christ from the dead? Do you trust in Him, believing that He both died and rose again for you? Do you place your entire dependence upon the merit of His blood certified by the fact of His rising again? If so, you have a foundation of fact and truth, a foundation against which the gates of hell shall not prevail."

STEWARDS

MEMORY VERSE: *Moreover it is required in stewards, that a man be found faithful* (1 Corinthians 4:2).

When one is born again, he is bound for heaven.
Why doesn't God take him to heaven right that moment?
He has work to do (see Ephesians 2:10).
He has become a steward for his Lord.
And stewards for the Lord are to be faithful.

Those who are faithful stewards give of themselves in the service of Christ in whatever area He places them. A woman who wanted Gypsy Smith to speak at a meeting in London, wrote to him and said, "I have a meeting I want you to come and speak to. It is only a small meeting and will take nothing out of you." Smith answered, "I cannot come, and it would be of no use if I did come. If it takes nothing out of me it will do nobody any good."

Service costs.

Someone asked John Wanamaker: "How do you get time to run a Sunday school for four thousand scholars, in addition to the business of your stores, your work as Postmaster General, and other obligations?" He replied, "Why, the Sunday school is by business! All the other things are just things. Forty-five years ago I decided that God's promise was sure: *Seek ye first the kingdom of God, and His righteousness; and all these things shall be added unto you* (Matthew 6:33).

Stories about stewardship abound...but what about our stewardship? We may find it thrilling to glory in all that God is doing through others but the accomplishments of our friends or heroes will not be of any value to us at the Judgment Seat of Christ. Each one must give an account of himself. Seize the day for Jesus.

FOOLS FOR CHRIST

MEMORY VERSE: *We are fools for Christ's sake, but ye are wise in Christ; we are weak, but ye are strong; ye are honourable, but we are despised* (1 Corinthians 4:10).

Paul had been a man of position before his conversion to Christ. Now, as a servant of the Lord, he often suffered because of his faith. Wava Campbell has enlarged upon this message in her poem:

THE WALK WITH GOD
The walk with God is a lonely walk,
For few believers care
To tread the rough and rugged path
Of service, love, and prayer.
And few will leave their pleasures,
And the silly toys of earth
To seek the things that matter most,
That have eternal worth.
The walk with God is a lonely walk,
For then, and then alone,
Will others judge your motives
And claim you seek your own.
The walk with God is a lonely walk,
But fellowship is sweet,
And only on that lonesome road
Is rest and joy complete.
The world may choose to shun me,
And think of me as odd,
But I will walk that lonesome road
In fellowship with God.

...Wava Campbell

THE OLD LEAVEN

MEMORY VERSE: *Purge out therefore the old leaven, that ye may be a new lump, as ye are unleavened. For even Christ our passover is sacrificed for us* (1 Corinthians 5:7).

In the Bible, leaven symbolizes sin.

Christians are new creatures in Christ and ought to demonstrate this by righteous living: *Therefore if any man be in Christ, he is a new creature: old things are passed away; behold, all things are become new* (2 Corinthians 5:17).

One cannot sin and win.

When Chrysostom was arrested by the Roman Emperor, the powerful ruler tried to make Chrysostom recant, but without success. Frustrated, the Emperor questioned his advisors about what could be done with the prisoner.

"Shall I put him in a dungeon?" the Emperor asked.

"No," one of his counselors replied, "for he will be glad to go. He longs for quietness wherein he can delight in the mercies of his God."

"Then he shall be executed!" said the Emperor.

"No," was the answer, "for he will also be glad to die. He declares that in the event of death he will be in the presence of his Lord."

"What shall we do then?" the ruler asked.

"There is only one thing that will give Chrysostom pain," the counselor said. "To cause Chrysostom to suffer, make him sin. He is afraid of nothing except sin."

Sin brings suffering.

Christians are equipped for daily victory over sin.

Purge out the old leaven.

You've been defeated long enough.

TAKE WRONG

MEMORY VERSE: *Now therefore there is utterly a fault among you, because ye go to law one with another. Why do ye not rather take wrong? why do ye not rather suffer yourselves to be defrauded* (1 Corinthians 6:7).

Here is a forgotten verse. Few obey its teaching. But think of the conflicts that would be settled if a revival would bring this verse into daily experience. Lawsuits would be dropped. Feuds would be ended. Church quarrels would be forgotten.

Meditate on these life changing questions: *Why do ye not rather take wrong? why do ye not rather suffer yourselves to be defrauded?*

Most professing Christians react just like the world reacts: demanding their rights. No wonder so few are moved to salvation by observing Christians in action.

How will your life change if you decide to take wrong and allow yourself to be defrauded?

Will you drop a lawsuit?

Will you forget an old debt?

Will you forego sending a blistering letter?

Will you be reconciled to one who has wronged you?

Will you stop fighting over an inheritance?

Will you stop telling your sob story about being cheated by others?

Notice Paul's interesting advice. He says certain Christians at Corinth are defrauding others by not allowing themselves to be defrauded.

How so?

When we react in the flesh...demanding our rights...we defraud those who are watching our lives and hoping to find an example of genuine Christian living.

Stop defrauding those who need your witness....take wrong...thankfully.

April 11   1 Corinthians 6:12-20

LIBERTY

MEMORY VERSE: *All things are lawful unto me, but all things are not expedient: all things are lawful for me, but I will not be brought under the power of any* (1 Corinthians 6:12).

We are saved by grace...not by works. Even law keeping fails in gaining or keeping salvation. When the Galatian Christians became confused on this issue, Paul reminded them of their liberty in Christ: *Stand fast therefore in the liberty wherewith Christ hath made us free, and be not entangled again with the yoke of bondage* (Galatians 5:1).

Nevertheless, there are limits on Christian liberty.

Christian liberty is limited by love. Paul declares that all things are lawful but all things are not expedient...helpful...profitable. Christians limit their liberty so as to be helpful to others...to help along brothers or sisters in Christ.

What should you leave out of your life for the sake of others?

What should you decline in order to keep from being a stumbling block to young converts?

Do weaker ones fall because you demand unbridled liberty?

Paul adds that his liberty is limited by anything that might bring him under its power. Claiming liberty in order to partake of something that enslaves is a contradiction...hypocritical. Those who take part in social drinking need to read this vital verse again. Any enslaving agent is outside the bounds of Christian liberty.

Christian liberty frees us to live for Christ and others.

Limit liberty with love.

HUSBANDS AND WIVES

MEMORY VERSE: *For what knowest thou, O wife, whether thou shalt save thy husband? or how knowest thou, O man, whether thou shalt save thy wife?* (1 Corinthians 7:16).

The Bible contains common sense advice for married people that makes happy homes and lasting marriages. Husbands and wives are to give of themselves to one another unselfishly. Each one is to live for the other with neither holding back in showing affection and love.

Writing on this text many years ago, Dr. Oswald J. Smith explained: "Your body, God says, is not your own. You thought it was. You withheld it when you should have given it. Husband and wife are one. That body of yours belongs to your husband and his to you, so both have privileges that neither has any right to deny. Have you learned to yield? If there is love, you will."

He continues: "You say you are too busy, too weary, and too old. Too busy for love? Too weary to express your affection? Too old to yield yourself to the one who loves to hold you in his arms and enjoy your response? Too cold to appreciate the touch of a lover's hand and to express a little of the affection of your heart?"

What searching questions! How will you answer them?

And there is another dimension to these responsibilities. The Christian husband or wife who is faithful and responsive may win an unbelieving mate to Christ. Christians are not to leave unbelievers because the continued contact is liable to result in the conversion of the one who is lost.

How are things at home?

Try living the Bible way.

The results will be heaven in your home...and your witness may reach your loved one so that some day you will share the joys of heaven.

NOT THE SERVANTS OF MEN

MEMORY VERSE: *Ye are bought with a price; be not ye the servants of men* (1 Corinthians 7:23).

Every Christian has a relationship with Christ that transcends his earthly position. Though he is a servant, in Christ he is free. And even though he is free, he is the servant of Christ. In view of this, a child of God can endure difficulties; his private walk with Christ enabling him to look beyond his present circumstances.

Many have difficult home situations.

Christ can give strength to endure.

Some have employment surroundings that are trying.

Christ can give strength to endure.

Health problems can make life hard to bear.

Christ can give strength to endure.

Financial problems may oppress.

Christ can give strength to endure.

No matter how distressing the Christian finds the view about him, he can be certain of safety because his Lord will care for him. One glance toward Calvary will remind him that he will never be forsaken. He belongs to his Lord, having been bought with the price of the ages: *Forasmuch as ye know that ye were not redeemed with corruptible things, as silver and gold, from your vain conversation received by tradition from your fathers; But with the precious blood of Christ, as of a lamb without blemish and without spot* (1 Peter 1:18,19).

Storms may sweep about the child of God but his Lord is over all and even the winds and the waves obey Him. When all seems lost, Jesus will speak peace.

Stand true...you are not a servant of men.

April 14   1 Corinthians 8

STUMBLINGBLOCKS

MEMORY VERSE: *But take heed lest by any means this liberty of yours become a stumblingblock to them that are weak* (1 Corinthians 8:9).

This chapter raises an interesting question of conduct. The Christians in Corinth were facing the issue of whether or not to eat meat that had been offered to heathen idols. There was nothing wrong with the meat and it was often priced very reasonably. What was the proper attitude for the church?

In his book, *Studies in First Corinthians*, Dr. M. R. DeHaan sums up Paul's answer as follows: "The question then is never, Have I a right to do this or that, or is this or that in itself a sin? But the question is, Does my conduct glorify God, and does it help or hinder my testimony, and is it a help or a stumblingblock to my weaker brethren? This, then, would at once settle the question of amusements, dress, business practices, and games, and all our Christian privileges. The Lord lays down the rule specifically: *And whatsoever ye do in word or deed, do all in the name of the Lord Jesus* (Colossians 3:17).

"That is the test by which we are to evaluate everything which is of a questionable nature. It is not a matter of legality, but a matter of honestly facing the question, Is this thing which we are doing to the glory of God, and is it a help or hindrance to those round about us?"

Not one of us will have to deal with the question of eating meat that has been offered to idols in heathen temples. That was a question pertaining especially to Paul's day and to a particular area. But every decision concerning Christian conduct requires the same basic question. Is this thing to the glory of God, and is it a help or hindrance to others?

Facing a decision about conduct? Give it the "stumblingblock" test.

PAY FOR PREACHERS

MEMORY VERSE: *If we have sown unto you spiritual things, is it a great thing if we shall reap your carnal things?* (1 Corinthians 9:11).

A secretary of a British Missionary Society called on a Calcutta merchant and asked him to help in the work. He wrote a check for $250 and handed it to the visitor. At that moment a cablegram was brought in. The merchant read it and looked troubled. "This cablegram" he said, "tells me that one of my ships has been wrecked and the cargo lost. It makes a very large difference in my affairs. I shall have to write you another check."

The secretary understood perfectly and handed back the check for $250. The checkbook was still open and the merchant wrote another check and handed it to him. He read it with amazement. It was for $1,000. "Haven't you made a mistake?" the secretary asked. "No," said the merchant, "I haven't made a mistake." And then, with tears in his eyes, he said, "That cablegram was a message from my Father in heaven. It read, *Lay not up for yourselves treasures upon earth* (Matthew 6:19).

Most understand the importance of giving but some wonder whether gifts given to the work of Christ should ever be donated to pastors, missionaries, or evangelists. Should ministers of the gospel be paid?

Paul puts the question to rest. He explains that the principle of sharing gifts given to the Lord with the servants of the Lord was true in the Old Testament and that this practice is to be continued in the age of grace.

Giving is spiritual...a part of Christian service.

Remember that a part of your giving is to go to those who minister to you.

Support God's man so that he can serve well.

God will honor your gifts of love.

WOE IS ME!

MEMORY VERSE: *For though I preach the gospel, I have nothing to glory of: for necessity is laid upon me; yea, woe is unto me, if I preach not the gospel* (1 Corinthians 9:16).

Paul couldn't keep from preaching.

Jeremiah had the same problem. One day he became so discouraged that he declared he was all through speaking for the Lord but he couldn't keep his resolution. Hear him: *Then I said, I will not make mention of him, nor speak any more in his name. But his word was in mine heart as a burning fire shut up in my bones, and I was weary with forbearing, and I could not stay* (Jeremiah 20:9).

Many have been called to preach and have disobeyed God's call. Often later in life they have been filled with regret, having missed out on God's will for their lives.

Preaching the gospel is the most important work on earth. All other occupations deal with temporal things. Preaching the gospel deals with eternal issues.

Not all preaching is reserved for pastors or evangelists. Phillip was an officer in the Early Church but was a powerful preacher. Actually every Christian is charged to carry the gospel to others and in that sense has a preaching responsibility and opportunity.

If God has called you to preach...preach.

If your responsibility in the work of Christ is to teach a Sunday school class...teach.

If God has called you to a ministry of organization or tract distribution...carry out His will in your life.

Be so surrendered to the Holy Spirit that you know what He wants you to do and so dedicated that you must carry out His commission.

In the Christian life, "Go" or "Woe" are the choices for us all.

DISCIPLINE

MEMORY VERSE: *But I keep under my body, and bring it into subjection: lest that by any means, when I have preached to others, I myself should be a castaway* (1 Corinthians 9:27).

Paul was like a man in training...ever prepared to give his best in the race. He understood that this demanded discipline...self-control. But he wanted the prize and counted all sacrifices worthwhile. Eternal rewards meant more to him than momentary gratification. Until we come to this same conviction, we are poor candidates for victory in the race of life.

In his letter to the Philippians, Paul again alludes to his effort in the race: *Brethren, I count not myself to have apprehended: but this one thing I do, forgetting those things which are behind, and reaching forth unto those things which are before, I press toward the mark for the prize of the high calling of God in Christ Jesus* (Philippians 3:13,14).

Discipline holds an important place in the successful Christian life. It is essential in maintaining daily Bible reading. There will be times when one does not feel like reading; times when some relaxing pastime appeals right at the time for personal devotions. But no one can have victory over sin without a regular intake of God's Word. Discipline takes the tempted one to his Bible where he can receive the life-giving milk and meat that provides spiritual health.

Consistency in prayer comes through discipline. How glibly we recite our learned prayers and then wonder why answers do not come!

Discipline demands regular attendance at the services of the church where fellowship and Bible teaching combine to develop the abundant life.

We all need discipline to guarantee spiritual growth.

April 18   1 Corinthians 10:1-12

DANGER ZONE

MEMORY VERSE: *Wherefore let him that thinketh he stand-eth take heed lest he fall* (1 Corinthians 10:12).

Temptation is always a danger.

Pride prepares us for falling into temptation's trap.

Dr. Vance Havner said: "We are a generation of proud, fussy little Christians—experts but not examples. We know too much, or we think we do. We have heard all the preachers and read all the books. It is hard these days to be converted and become like little children. We want to be thought philosophers and scholars—brilliant but not childlike. So we miss the secrets God has hidden from the wise and prudent and revealed unto babes. How often, even among the saints does some simple soul learn the deeper things of God and press through to heaven's best while 'the wise and the prudent' utterly miss them!"

We never outgrow the peril of pride.

And temptation besets us all.

An elderly man asked a boy to go with him into the woods to cut down some hickory trees to make ax handles. They soon came to several young hickory trees and the boy suggested that they cut them down. The old man said, "These trees in the lowlands have been protected from the storms which rage higher up. Let's go to the heights where the trees have been rocked back and forth by fierce winds. Those trees have been hardened by the tempest and they will make much stronger ax handles."

The tempests that bend us may be part of God's great plan to make us strong. In bending low, we see the folly of pride and learn to look to the Lord in times of trouble.

Do you think you have arrived?

If so, you are in the danger zone.

Look to Jesus for protection when temptation comes your way.

TEMPTATION'S LIMIT

MEMORY VERSE: *There hath no temptation taken you but such as is common to man: but God is faithful, who will not suffer you to be tempted above that ye are able; but will with the temptation also make a way to escape, that ye may be able to bear it* (1 Corinthians 10:13).

Two alcoholics were converted. One testified, "From the moment I trusted Christ to save me, and deliver me from the enslaving habit of strong drink, I have never had the slightest desire to drink anything of alcoholic content. I would have to learn all over again to love the evil which, for more than thirty years, was the greatest love of my life." The second said, "How I wish my experience corresponded with the experience of the brother who has just testified. Every day I have a terrific struggle not to partake of the evil which for years all but wrecked my life. I am depending solely upon the mighty Saviour to keep me from temptation. Pray for me!"

God may deal differently with His children concerning temptation but He has promised that all temptation is limited. Every Christian can overcome any temptation. Our Lord guarantees our ability to conquer is greater than temptation's power. He allows no temptation to come to us that is too strong for us to defeat. And He always provides an escape.

So, your excuse for yielding doesn't stand.

The power of the Holy Spirit within and the Word of God at your disposal equips you to conquer. Prayer taps the resources of God making you invincible.

Others have faced the same temptation.

And you are equipped to win.

TO THE GLORY OF GOD

MEMORY VERSE: *Whether therefore ye eat, or drink, or whatsoever ye do, do all the glory of God* (1 Corinthians 10:31).

Here's a rule that governs conduct,
        that brings peace of mind,
        that is unselfish,
        that defeats pride,
        that sanctifies motives,
        that cultivates humility,
        that eliminates hypocrisy,
        that builds faith,
        that increases thankfulness,
        that changes priorities,
        that settles arguments:
        do all to the glory of God.
Here's a rule that gives a song,
        that conquers depression,
        that fosters unity,
        that promotes revival,
        that produces praise,
        that destroys divisions,
        that brings rewards,
        that brightens a home:
        do all to the glory of God.
Here's a rule you can use today; a rule that will take your burdens away; a rule that is right whatever men say; a rule that is proper at home or away: DO ALL TO THE GLORY OF GOD!

April 21   1 Corinthians 11:1-17

FOR BETTER OR WORSE?

MEMORY VERSE: *Now in this that I declare unto you I praise you not, that ye come together not for the better, but for the worse* (1 Corinthians 11:17).

Coming together in the local church meetings should always be edifying. In Corinth, there were so many divisions and so much backsliding that their meetings were unprofitable. Many were worse for their coming.

Today, with so much emphasis on organization and buildings, we are apt to forget that the Church is made up of people. Buildings are only meeting places for the Church. And when the Church meets, Christ should be honored and His people strengthened in the faith. Wava Campbell has written:

THE PERFECT CHURCH
I care not if your church is long or square,
But is the name of Jesus honored there?
I care not if it's made of brick or stone,
But do its members live for Christ alone?
No lovely stained glass window can compare
With the beauty of a house of fervent prayer;
Give me a church that sends o'er land and sea
The Word, the life, that sets the sinner free.

If your church is not all it ought to be, perhaps you are the key to change. Revival may rest in your hands. Are you the one to forgive old wrongs? Are you the one to lead the way?

All Christians are commanded to attend their local church regularly (see Hebrews 10:25). Do your part to make the meetings profitable.

COMMUNION

MEMORY VERSE: *And when he had given thanks, he brake it, and said, Take, eat: this is my body, which is broken for you: this do in remembrance of me* (1 Corinthians 11:24).

Salvation does not come through taking Communion. This Christian experience is, rather, the celebration of sins forgiven through the death of Christ on the cross.

The Communion service looks both backward and forward. In it we look back to the cross and ahead to His return: *For as often as ye eat this bread, and drink this cup, ye do shew the Lord's death till he come* (1 Corinthians 11:26).

This ordinance is one of joy and judgment.

We rejoice in the great love of God that has caused Him to send His Son to die for us. We anticipate meeting our Saviour. We feel the warmth of Christian fellowship, and thank God for "the tie that binds our hearts in Christian love."

Yet there is a solemn note to this sacred time. We are to judge ourselves. A stern warning accompanies the instruction for communion: *Wherefore whosoever shall eat this bread, and drink this cup of the Lord, unworthily, shall be guilty of the body and blood of the Lord* (1 Corinthians 11:27).

Frightening? Yes, if we must become worthy through our own spiritual accomplishment. Thank God that is not the case. While we have all failed in many ways, we become worthy in Christ. Each Christian must judge himself and confess his sins to Christ (see 1 Corinthians 11:31). In confession spiritual communion is restored, and the ordinance of communion can be shared. *If we confess our sins, he is faithful and just to forgive us our sins, and to cleanse us from all unrighteousness* (1 John 1:9).

April 23   1 Corinthians 12:1-12

DIFFERENCES

MEMORY VERSE: *Now there are diversities of gifts, but the same Spirit* (1 Corinthians 12:4).

Christians do not all have the same gifts. And much harm has been done by some members trying to copy the ministry of others rather than using their own gifts. The consequence is often frustration and fruitlessness.

When I was a boy I lived on a grain and dairy farm. The soil was heavy and quite fertile and usually produced fine crops. Even when the summer was very dry, our fields looked comparatively green and healthy because the soil retained moisture so well. A few miles west of our farm, nearer Lake Michigan, the soil was light and sandy. There the farming was very poor, especially during a dry season. Many summers the corn browned and curled, a discouraging sight for the struggling farmers who lived there.

Today, however, this area is a prosperous farming community, which ships its produce to many distant places. It is one of the most productive blueberry areas in the United States.

The secret of this agricultural success story was simply planting a crop for which the soil and climate were well-suited. And that is a good lesson for life.

If you want to be effective as a member of the body of Christ, serve with the gifts that God has given to you. Stop trying to be someone else. Diversity is part of God's wonderful plan.

Consult with your pastor about a work in your church for which you are gifted. Determine to use what God has given you for His glory. Though your service may differ from your most admired Christian worker, do not be discouraged. God delights in diversity. You are special to Him.

April 24   1 Corinthians 12:13-31

WE NEED EACH OTHER

MEMORY VERSE: *And the eye cannot say unto the hand, I have no need of thee: nor again the head to the feet, I have no need of you* (1 Corinthians 12:21).

Christians need each other. There is no room for carnal rivalry in the body of Christ. We have been commissioned to take the gospel to the world and there is work for all to do.

Paul drives this message home in seeking to squelch the discord among the Christians in Corinth. He reminds his readers that every member of the human body is important. We do not choose one part over another but are grateful for every part. This should also be true in the Church.

Does some member or the work of some member of your church seem insignificant?

Have you been looking down on someone in your fellowship?

Ask the Lord to forgive you. The root of your problem is pride.

Perhaps you have no problem in looking down on others but you feel that your own work is unimportant. You continually put yourself down, thinking your gifts are few and practically useless. You suffer from low self-esteem. You think the work of Christ would move on just as well without you.

How sad.

Your outward humility is not humility at all but rebellion against the all-wise God who gave you life and gifted you according to His will. Thank God for His blessings and for making you the person you are. Say with Paul, *But by the grace of God I am what I am* (1 Corinthians 15:10).

THE GREATEST OF THESE

MEMORY VERSE: *And now abideth faith, hope, charity, these three; but the greatest of these is charity* (1 Corinthians 13:13).

No one would question the importance of love in the Christian life. Love is the very heart of the gospel. The good news is that God loves us and has given His Son for our salvation.

There is, however, another side to this love story. John puts it well: *Beloved, if God so loved us, we ought also to love one another* (1 John 4:11).

Simple, you say?

Perhaps. Yet sometimes difficult.

To live above with saints in love
Will be eternal glory;
To live below with saints we know
Is quite another story.

What will happen to our relationships with other Christians if we allow the love of Christ to rule in our hearts?

We will be quick to forgive. We will be slow to wrath. We will be careful with our words. We will shut our ears to gossip and grumbling. We will want to share our blessings. We will find it more blessed to give than to receive.

And that's only the beginning! The Lord will continually give opportunities to show His love to others.

By this shall all men know that ye are my disciples, if ye have love one to another (John 13:35).

D. L. Moody said: "There are two ways of being united—frozen together, and melted together. What Christians need most is to be united in brotherly love."

Amen, Mr. Moody. Amen!

HOLY SPIRIT POWER FOR BELIEVERS

MEMORY VERSE: *But ye shall receive power, after that the Holy Ghost is come upon you: and ye shall be witnesses unto me both in Jerusalem, and in all Judaea, and in Samaria, and unto the uttermost part of the earth* (Acts 1:8).

Power is released in a Christian as the indwelling Holy Spirit is allowed to take full control. Do not misunderstand—every saved person has the Holy Spirit indwelling him. [We] *have been all made to drink into one Spirit* (1 Corinthians 12:13). All means ALL. In fact, it is correct to say that it is impossible to be a child of God if one does not have the Holy Spirit, for *if any man have not the Spirit of Christ, he is none of his* (Romans 8:9).

While it is true that every believer has the Holy Spirit (and has all of Him, for He does not enter in percentage portions), this does not guarantee that He has all of us. Therefore, subsequent to salvation, every believer needs the filling of the Spirit. Ephesians 5:18 says, *Be filled with the Spirit.*

When one is filled, power for witnessing will be evident so that one may win the lost to Christ...*ye shall receive power, after that the Holy Ghost is come upon you:* [the result] *and ye shall be witnesses unto me.* So seek the power the apostles had to witness as they bore ridicule, hatred, persecution, and death for the Lord Jesus Christ.

April 27   1 Corinthians 14:18-40

CONFUSION

MEMORY VERSE: *For God is not the author of confusion, but of peace, as in all churches of the saints* (1 Corinthians 14:33).

God approves order. This is evident on every hand. Notice that the sun comes up in the East every day and sets in the West. Laws of the universe are so orderly and dependable that scientists can depend on them in conducting experiments. Mathematics as a science is unchanging because God has created an orderly universe.

How strange then that some think of God's order in the Church as being disorganized. The Church and the life that moves in the perfect will of God is characterized by order as well as power.

The Corinthian church conducted disorderly meetings. And their members lived disorderly lives. Paul urged them to put away their differences (*in malice be ye children*) and to lay down some rules for worship. *Let all things be done decently and in order*, he pleads.

Perhaps your life is disorderly. You have somehow con- cluded that by never making a firm decision you are following the leading of the Lord. Nothing could be further from the truth. It is true that there are times for waiting and seeking God's will, but when His will is clear it is time to act. God does not intend that we dwell forever in a state of confusion. *God is not the author of confusion, but of peace.* And life that is cluttered cannot know real peace.

Begin today to organize your life. Set up a schedule for devotions and for your daily responsibilities. Settle on God's will for your life and do it. You've been indecisive long enough.

Set some goals. Chart a course.

God will guide you all the way.

April 28   1 Corinthians 15:1-27

THE GOSPEL

MEMORY VERSE: *For I delivered unto you first of all that which I also received, how that Christ died for our sins according to the scriptures; And that he was buried, and that he rose again the third day according to the scriptures* (1 Corinthians 15:3,4).

Many are confused about the gospel.

Paul ends the confusion by stating that gospel clearly.

We are commissioned to preach the gospel.

Dr. George Truett wrote: "The superintendent of a city cemetery lived in a small cottage just inside the cemetery gate through which entered several funeral processions daily. 'Does not this daily scene of sadness get on your nerves and interfere with your sleep?' someone asked the superintendent. 'Oh, no,' he said. 'When I first began to work here, I often could not sleep, and when I did drop off to sleep, it was a fitful, restless sleep. I seemed to see the endless processions, and the caskets of all lengths. Now I have become so hardened to these things that I could lie down and sleep soundly in the midst of the tombstones!'

"Was there a time in your experience when the preaching of the simple gospel of the grace of God set aglow God's love in your heart and made you dissatisfied with the smallness of your sacrifice and service for Christ? Have the 'spirit of the times' and the 'cares of this life' blunted the keen sensitive edge you formerly had for the things of God?"

What are your answers to Dr. Truett's questions?

What does the gospel mean to you?

Do you care about others hearing it?

Have you become hardened to the greatest news on earth?

April 29   1 Corinthians 15:27-58

BE STEDFAST

MEMORY VERSE: *Therefore, my beloved brethren, be ye stedfast, unmoveable, always abounding in the work of the Lord, forasmuch as ye know that your labour is not in vain in the Lord* (1 Corinthians 15:58).

It has been said that when the word "therefore" appears in the Bible one should always consider what it is there for. Here, this word looks back to all the truths just presented and in view of them calls for faithful service for Christ.

Because Christ is risen, be *stedfast, unmoveable, always abounding in the work of the Lord.*

Because Christ is coming to raise the Christian dead and catch away His bride, be *stedfast, unmoveable, always abounding in the work of the Lord.*

To be *stedfast* is "to be firm in your own convictions." To be *unmoveable* is "to be firm against the influences of others." The Pulpit Commentary says: "There are some works of the Lord in which we cannot engage. We cannot help to control the ocean, guide the stars, or even create a blade of grass, but here we are 'labourers together with Him.'"

What a privilege!

Let us stand firm against evil and abound in service for Christ.

He lives.

And He is coming again.

Our work for Jesus will not be in vain. When He comes He will reward all who have been *stedfast, unmoveable, and always abounding in the work of the Lord. And, behold, I come quickly; and my reward is with me, to give every man according as his work shall be* (Revelation 22:12).

THE OPEN DOOR

MEMORY VERSE: *For a great door and effectual is opened unto me, and there are many adversaries* (1 Corinthians 16:9).

One Sunday morning in 1856, a congregation of well-dressed people had been ushered to their rented pews in Chicago's Plymouth Congregational Church. Suddenly there was a commotion near the door. Many turned and looked. Something occurred which had never before been seen by that elite congregation. In walked a young man—a 19-year-old salesman. Following him was a poorly dressed group of people that he had gathered off the streets. The young man let them into four pews he had personally rented for the visitors. He continued to do this important work each Sunday until God called him into a world-wide ministry. His name was Dwight L. Moody.

God opens doors of service to those who are willing to serve. But there are always obstacles to overcome in the service of Christ.

Phillips Brooks said: "Oh, do not pray for easy lives. Pray to be strong men and women. Do not pray for tasks equal to your powers. Pray for powers equal to your tasks. Then the doing of your work will be no miracle; but you shall be a miracle. Every day you will wonder at yourself, at the richness of life which has come to you by the grace of God."

Has God opened a door of service for you?

What is holding you back?

Are there adversaries...problems...obstacles?

They are to be expected, but God is able.

The opportunity is brief—do not delay.

The prize is glorious—do not faint.

Walk through that open door.

May

THIS MONTH'S STUDY

The Tongue

Days 8,9,11,21,24,26,28,30, and 31 contain quotes or infor-mation from "Three Thousand Illustrations for Christian Ser-vice," "Knight's Master Book of New Illustrations," and "Knight's Treasury of Illustration" all by Walter B. Knight, pub-lished by Wm. B. Eerdmans Publishing Company, Grand Rapids, Michigan. Used by permission. Day 31 is from "Knight's Up-to-the-Minute Illustrations," published by Moody Press, Chicago, Illinois. Used by permission. Days 8,10,22,25, and 27 contain quotes or poems from "Let's Communicate," by Roger F. Campbell, published by Christian Literature Crusade, Fort Washington, Pennsylvania.

WHAT SHALL I SAY?

MEMORY VERSE: *And God said unto Moses, I AM THAT I AM: and he said, Thus shalt thou say unto the children of Israel, I AM hath sent me unto you* (Exodus 3:14).

A team of market researchers recently asked 3,000 people, "Of what are you the most afraid?" The number one fear was speaking before a group. Had the survey been conducted on the backside of the desert where Moses was tending sheep, the results would have been the same. When God called Moses to lead His people out of slavery, he doubted his ability as a speaker. "What shall I say unto them?" he asked.

Moses' question has been repeated through the centuries by those called upon to serve the Lord. Challenged to teach, many have asked, "What shall I say unto them?" Christians convicted about their responsibility to do visitation work in their communities have echoed the question. Young ministers facing their first preaching responsibilities have joined the chorus. Perhaps no question has ascended to heaven as often as this one. You may have voiced it this very week when preparing for some ministry in your church.

God's answer to Moses reveals that success in carrying out a mission depends more on the sender than on the speaker. And in every work of God—He is the sender. Moses would not go in his own strength nor by his own authority. He would be sent by the Eternal God.

We must remember that all Christian service is empowered by the One who said, *All power is given unto me in heaven and in earth* (Matthew 28:18).

Go to your task in confidence. You do not go alone.

You have been sent by the all-powerful One.

Approach your mission with assurance. Repeat these words: "The Lord has sent me to serve." He will tell you what to say!

NOT ELOQUENT

MEMORY VERSE: *And the LORD said unto him, Who hath made man's mouth? or who maketh the dumb, or deaf, or the seeing, or the blind? have not I the LORD?* (Exodus 4:11).

Moses wanted his people to be delivered from bondage, but when he was called to be the deliverer, he began to make excuses: "I am slow of speech, and of a slow tongue," he complained.

Many are like him!

They want the community evangelized—as long as they do not have to go to their neighbors with the gospel.

They long for the church to be filled each Sunday—as long as the pastor doesn't call on them to get involved in the visitation program.

They are in favor of revival in the land—as long as they do not have to give up their favorite sins.

They cry for a return of prayer and Bible reading to the classrooms of the land—but do not take time to read the Bible to their families.

They talk of the importance of missionary giving and complain because other churches have larger missionary budgets than their own—but they do not dare trust God for the future and selfishly hold back their own money rather than investing it in reaching the lost for Christ.

God had an answer for reluctant Moses. *Now therefore go, and I will be with thy mouth, and teach thee what thou shalt say* (Exodus 4:12). Moses obeyed and became part of the great miracle of the deliverance of his people. He was there to see the plagues fall on Egypt. He raised his rod and the Red Sea opened. He saw water flow from a rock and witnessed the feeding of his people with manna from heaven.

Because Moses obeyed God he witnessed the power of God in his life. Put away your excuses. God will use you today!

TALK

MEMORY VERSE: *And he answered and said, Must I not take heed to speak that which the LORD hath put in my mouth?* (Numbers 23:12).

Balaam said a lot of good things.

Too bad his walk didn't match his talk.

When Balaam was offered a bribe to come and curse Israel, he took a solid stand. Hear and admire him: *And Balaam answered and said unto the servants of Balak, If Balak would give me his house full of silver and gold, I cannot go beyond the word of the LORD my God, to do less or more* (Numbers 22:18). Some speech! Yet, the next morning he was on his way with the messengers of Balak to cooperate with the enemy.

Because Balaam was inconsistent, he became a symbol of disobedience. The Scofield Reference Bible says of Him: "Balaam was a typical hireling prophet, anxious only to make a market of his gift. This is the 'way' of Balaam." And what does the Bible say about the way of Balaam? *Which have forsaken the right way, and are gone astray, following the way of Balaam the son of Bosor, who loved the wages of unrighteousness* (2 Peter 2:15); and *Woe unto them! for they have gone in the way of Cain, and ran greedily after the error of Balaam for reward, and perished in the gainsaying of Core* (Jude 11), and again *But I have a few things against thee, because thou hast there them that hold the doctrine of Balaam, who taught Balac to cast a stumblingblock before the children of Israel, to eat things sacrificed unto idols, and to commit fornication* (Revelation 2:14).

Strong words!

Better not trifle with God!

Be sure that your walk measures up to your talk!

Order Rexella's book, *Mirror, Mirror, On the Wall, Who am I Fooling?*

THE GREAT PROPHET

MEMORY VERSE: *I will raise them up a Prophet from among their brethren, like unto thee, and will put my words in his mouth; and he shall speak unto them all that I shall command him* (Deuteronomy 18:18).

Commenting on this text, Matthew Henry said, "It is here promised concerning Christ, that there should come a Prophet, great above all prophets; by whom God would make known himself and His will to the children of men, more fully and clearly than He had ever done before...He should be like Moses, only above him. This Prophet is come, even JESUS: and is 'He that should come, and we are to look for no other.'"

When Jesus came, His hearers marveled at His words. He spoke with authority. They said of Him, *Never man spake like this man* (John 7:46).

He spoke to the wind and waves and they obeyed Him.

He spoke to the demons and they were subject to Him.

He spoke to little children when others thought He was too busy for them.

He spoke to lepers and made them clean—to the lame and made them whole.

He spoke to the dead and raised them to life again.

He spoke to the Samaritan woman at the well, breaking through the social barrier that divided the Jews from the Samaritans.

He spoke to a dying thief and guaranteed him Paradise.

He spoke words of forgiveness to the woman taken in adultery and rebuked her accusers.

He spoke to the weary and called them to rest.

Listen. Jesus is speaking today. Read the Bible to hear His voice. Obey it to experience the abundant life.

His Word will abide forever!

CHECK YOUR TONGUE

MEMORY VERSE: *Is there iniquity in my tongue? cannot my taste discern perverse things?* (Job 6:30).

The doctor may want to check your tongue to diagnose your physical condition. Job says the tongue check also reveals the condition of the heart toward God. If there is sin in one's heart it will show in the way he uses his tongue.

And the tongue has great potential for both good and evil.

A Greek philosopher asked his servant to provide the best dish possible. The servant prepared a dish of tongue, saying, "It is the best of all dishes, because with it we may bless and communicate happiness, dispel sorrow, remove despair, cheer the faint-hearted, inspire the discouraged, and say a hundred things to uplift mankind."

Later, the philosopher asked the servant to provide the worst dish possible. Again, the servant prepared a dish of tongue. The philosopher questioned his servant about his decision and received this answer: "It is the worst because with it we may curse and break human hearts, destroy reputations, promote discord and strife, set families, communities, and nations at war with each other."

Job invited his friends to check his tongue to see whether he was wicked or righteous. The condemnation of these supposed comforters moved this man of God to a challenge. Had they been able to determine that he was evil by this speech? He was confident that he could pass the tongue test.

How would you do in a checkup of your tongue? What would it reveal about your heart? Though you may not realize it, others are checking your tongue regularly. What will they conclude about your walk with God?

Are you starting to backslide? Check your tongue and see!

Read James chapter 3.

RESOLUTION

MEMORY VERSE: *My lips shall not speak wickedness, nor my tongue utter deceit* (Job 27:4).

In times of despair, many have lost control, saying things that violate their convictions. Job was determined not to allow that to happen to him. Though covered with boils and grieving the loss of home and family, he would not compromise his testimony. An acceptable excuse did not open the door to a flow of words that were inconsistent with Job's character.

The good man was even careful of speech when responding to his wife upon her suggestion that he curse God and die. Preachers and Bible teachers have often pounced on her statement to illustrate a lesson on frail faith or a critical attitude, but Job answered her tenderly. Taking into consideration her feelings in the loss of their loved ones and their wealth, Job said warmly, *Thou speakest as one of the foolish women speaketh* (Job 2:10). Note that this understanding husband did not call his wife a fool nor respond to her awful urging harshly. He was saying, "You're not yourself today. You're talking like one of the foolish women. And I know why. It's all this grief and pressure. But let's remember that God is in control."

Now while battered by the criticism of his self-appointed comforters, Job retains control of his tongue. Although their accusations have been false, he will not be shaken by them to the point of answering wickedly. His resolution to be faithful in his speech is an example to all.

Perhaps you are going through trials and this is affecting your conversation. Barriers of decency and pure speech have been falling. You've been given to pouting and complaining since the trouble began. Your language has become like of the the foolish ones.

Join Job. Let Christ control your tongue!

CONVICTION

MEMORY VERSE: *Behold, I am vile; what shall I answer thee? I will lay mine hand upon my mouth* (Job 40:4).

Confronted by the Lord, Job was convicted of his sin. *All have sinned, and come short of the glory of God* (Romans 3:23), and Job was no exception. Conviction is the result of comparing one's sinful self with absolute righteousness. This allows us to see ourselves as God sees us.

Isaiah responded much like Job when he was given a vision of the Lord. Hear him: *Then said I, Woe is me! for I am undone; because I am a man of unclean lips, and I dwell in the midst of a people of unclean lips: for mine eyes have seen the King, the LORD of hosts* (Isaiah 6:5).

You may have escaped conviction because you have been comparing yourself to others. Since they have shortcomings, you feel quite comfortable in the comparison. You measure up about as well as the next person. You are reasonably honest. You pay your bills. You take care of your family. You hold a respectable place in the community.

Sounds like you might make it to heaven.

Better look again! And this time look in the mirror supplied by the Lord—the Bible. There you will see yourself as God sees you. He will give you a glimpse of His holiness.

Now, what is your need?

Do you need to be saved? *Believe on the Lord Jesus Christ, and thou shalt be saved* (Acts 16:31). Then tell others of your salvation.

Are you a Christian but convicted of wrongs in your life? *If we confess our sins, he is faithful and just to forgive us our sins, and to cleanse us from all unrighteousness* (1 John 1:9).

What a good use for man's tongue! *Responding to God's conviction!*

BACKBITERS

MEMORY VERSE: *Lord...who shall dwell in thy holy hill? He that backbiteth not with his tongue, nor doeth evil to his neighbour, nor taketh up a reproach against his neighbour* (Psalm 15:1,3).

The dictionary says that backbiting means to slander an absent person or persons. The old sinful nature of man is easily lured into that trap.

When we criticize others we turn attention away from our own faults. At least we think so. However, Judge Harold Medina saw it another way. He said, "Criticizing others is a dangerous thing, not so much because you may make mistakes about them, but because you may be revealing the truth about yourself."

Oliver Wendell Holmes said, "The human race is divided into two classes—those who go ahead and do something and those who sit still and inquire why it wasn't done the other way."

If you find that someone has been criticizing you, don't ever let it defeat you. If the criticism is untrue, disregard it. If it is unfair, keep from irritation. If it is ignorant, smile. If it is justified, learn from it.

But how about those who eat away at others in your presence. What can you do about them? You will never escape them for the world is full of such little people. You must simply let them know that you disapprove of their backbiting. Refuse to listen to their tirades against others. Do not allow them to deposit their poisonous thoughts in your mind. Object to being a party to their sin.

The psalmist declares that those who are close to the Lord are not backbiters. Regardless of how righteous they may sound, backbiters need to get right with God!

PURPOSE

MEMORY VERSE: *Thou hast proved mine heart; thou hast visited me in the night; thou hast tried me, and shalt find nothing; I am purposed that my mouth shall not transgress* (Psalm 17:3).

John Wesley was preaching and wearing a new bow tie with two streamers hanging down from it. There was a sister in the meeting who didn't hear a word about Jesus, but sat with a long face and saw nothing but those two streamers.

When the service was over the critic went up to Wesley and said, "Pardon me, Mr. Wesley, will you allow me to give you a little criticism?"

"Yes," replied the preacher.

"Well," she said, "your bow tie is too long and it is an offense to me."

"Have you any shears?" asked Wesley.

Upon receiving a pair of shears from one in the gathering, Wesley handed them to the offended lady, saying that she would know best how to fix the tie.

Eagerly, she clipped off the streamers.

"Is that all right now?" asked Wesley.

"Yes," she said, "that is much better."

Then Wesley asked for the shears. "Would you mind me giving you a little criticism?" he asked. "Your tongue is a great offense to me—it is a little too long. Please stick it out while I take some off."

Many who self-righteously criticize outward things, are guilty of transgressing with their tongues. And according to the Bible, tongues are far more likely to offend the Lord than ties (see James 1:26).

Start the day with the psalmist's praiseworthy purpose: *I am purposed that my mouth shall not transgress.*

A PERFECT PRAYER

MEMORY VERSE: *Let the words of my mouth, and the medi-
tation of my heart, be acceptable in thy sight, O LORD, my
strength, and my redeemer* (Psalm 19:14).

The most dangerous beast in the world is the one that lives
in that den behind your teeth...your tongue!

James compares the tongue to a flame of fire. He warns that
it is full of wickedness and can poison every part of the body.

David prayed that the Lord would set a guard at his mouth:
*Set a watch, O LORD, before my mouth; keep the door of my
lips* (Psalm 141:3).

The tongue at its greatest potential is used to bring praise to
God. The dedicated Christian sings:

"Take my lips and let them move,
At the impulse of Thy love."

The Bible teaches that one of life's greatest contradictions is
to both praise God and curse men. In other words, it is the
height of hypocrisy to be given to both godliness and gossip.
Like oil and water, the two just do not mix.

Peter instructs us to lay aside all slanderings if we want to
mature in the Christian life (see 1 Peter 2:1,2).

If the use of your tongue is really that important to the Lord,
what guideline can you follow to be sure your words are
pleasing to Him?

A number of proverbs and sayings have been put together to
help us. One is:

"If your lips would keep from slips,
Five things observe with care:
Of whom you speak, to whom you speak,
And how and when and where."

But the best is given in the psalmist's perfect prayer contained in our memory verse. Let this be your prayer—today
and every day!

PRAISE THE LORD

MEMORY VERSE: *I will bless the LORD at all times: his praise shall continually be in my mouth* (Psalm 34:1).

In China, a missionary was living a defeated life. Everything seemed to be touched with sadness and although he prayed and prayed for months for victory over depression and discouragement, his life remained the same.

As a result, he decided to leave his work and go to an interior mission station and pray until victory came. He reached the place and was entertained in the home of a fellow missionary. On the wall hung a motto with these words, "Try Thanksgiving."

The words gripped his heart and he thought, "Have I been praying all this time and not praising?" He began to praise God and was so uplifted that instead of hiding away to pray and agonize for days, he immediately returned to his waiting flock to tell them that praise changes things. Wonderful blessings attended his simple testimony and the chains of depression that had bound others in his congregation were broken through praise.

And why shouldn't we praise God? He deserves it. He loves us. He has provided salvation for us. He promises to always be with us.

Praise is profitable.

You cannot pout and praise at the same time.

You cannot worry and praise at the same time.

You cannot grumble and praise at the same time.

You cannot give up and praise at the same time.

But you can rejoice and praise God at the same time.

Praise changes things!

GOOD TOPIC

MEMORY VERSE: *And my tongue shall speak of thy right-eousness and of thy praise all the day long* (Psalm 35:28).

Have you ever secretly longed to direct a great choir that was lifting voices in moving songs of praise? That must have been David's desire as he called for everyone to shout for joy and magnify the Lord for all His blessings.

Concluding the psalm, he says that his tongue will speak of the righteousness of the Lord all day long. In his book, *The Thousand Hours in Two Psalms*, Dr. Marion McHull wrote that the word translated "speak" here really means to croon. David is evidently not only urging others to lift their voices in songs of praise, but is saying that he is going to join the chorus and that the theme of his song will be the Lord's righteousness and praise.

God is so good that we could sing all day every day and never run out of reasons to continue singing. He has given life. He has loved us in spite of our sins. He has provided salvation. He works all things out for our good. He will take us to heaven at death. He will never leave us nor forsake us. His promises never fail.

Some look for reasons to cast doubt on the goodness of God, but the future will declare that their conclusions were the result of a lack of information. When we meet the Lord, we'll find that He has been completely righteous and we'll join in the song: *Blessing, and glory, and wisdom, and thanksgiving, and honour, and power, and might, be unto our God for ever and ever. Amen* (Revelation 7:12).

If you're tired of the problems of life, turn your thoughts to praise. Sing of His righteousness all the day long!

WISDOM AND JUSTICE

MEMORY VERSE: *The mouth of the righteous speaketh wisdom, and his tongue talketh of judgment* (Psalm 37:30).

This beloved psalm begins with two important words: *Fret not*. It ends with three words that are the key to carrying out the command: *Trust in him*.

There are a number of direct commands given in the psalm that have to do with faith in action: *Delight thyself also in the LORD* (vs. 4); *Commit thy way unto the LORD* (vs. 5); *Rest in the Lord* and *wait patiently for him* (vs. 7); and *Cease from anger* (vs. 8).

A heart that is conformed to these commands will be evidenced by a tongue that speaks of wisdom and justice. That's biblical: *A good man out of the good treasure of the heart bringeth forth good things: and an evil man out of the evil treasure bringeth forth evil things* (Matthew 12:35).

How the world needs to hear from those who can contribute wisdom! Theories abound for meeting the problems faced by the inhabitants of this imperiled planet. Hopes run high at seemingly successful moves toward peace and then are dashed by the inconsistencies of fallen men who seek their own profit rather than genuine justice.

But there are answers.

And they are found in the Bible.

Let us fill our minds with God's Word so that we have His wisdom to impart to troubled people. Though the world seems to be in chaos, God's plan is working out as scheduled. Christ will come and take His bride away. Following the seven years of Tribulation, He will come as King of Kings and will establish justice and peace.

Talk about it! Others need to hear.

THE BRIDLE

MEMORY VERSE: *I said, I will take heed to my ways, that I sin not with my tongue: I will keep my mouth with a bridle, while the wicked is before me* (Psalm 39:1).

Some things are better left unsaid, especially in the presence of those who are looking for some reason to doubt the reality of your faith in Christ. A watching world is far more likely to remember your lapse than your light. Christians are continually on display and careless words can spoil a testimony that has taken years to build.

A fit of anger can be forgiven at the moment you confess your sin to the Lord, but it will never be forgotten by those who witnessed your explosion. Your demand for your rights may seem perfectly justified but it would be far better to take wrong if your witness for Christ would be damaged by some indignant outburst.

Perhaps you remember a time when you lowered your standards of speech before others. You complained when you should have been thankful. You used near profanity to punctuate and emphasize an argument. You gave someone a piece of your mind over a trifle.

What can you do about it?

Probably nothing. Even apologies may accomplish little.

But you can bridle your tongue in the future. There are more important things than getting your way. If you are a Christian, you represent your Saviour. You are the best Christian somebody knows. Don't give the enemies of the Lord cause to rejoice.

When you feel like exploding, keep that bridle handy.

Don't disappoint Jesus by what you say.

Take heed...that you sin not with your tongue!

A NEW SONG

MEMORY VERSE: *And he hath put a new song in my mouth, even praise unto our God: many shall see it, and fear, and shall trust in the LORD* (Psalm 40:3).

Do you remember the pit? The one you were in when Christ saved you? You called and He answered. You came to Him and found that He would not cast you out. Your heart was overjoyed and you began to tell others about your Saviour. There was a new song in your mouth, even praise to your God.

But something has happened to your song.

Like many others, your most fruitful time of witnessing was right after your conversion. Your feet stood firm on the solid rock after having been lifted from the miry clay. You felt secure for the first time in your life. Your sins were gone and you knew it. Heaven was ahead and you rejoiced in it. All your old friends became prospects for witnessing. A number of them were saved as a result of your radiant testimony. You thought seriously about becoming a missionary, a pastor, a youth worker, or some other full-time Christian servant.

Then you began to take the Christian life for granted. Seeing others content to just go to church and take in without giving out, you concluded that must be a normal Christianity. Somehow, you settled down into a rut. Not the pit...but a rut. Now you're tired of living this way. You want to get back to the basics...reality...revival.

What can you do?

Glance back at the pit again. Don't dive in, but just remember what it was that Christ did to save you from that awful miry clay. He died for you...gave himself on the cross...shed His blood.

Now aren't you glad you're saved? If you are, start singing!

THE WRITER'S PEN

MEMORY VERSE: *My heart is inditing a good matter: I speak of the things which I have made touching the king: my tongue is the pen of a ready writer* (Psalm 45:1).

The psalmist begins here by saying that his heart is inditing a good matter, meaning his heart is overflowing (literally bubbling up) with good news. And no wonder. This is a psalm that prophecies the coming of Christ as King.

Doubts about that are erased by reading Hebrews 1:8,9 which repeat Psalm 45:6,7. See how they fit in the context of the book of Hebrews: *And again, when he bringeth in the firstbegotten into the world, he saith, And let all the angels of God worship him. And of the angels he saith, Who maketh his angels spirits, and his ministers a flame of fire. But unto the Son he saith, Thy throne, O God, is for ever and ever: a sceptre of righteousness is the sceptre of thy kingdom. Thou hast loved righteousness, and hated iniquity; therefore God, even thy God, hath anointed thee with the oil of gladness above thy fellows. And, Thou, Lord, in the beginning hast laid the foundation of the earth; and the heavens are the works of thine hands* (Hebrews 1:6-10).

This prophecy then—in the Psalms—declares the deity of Christ. Now we know why the psalmist said his heart was bubbling up with a good matter. He saw the truth of the incarnation and rejoiced in it.

Thrilled, he offers his tongue to the Lord and compares the availability of his tongue to tell the message to the pen of the ready writer. He is saying, "Here, Lord, use my tongue to get this message out to everyone."

How available are you?

THE WAY BACK

MEMORY VERSE: *Deliver me from bloodguiltiness, O God, thou God of my salvation: and my tongue shall sing aloud of thy righteousness* (Psalm 51:14).

Backsliders are silenced. Their testimonies are squelched. They feel unworthy to talk about the Lord to others. They ask, "Who am I?" Before they return to the Lord, their lives are barren—desert like. Hear David describe his feelings while in this condition: *When I kept silence, my bones waxed old through my roaring all the day long. For day and night thy hand was heavy upon me: my moisture is turned into the drought of summer* (Psalm 32:3,4).

But no one needs to dwell in that desert.

All backsliders are invited back to the open arms of Jesus.

Read David's description of his return: *I acknowledged my sin unto thee, and mine iniquity have I not hid. I said, I will confess my transgressions unto the LORD; and thou forgavest the iniquity of my sin* (Psalm 32:5). How blessed!

Psalm 51 is David's prayer of confession as he returns to the Lord. Note that he not only expected forgiveness but also knew that his song would return, as well as his usefulness: *Then will I teach transgressors thy ways; and sinners shall be converted unto thee* (Psalm 51:13).

Are you far from God? It is time now for you to rid yourself of that heavy load you have been carrying. Confess your sins to Christ and claim His forgiveness. Commit your life to Him and get busy in His service. Return to your church and let others know what has happened in your life!

Returning, your tongue will again sing aloud of His righteousness and love.

HIS FAITHFULNESS

MEMORY VERSE: *I will sing of the mercies of the LORD for ever: with my mouth will I make known thy faithfulness to all generations* (Psalm 89:1).

It is easy and natural to sing of the Lord's mercy and faithfulness when all is going well. But that is not the message of this psalm. Rather, the psalmist declares that he will use his tongue to magnify the Lord no matter what comes upon him. He will sing of God's mercies forever and will tell of His faithfulness to young and old.

To have that kind of consistent testimony, one must learn that God is sufficient even in difficult times. That is what Wava Campbell has expressed in her moving poem:

HIS GRACE IS SUFFICIENT FOR THIS
His grace is sufficient for this.
I wasn't quite sure it would be;
And often I've quaked at the thought
That this thing could happen to me.

But now in a special new way
I know He's enough, come what may;
This trial is surely not bliss,
But His grace is sufficient for this.

His grace is sufficient for this,
And therefore for other things too;
And so I can face without fear,
The things that He tells me to do.

Our Lord is unchanging. He always merciful, always faithful. Sing it forever. Tell it to all.

Sing and make melody to the Lord (see Ephesians 5:19).

PUBLIC HEARING

MEMORY VERSE: *I will greatly praise the LORD with my mouth; yea, I will praise him among the multitude* (Psalm 109:30).

The expression "greatly praise" does not occur anywhere else in the Psalms. It demonstrates an unusually strong feeling of thankfulness. David's heart is filled with praise and he is determined to find words to express his gratitude for God's goodness to him.

But he is not going to slip off to the mountains to yell his praise from peak to peak. Neither does he seek a quiet wooded spot where he can whisper his worship to the trees or to a rippling brook. David declares that he will praise God among the multitude. While we may sometimes need solitude, we must not abandon public worship.

Public worship is commanded in the Bible: *Not forsaking the assembling of ourselves together, as the manner of some is; but exhorting one another: and so much the more, as ye see the day approaching* (Hebrews 10:25). We have an obligation to God and to others to be in the place of public worship regularly. No one can stay strong and neglect the services of his local church.

One can praise God in singing with others in the congregation. Isn't it good that God has made music? And Christians have a song! It needs to be expressed in public worship. We should lift our voices with others who know the Lord and love to praise Him.

One can praise the Lord through a public testimony. When the opportunity is given, be one of the first to tell what God is doing in your life.

One can praise the Lord with his mouth in teaching the Bible to others. Use your knowledge of God's Word to help others grow.

Praise the Lord among the multitude.

CHRISTIAN CONVERSATION

MEMORY VERSE: *My tongue shall speak of thy word: for all thy commandments are righteousness* (Psalm 119:172).

Christians are often guilty of making conversation about everything but the Bible. Gatherings after church services may cover everything from sports to the faults of the preacher without ever getting around to sharing blessings from God's Word. Let's stop neglecting God's great Book.

THIS BOOK

This Book, whose words are God's own breath,
Tells me of Christ my Saviour's death;
I find within these pages dear
The message to remove my fear.
When troubles come in like a flood,
I think of how He shed His blood;
And then as at the Cross I look,
I give Him thanks for such a book.
This Book reveals the sins of man,
And yet unfolds God's wondrous plan,
It brings to all this fallen race
The message of God's love and grace.
So as I travel on my way,
In dark of night, or light of day,
I find that whether weak or strong,
This Book will give my heart a song.
The Bible, that's the book I mean,
The book that makes a man's life clean,
That plants God's message deep within,
Of Christ, who came to save from sin.

—Roger F. Campbell

CHRISTIAN JOY

MEMORY VERSE: *Then was our mouth filled with laughter, and our tongue with singing: then said they among the heathen, The LORD hath done great things for them* (Psalm 126:2).

Christian joy is a powerful witness.

One Sunday morning a man from Louisville, Kentucky, walked down a street in St. Louis, Missouri, trying to find a church to attend. The streets were rather deserted, but he saw a police officer; so he went up to him and said, "Officer, I'm a stranger in St. Louis and I want to go to church to worship. Could you suggest a place?"

The officer named a church and gave him directions to find it. The man thanked him and started to go; then suddenly he stopped, turned around, and said, "By the way, officer, there must be several churches on your beat. Why have you named this particular one?"

The officer said, "I'll tell you why! I'm not a very religious man; I'm not a church man. There are several churches on my beat. I'm sending you to this one because I've observed for years that the people who come out of that church are the happiest looking church people in St. Louis!"

Probably no one in that congregation realized that his outward evidence of Christian joy had influenced the officer. Yet a visitor came to the church that Lord's Day because he had been told that the joy of the Lord was there.

Nehemiah knew the power of this neglected area and wrote: *For the joy of the LORD is your strength* (Nehemiah 8:10).

So, what do you talk about? Burdens or blessings? Troubles or triumphs? Clouds or sunshine? Roadblocks or opportunities?

Your daily conversation will impress someone. Will your listeners today say, "God is at work in that life"?

A GOOD WORD

MEMORY VERSE: *Heaviness in the heart of man maketh it stoop: but a good word maketh it glad* (Proverbs 12:25).

Recently I read a letter of appreciation from a Christian friend. I cannot tell you how much that kind word meant to me. I was lifted and encouraged.

There are too many times in life that I have not taken time to give a good word to others when it was in order. How easy it is to take one another for granted.

A wife keeps her house in order for years and her husband just expects it to be that way. He seldom takes her in his arms to whisper words of appreciation. What a waste of opportunity!

A husband and father labors hard and provides for his family. Finally, after life is past, the children gather at his funeral to talk about what a good man he was. That's too late! There were a thousand times when one of those kind comments would have rebuilt his confidence and recharged his vitality.

A family works in the church. He serves on the board. She teaches and sings in the choir. They are faithful in their place at every opportunity. Then, one day they are gone. Why? They've decided to try another church. Diagnosis? Discouragement! A good word might have improved their service and kept the fires burning in their hearts.

We are all just human enough to need a good word once in a while. Heaviness comes to all from time to time. Smiles may cover inner turmoil and depression. That seemingly radiant person who works next to you may be hiding a burdened heart.

Lift a stooping heart. Give a good word to someone you meet today.

A WHOLESOME TONGUE

MEMORY VERSE: *A wholesome tongue is a tree of life: but perverseness therein is a breach in the spirit* (Proverbs 15:4).

A wholesome tongue heals.

A perverse tongue wounds.

Dr. H. A. Ironside wrote: "How much more common is the tongue of perversity than the healing tongue! The one separates brother from brother, and makes breach upon breach; the other binds together, giving cheer and gladness, and is a tree of life to those who meditate upon its utterances. The healing tongue is the tongue of the peacemaker. The perverse tongue belongs to him who sows discord among brethren. May it be ours to covet the former and flee the latter."

What does a peacemaker do?

He forgets the gossip that he hears about others.

When the faults of his friends become the topic of discussion, he maneuvers the conversation to another subject.

When he hears something negative about another, he doesn't feel it his duty to report what was said.

When he is approached by two who are at odds, he refuses to allow his ear to become a dumping ground for criticism.

When he hears a complimentary comment concerning someone, he is eager to pass the good word along.

He is willing to meditate between those who are in a disagreement.

He has understanding about the weaknesses of all people, but doesn't major on them.

He would rather discuss ideas or events than people.

He is *swift to hear, slow to speak, slow to wrath* (James 1:19).

A spiritual person is a peacemaker.

Blessed are the peacemakers!

May 24   Proverbs 16:1-11

WHO HAS THE ANSWER?

MEMORY VERSE: *The preparations of the heart in man, and the answer of the tongue, is from the LORD* (Proverbs 16:1).

Too many never witness for Christ because they are afraid that when the opportunity comes they will not know what to say. Openings to speak or teach are refused and confrontations with those who have questions about the Bible are avoided for fear of becoming speechless at the crucial moment.

Relax.

The One within you has the answer. And He will give it to you when you need it. Even in difficult times, Christians are promised words for the occasion: *And when they bring you unto the synagogues, and unto magistrates, and powers, take ye no thought how or what thing ye shall answer, or what ye shall say: For the Holy Ghost shall teach you in the same hour what ye ought to say* (Luke 12:11,12).

Bible verses may be difficult to remember. You've studied the Bible for years but shrink from engaging in conversation about it because you don't want to appear ignorant of the Scriptures. Consider this thrilling promise concerning the work of the Holy Spirit: *But the Comforter, which is the Holy Ghost, whom the Father will send in my name, he shall teach you all things, and bring all things to your remembrance, whatsoever I have said unto you* (John 14:26). Step out in faith and see what the Lord does through you.

There is one important requirement.

The heart must be right.

All opportunities to speak for Christ call for prepared hearts. Is your heart right with God? Have you confessed all known sin to Him? Are you grieving the Holy Spirit? Are you quenching the Holy Spirit?

If your heart is right, speak up! The Lord will speak through you.

SPEAKING TO GOD

MEMORY VERSE: *Call unto me, and I will answer thee, and shew thee great and mighty things, which thou knowest now* (Jeremiah 33:3).

Five men were entrapped in a spar and zinc mine in Salem, Kentucky. They had nothing to eat and were in utter darkness. One of the men could have escaped had he not run back to warn the others.

When the entombed men discovered that they could not escape, they began to pray and sing. Their prayer and praise service lasted for fifty-three hours. Then they were rescued.

After the ordeal, one of the men said, "We lay there from Friday morning till Sunday morning. We prayed without ceasing. When the rescuers reached us, we were still praying."

When the men were brought up out of the mine, on the caps of each one were scrawled these words: "If we are dead when you find us, we are all saved."

God answered the prayers of the desperate miners. Undoubtedly many relatives and friends were also praying for their rescue. Reflecting on their experience, they must have felt they had used their time and tongues wisely...praying and singing praises to God.

But a question rises: "What would they have been talking about had the emergency not occurred?" And that begs another, "What miracles are missed because we do not pray?"

Had those miners used the same amount of time praying on another day when not facing death, what might the results have been?

If you are faced with a crisis today, do you believe that God will answer your prayer and bring you safely through? Do you need a crisis to cause you to speak to God?

Claim His promise. Call upon Him. See what great and mighty things are wrought by earnest prayer!

ACCOUNTABLE

MEMORY VERSE: *For it is written, As I live, saith the Lord, every knee shall bow to me, and every tongue shall confess to God* (Romans 14:11).

We're accountable for our words.

The Judgment Seat of Christ will test our words as well as our works.

Dr. Wilber Penfield, director of the Montreal Neurological Institute, in a report to the Smithsonian Institute, said: "Your brain contains a permanent record of your past that is like a single continuous strip of movie film, complete with sound tract. This 'film library' records your whole waking life from childhood on. You can live again those scenes from your past, one at a time, when a surgeon applies a gentle electrical current to a certain point on the temporal cortex of your brain." The report goes on to say that as you relive the scene from the past, you feel exactly the same emotions that you did during the original experience.

Could it be that the human race will be confronted with this irrefutable record in judgment when *God shall judge the secrets of men by Jesus Christ* (Romans 2:16)?

Signs of the times indicate the return of Christ for His Church is very near. Remember—the Christian's first appointment at the Rapture is the Judgment Seat of Christ. We will give an account of all our words and works as they affected our service since we were born again.

On that great day we will gladly own Him as Lord.

Let us prepare for that day by speaking for Him at every opportunity.

At the Judgment Seat of Christ, we'll be glad we were faithful.

May 27   Ephesians 5:18-21

SPIRIT FILLED

MEMORY VERSE: *Speaking to yourselves in psalms and hymns and spiritual songs, singing and making melody in your heart to the Lord* (Ephesians 5:19).

The tongue of man reaches its highest potential when praising the Lord. Filled with the Holy Spirit, Christians lay aside their differences and praise the Lord together. When that happens in any local church a revival is taking place.

Music is an important part of the Christian life. It always has been. The Early Church lacked our music-making equipment, but they made up for these helps to harmony with joyful hearts and voices.

Revival speaks of the return of life, and that wouldn't hurt the music in most churches. There are some great hymns in our hymnals, but mouthing the words of a song means nothing at all. Songs of dedication are generally prayers of commitment set to music. Realizing that should make us sing with care.

When the soul is refreshed by personal revival, singing follows. Choir members do not have to be coaxed. Congregations do not have to be talked into doing their best. Music flows naturally from a revived heart.

The tone of the music changes. Songs about the difficulties of the Christian life are replaced with songs of praise. Luther said: "The devil is a chronic grumbler. The Christian ought to be a living doxology."

Paul said it all: *Let the word of Christ dwell in you richly in all wisdom; teaching and admonishing one another in psalms and hymns and spiritual songs, singing with grace in your hearts to the Lord* (Colossians 3:16).

Is your heart in tune today?

GREAT DAY

MEMORY VERSE: *And that every tongue should confess that Jesus Christ is Lord, to the glory of God the Father* (Philippians 2:11).

What does the name "Jesus" mean to you?

Mrs. Booth used to tell a beautiful story of a man whose consistent Christian life left a permanent impression on her own. He seemed continually to grow in grace and at last he could speak of nothing but the glories of his Saviour and his face was radiant with awe and affection whenever he spoke that name.

When he was dying, a document was discovered that required his signature and it was brought to him. He held the pen for one brief moment, wrote, and fell back upon the pillows, dead. On the important paper, he had not written his own name, but the name that is above very name. Within sight of heaven, the name of Jesus was all that mattered to him.

To some the name of Jesus is but a means of emphasizing a point...a word to use in a tirade of profanity. To others the mention of the name brings to mind a prophet or a good man, perhaps a martyr to a cause. But to the Christian the name of Jesus speaks of salvation, heaven, resurrection, and a kingdom that will never be destroyed.

The name Jesus may call to mind His love for the outcasts, His tenderness with children, His compassion for all people, or His outpouring of love on the cross.

There is a day coming when at the name of Jesus every knee shall bow and every tongue confess that He is Lord, to the glory of God the Father.

That day is fast approaching.

Get ready.

Let Him be Lord of your life today!

VAIN RELIGION

MEMORY VERSE: *If any man among you seem to be religious, and bridleth not his tongue, but deceiveth his own heart, this man's religion is vain* (James 1:26).

The ability to communicate is one of God's greatest gifts to us. We can express the deep feelings of our hearts in words and songs of praise and thanksgiving. When we hurt, we can describe our pain to another who may be able to help. Love would be frustrated without means of communication. Poets and writers have capitalized on this and a never-ending stream of books and songs flow from their pens.

Some overcommunicate.

A woman once said to John Wesley, "My talent is to speak my mind." He answered, "God won't object if you bury that talent."

There is no sin quite so destructive as gossip. Churches have been divided, homes broken, and reputations ruined through careless words. Washington Irving said, "A sharp tongue is the only edge tool that grows sharper with constant use."

But the Christian has been given power to control his tongue and to use it for the glory of God. When he does not do so but continues to use his tongue to slander and divide, he is on dangerous ground. James casts doubt on the salvation of such a person by saying that his religion is vain...useless.

Heaven will hold many surprises. One of them will be the absence of many who claimed to be saved but had no real walk with God through faith in Christ. A mark of such people, according to the Bible, is their inability to bridle their tongues.

Don't follow a gossip.

He may be mistaken about his destination!

UNTAMED THOUGHTS

MEMORY VERSE: *Out of the same mouth proceedeth bless-ing and cursing. My brethren, these things ought not so to be* (James 3:10).

Dr. Bob Jones Sr. wrote: " 'If any man offend not in word, the same is a perfect man, and able also to bridle the whole body.' That is what the Holy Spirit said through James in the third chapter of the book he wrote.

"This statement we should know to be true even if it were not in the Bible. All of us know, if we stop to think, that our most difficult task is to control our tongues. There is nothing today that is doing more to deaden the spiritual testimony of orthodox Christianity than the long, backbiting, mean tongues of some supposedly orthodox Christians.

"There are Christians that talk much about a separated life, and boast about what they do and do not do, and speak with great pride about their loyalty to orthodoxy, who spend their time dipping their tongues in the slime and slander and speaking the death warrant to the reputation of other orthodox Christians.

"The Bible is filled with condemnation of people that slander other people. It condemns with great severity people who even take up a reproach about other people. It is just as bad to carry a rumor around after it starts as it is to start it."

You may be rebuked by this strong statement. You feel uncomfortable. Convicted. You've been unkind with your tongue.

What can you do?

Confess your unkind words to the Lord. Claim His forgiveness.

Stop grieving over past failures. But don't travel that same road again. Give Christ control of your life...including that dangerous tongue!

SAY COME

MEMORY VERSE: *And the Spirit and the bride say, Come. And let him that heareth say, Come. And let him that is athirst come. And whosoever will, let him take the water of life freely* (Revelation 22:8-21).

A Christian railroad engineer said, "I always found it easy to justify my lack of results in witnessing to my fellow workers on an industrial railroad. I didn't associate with them, but they knew where I stood as a Christian. I didn't drink, smoke, or swear, so getting my reputation as being 'religious' was easy. One night, however, one of the men of my crew said to me, 'If you have the answers to our spiritual needs, why don't you share them with the rest of us? Or don't you care about us?'

"His question struck home. I confessed, 'You are right! If I were really concerned about you like I pretend, I wouldn't let any opportunity pass to show my concern. What an inadequate representative of Christ I've been!'"

The last invitation in the Bible calls for the Bride (Christians) to say, "Come." What does that mean?

You can invite people to come and be forgiven all their sins: *Come now, and let us reason together, saith the LORD: though your sins be as scarlet, they shall be as white as snow; though they be red like crimson, they shall be as wool* (Isaiah 1:18).

You can invite people to come with their burdens and find rest: *Come unto me, all ye that labour and are heavy laden, and I will give you rest* (Matthew 11:28).

You can assure those whom you invite that Christ will receive them: *All that the Father giveth me shall come to me; and him that cometh to me I will in no wise cast out* (John 6:37).

Say, "COME!"

June

THIS MONTH'S STUDY

Fear

Days 2,8,13,15,17,19, and 25 contain quotes or information from "Three Thousand Illustrations for Christian Service," "Knight's Master Book of Illustrations," and "Knight's Treasury of Illustrations" all by Walter B. Knight, published by Wm. B. Eerdmans Publishing Company, Grand Rapids, Michigan. Used by permission. Days 3 and 6 contain quotes from "The Root of the Righteous" by A. W. Tozer, published by Christian Publications, Inc., Harrisburg, Pennsylvania. Day 28 contains a quote from "Hope Thou in God" by Vance Havner, published by Fleming H. Revell, Old Tappan, N.J.

THE REWARD

MEMORY VERSE: *After these things the word of the LORD came unto Abram in a vision, saying, Fear not, Abram: I am thy shield, and thy exceeding great reward* (Genesis 15:1).

Those who sacrifice to do the will of God will be rewarded.

Abraham had left his homeland not knowing his destination but sure of the call of God. To their sorrow, he and Sarah, his wife, were childless. And they were up in years. There seemed no human hope that they would have descendants. Now they were in a strange land and had been in battle to rescue their relatives who had been taken captive by heathen kings.

In spite of many difficulties, Abraham remained faithful. He was confident that God would repay his obedience. He believed God and anticipated rewards ahead. Nevertheless, he must have wondered how long it would be before he began to receive dividends on his investment of sacrifice and obedience.

Then came this revelation: THE LORD WAS HIS REWARD. It might be a great distance from the place of his call to his unknown destination, but in the meantime, God was with him. That was his reward.

Today, you are weary in the race of life. The journey seems long. You have no doubt about your salvation or the certainty of your final destination, heaven. But you are tired, discouraged, about to yield to temptation, wondering if heavenly rewards are worth your present trials.

And here you are dreading the remainder of the year.

Don't be afraid. The Lord is your reward. He will go with you to protect you—be your shield. His presence will fill the year with joy!

June 2

Genesis 21:9-21

WHAT AILETH THEE?

MEMORY VERSE: *And God heard the voice of the lad; and the angel of God called to Hagar out of heaven, and said unto her, What aileth thee, Hagar? fear not; for God hath heard the voice of the lad where he is* (Genesis 21:17).

Needy miners and settlers in British Columbia, engaged in stripping abandoned Fort Alcan of lumber, electrical appliances, and plumbing, made an amazing discovery. While dismantling the jail they found that though mighty locks were attached to the heavy doors and two inch bars covered the windows, the walls of the prison were only patented wallboard made of clay and paper, painted to resemble steel. A good heave against any of the walls would have burst them out.

Nobody ever escaped from the jail at Fort Alcan by breaking down a wall because all thought it impossible. Many are prisoners of fear and doubt when a push of faith would bring freedom.

Hagar, Abraham and Sarah's banished maid, wandered in the desert and despaired for the life of her child. When her meager supply of water was exhausted, she placed the young boy under a shrub and went some distance away to weep so that she wouldn't witness his death. God's question, "What aileth thee, Hagar?" let this troubled mother know that He was aware of her problem. As soon as her eyes were opened she saw that He had already provided the solution—life-giving water. Now His promise assured the future of her son.

What aileth thee? What is bothering you? Why are you troubled?

Put away your fears. Your problem has not taken God by surprise. There is a design in your present difficulties.

Open your eyes and you will see that God has a solution. Rest your future in His hands!

THE PROMISES

MEMORY VERSE: *And the LORD appeared unto him the same night, and said, I am the God of Abraham thy father: fear not, for I am with thee, and will bless thee, and multiply thy seed for my servant Abraham's sake* (Genesis 26:24).

God reminded Isaac that he did not need to be afraid. Certain promises that had been made to his father Abraham included him in their benefits. God's agreement—covenant—with Abraham was reported to dispel Isaac's anxiety. Remembering the promises of the Bible will aid us when facing obstacles that make us afraid.

God's promises encourage faith. Faith is developed by exposure to the Bible: *So then faith cometh by hearing, and hearing by the word of God* (Romans 10:17). As you take time to study the Bible you will find guarantees of strength, peace, courage, salvation, power, victory, and answered prayer. Consequently, your faith will grow. Depression will depart. Fears will flee.

We need to trade our fears for faith. A. W. Tozer wrote: "Many of us Christians have become extremely skillful in arranging our lives so as to admit the truth of Christianity without being embarrassed by its implications. We arrange things so that we can get on well enough without divine aid, while at the same time ostensibly seeking it. We boast in the Lord but watch carefully that we never get caught depending on Him."

God's promises hold true today.

And they are given for our times of need.

Stop trembling and start trusting. Those good words, *Fear not*, are for you. His promises will bring you through your present test!

A MAJOR MOVE

MEMORY VERSE: *And he said, I am God, the God of thy father: fear not to go down into Egypt; for I will there make of thee a great nation* (Genesis 46:3).

Being uprooted can be frightening. Jacob lived in Canaan, the land of promise. The famine there had forced his family to go to Egypt to find food and while there they had discovered Jacob's son Joseph who had been sold into slavery many years before by his jealous brothers. Joseph now held high office in Egypt and invited his father and brothers to come there and live. An old man now, Jacob must have found it difficult to make the journey and to relocate his family.

There are many fears connected with moving. You may be wrestling with some of them: Will I ever feel at home there? Will the neighbors be friendly? Will I be accepted? Will the children be happy?

But we must remember that Christians do not move alone! Our walk with God is not confined to a geographical location. The Lord promised to go with Jacob and urged him to put away his fears.

On the other hand, conditions may not always be easy in a new home. Egypt was to become a difficult place for the descendants of Jacob, the Children of Israel. But their deliverance from that land would become a central miracle of the Bible.

The future may hold a major move for you. Remember— changing locations does not separate a child of God from his Heavenly Father. And your obligations to worship and pray will be just as important in that new area as in the old one where everyone knows you.

Whatever the future, allow the promises of God to dispel your fears. If you have been born again, you will never move alone. His love knows no boundaries.

GROUNDLESS FEARS

MEMORY VERSE: *Now therefore fear ye not: I will nourish you, and your little ones. And he comforted them, and spake kindly unto them* (Genesis 50:21).

Joseph's brothers were afraid. And there seemed to be good reason for their anxiety. They had conspired to do away with their brother because they were jealous of him. Having sold him into slavery, they thought they were through with him. But God had protected Joseph and had elevated him to great power in Egypt. Speaking to his brothers, Joseph explained it well: *But as for you, ye thought evil against me; but God meant it unto good, to bring to pass, as it is this day, to save much people alive* (Genesis 50:20).

This good news was related to Joseph's brothers while they were kneeling before him seeking forgiveness. They had expected judgment and instead received grace. They must have lived through this scene a thousand times on the way to Egypt, each time characterized by some variation of expected revenge. Perhaps Joseph would devise some means of paying them back for their meanness that would cost them their freedom or their families. He had seemed forgiving, but how could they be sure of his true feelings? The miles to Egypt must have been long, and the mileage rolled up on their bodies and emotional systems immense. That journey may have found them in imaginary Egyptian jails, serving as slaves for the rest of their lives, or experiencing some punishment practiced in Egypt that was unknown to them.

Now they were being told to stop being afraid. They would be treated kindly and both they and their children would be nourished by the one they had wronged. Their worries and fears were in vain.

Too often, like Joseph's brothers, we stew over imaginary fears. Our Lord will nourish and care for His own!

STAND STILL

MEMORY VERSE: *And Moses said unto the people, Fear ye not, stand still, and see the salvation of the LORD, which he will shew to you to day: for the Egyptians whom ye have seen to day, ye shall see them again no more for ever* (Exodus 14:13).

The Children of Israel were understandably afraid. They had fled from their cruel taskmasters in Egypt at the call of Moses and now their capture and return seemed certain. Pharaoh's soldiers were in hot pursuit and they had come to a dead end. There were mountains on either side and the Red Sea lay before them.

They began to complain, blaming Moses for their plight: *And they said unto Moses, Because there were no graves in Egypt, hast thou taken us away to die in the wilderness?* (Exodus 14:11).

At that panic point, Moses gave this surprising instruction: *Fear ye not, stand still, and see the salvation of the Lord* (14:13).

Stand still? What a difficult thing to do when collapse or tragedy seems imminent. We are more likely to run to and fro trying to find some saving solution. But it is in these trying times that our faith is tested. Writing about the difference between genuine faith and pseudo (false) faith, A. W. Tozer explained: "Pseudo faith always arranges a way out to serve in case God fails it. Real faith knows only one way and gladly allows itself to be stripped of any second way or makeshift substitutes. For true faith, it is either God or total collapse. And not since Adam first stood up on earth has God failed a single man or woman who trusted Him."

Are you in a corner? Does it seem there is no way out?

Stand still and see the salvation of the Lord!

OBSTACLES

MEMORY VERSE: *Only rebel not ye against the LORD, neither fear ye the people of the land; for they are bread for us: their defence is departed from them, and the LORD is with us: fear them not* (Numbers 14:9).

Opportunities are often lost because of fear. Hindsight reminds us of investments that would have made us wealthy had we dared risk a purchase. But fear kept our savings under lock and key. Now the opportunity is lost.

The Children of Israel had witnessed the power of God in the Exodus from Egypt. The Red Sea had opened before them. Food and water had been provided for their journey. God had been faithful. Now, at the very edge of the Promised Land, their faith faltered. Their spies returned from investigating the land with a mixed report. And the majority predicted defeat in entering the land.

They were afraid!

Two men of faith, Caleb and Joshua, urged the people to move forward in faith. These giants for God were not ruled by fear as were the others. Ten of the twelve spies saw the obstacles. Two saw the Lord. Because the people followed their fears, they wandered in the wilderness for forty years. During that time, all of that generation died except Caleb and Joshua. Only these two were allowed to seize the opportunity offered forty years earlier. And all because they were not afraid.

Every great opportunity has its obstacles. Futures and fortunes are lost by those who are afraid of those temporary roadblocks. Some dare to trust God and go ahead in faith.

What will you do with the adventure offered you today?

THE UNFAILING ONE

MEMORY VERSE: *And the LORD, he it is that doth go before thee; he will be with thee, he will not fail thee, neither forsake thee: fear not, neither be dismayed* (Deuteronomy 31:8).

George Frederick Handel, the great musician, lost his health; his right side was paralyzed; his money was gone; and his creditors seized and threatened to imprison him. Handel was so disheartened by his tragic experiences that he almost despaired. But his faith prevailed. In his affliction, he composed his greatest work, *The Hallelujah Chorus*, which is part of his great, *Messiah*.

The list is long of those who have overcome handicaps and gone on to achievement and success through trust in the Lord. Annie Johnson Flint, afflicted with pain and suffering, wrote the much used "He Giveth More Grace," and many other wonderful poems. Fanny Crosby was blind but composed more than 8,000 published hymns. Helen Keller, shortly before her sixteenth birthday, expressed pity for the real unseeing, for those who have eyes still often do not see. She said, "If the blind put their hand in God's, they find their way more surely than those who see but have not faith or purpose."

What has been the secret of these conquerors?

They have understood that God is still in charge of the future. Refusing to be defeated by their fears, they have dared trust Him to accomplish great things in spite of their problems. And He has rewarded their faith.

Some choose to major on their problems, drawing back from contacts with other people and choosing the imprisonment of fear. Perhaps you are one of them. What a good day to place your future in the hands of the Unfailing One. He will not forsake you.

And you will not fail!

LIFE

MEMORY VERSE: *And the LORD said unto him, Peace be unto thee; fear not: thou shalt not die* (Judges 6:23).

Death is a universal fear. And with good reason: *It is appointed unto men once to die, but after this the judgment* (Hebrews 9:27). The Bible calls death an enemy: *The last enemy that shall be destroyed is death* (1 Corinthians 15:26).

Salvation through faith in Christ gives positive assurance of heaven at the moment of death: *We are confident, I say, and willing rather to be absent from the body, and to be present with the Lord* (2 Corinthians 5:8). Nevertheless, the experience of death itself is not pleasant. God has placed a desire for life within us all.

Gideon was afraid he might die. Let him tell the reason: *Because I have seen an angel of the LORD face to face* (Judges 6:22). Your fears about death may be rooted in a number of possibilities. You haven't been feeling well and suspect some serious illness. Near relatives died young as a result of some family affliction and you think you may be next. A neighborhood tragedy has affected you and you fear for your sanity or your life. You have committed some sin and fear that it may be the sin of death. You expect an attack upon our country by another nation or by terrorists. You suspect contamination of food or water because of chemical waste experiments or acts of terrorism.

Gideon's fear of death was ended by a reminder that life is limited or extended by the Lord. It was not time for him to die because God had a work for him to do. Christians who are living in God's will do not need to fear death. Their lives will not end on this earth until their work is done.

NOT FORSAKEN

MEMORY VERSE: *And Samuel said unto the people, Fear not: ye have done all this wickedness: yet turn not aside from following the LORD, but serve the LORD with all your heart* (1 Samuel 12:20).

Reviewing your Christian life, you're frightened. There have been so many failures. In spite of good intentions, you've yielded to the same temptations over and over again.

You've been a complainer. Your pastor and others in the church have been the victims of your disgust. And you've let others know all about it. Weaknesses in others have been your specialty; gossip, your pastime.

Giving has been another disappointing area of your life. At the annual missionary conference your faith runs high but when the first of the month rolls around, all your resources take flight in just paying the bills. Since the Lord's share of your incomes comes out last, all is often gone before you can give as you had intended.

Devotional life for you has been a roller-coaster experience. Sometimes you're regular in reading the Bible and praying. More often, you're not. Time is a premium and since the Lord isn't first in your priorities, consistency in your devotional life escapes you.

And then there's witnessing. You seem to be able to talk about everything but the gospel. Few have been helped by your concerned sharing of the message of eternal life because you haven't been that concerned.

Taking inventory, you're afraid God is through with you.

Fear not. God is faithful. *The Lord will not forsake his people* (1 Samuel 12:22). Confess these sins and failures to Him. Start new today. And serve the Lord with all your heart!

FOR JONATHAN'S SAKE

MEMORY VERSE: *And David said unto him, Fear not: for I will surely shew thee kindness for Jonathan thy father's sake, and will restore thee all the land of Saul thy father; and thou shalt eat bread at my table continually* (2 Samuel 9:7).

Mephibosheth was the son of Jonathan. He was lame and had been in hiding since David had become king. When he was brought before David he feared for his life. But David had sought him out to show him kindness...to do him good...to extend grace. David brought Jonathan's lame son into his house and Mephibosheth ate continually at the king's table, placing his lame feet out of sight and enjoying the king's fellowship and bounty.

Some flee the call of God to salvation. They are afraid that God will condemn them or take the joy out of life. Actually, all who have not been saved are already condemned: *For God sent not his Son into the world to condemn the world; but that the world through him might be saved. He that believeth on him is not condemned: but he that believeth not is condemned already, because he hath not believed in the name of the only begotten Son of God* (John 3:17,18).

And as to taking the joy out of life, man's highest joy is found in fellowship with Christ. The poet said it well: "Jesus is the joy of living."

The fears of Jonathan's son were groundless. David wanted to do him good for Jonathan's sake. And the fears of those who resist salvation, expecting to lose out in life, are groundless. The Father wants to do them good for Jesus' sake.

Come and place your lame feet under the King's table and eat there continually!

UNSEEN ALLIES

MEMORY VERSE: *And he answered, Fear not: for they that be with us are more than they that be with them* (2 Kings 6:16).

Christians have immense resources in times of trouble. Sadly, we often forget this truth and react as if we had to face our problems alone. Angels must wonder at our frail faith. We have been promised protection and care, yet we fret and worry as if God did not exist. And worry is but another form of atheism.

Elisha and his servant found themselves surrounded by an army with horses and chariots bent on their destruction. The shaking servant seemed justified in his fears. But Elisha put away his fright by increasing his sight: *And Elisha prayed, and said, LORD, I pray thee, open his eyes, that he may see. And the LORD opened the eyes of the young man; and he saw: and, behold, the mountain was full of horses and chariots of fire round about Elisha* (2 Kings 6:17).

One of the surprises of heaven will be the revelation of God's goodness to us while we were on earth. When we get the answers to life's questions, it will amaze us to know how many times our Father has sent His angels to protect and help us in times of need.

Throwing in the towel when faced with difficulties disregards the effectiveness of our unseen allies. Christians ought not surrender, in view of their heavenly resources. We do not face obstacles alone.

The next time you're overwhelmed in a forest of fears, remember your unseen allies.

The woods are full of them. And their mission is for your good: *Are they not all ministering spirits, sent forth to minister for them who shall be heirs of salvation?* (Hebrews 1:14).

NOT AFRAID

MEMORY VERSE: *The LORD is my light and my salvation; whom shall I fear? the LORD is the strength of my life; of whom shall I be afraid?* (Psalm 27:1).

Chrysostom of Constantinople, threatened with exile or death, stated in a sermon at the time of his banishment: "What can I fear? Will it be death? But you know that Christ is my life. Will it be exile? But the earth and all its fullness is the Lord's. Will it be loss of wealth? But we brought nothing into the world and can carry nothing out. Thus all the terrors of the world are contemptible in my eyes, and I smile at all its good things."

He continued: "Poverty I do not fear. Riches I do not sigh for. Death I do not shrink from, and life I do not desire to save only for the process of souls. And so be if they banish me, I shall be like Elijah! If they throw me in the mire, more like Jeremiah. If they plunge me in the sea, like the prophet Jonah! If into the pit, like Daniel! If they stone me, it is Stephen I shall resemble! John the forerunner, if they cut off my head! Paul, if they beat me with stripes! Isaiah, if they saw me asunder."

The man of God had captured the meaning of David's question: *Whom shall I fear?*

Of whom are you afraid? Your boss? Your hot-tempered associate at work? Your husband? Your wife? Your creditors? Criminals? Communists?

They are but people. In Christ, you have the strength of the Lord. You do not need to be afraid!

OUR REFUGE

MEMORY VERSE: *Therefore will not we fear, though the earth be removed, and though the mountains be carried into the midst of the sea* (Psalm 46:2).

In his book, *Two Thousand Hours in the Psalms*, Dr. Marion Hull says of Psalm 46, "No wonder the psalmist says 'therefore will not we fear.' What could man do to anyone who has such a source of strength and help as this?"

He explains that *refuge* means "a place to go quietly for protection." And that the Hebrew word translated *trouble* means "in tight places." When we get in tight places we can go to the Lord and find a place of quiet protection.

This place of safety belongs to the children of God and is available even in convulsions of nature. One lady who slept through an earthquake was asked how she had such peace in the crisis. She replied that she rejoiced to have a God strong enough to shake the world.

Some are terrified at storms. The disciples expected to die in a watery grave during the storm that swept the Sea of Galilee. Jesus rebuked them for their lack of faith and also rebuked the wind and the waves. When they had entered the boat Jesus had said: *Let us pass over unto the other side* (Mark 4:35). His statement of sure crossing made the boat unsinkable in the face of any storm. Their fears were a waste of energy and a useless drain on their emotions. The Master of nature was on board. And in spite of their anxiety, all was well.

In all the storms of life, Christians have a refuge.

Flee to Him and leave your fears behind!

June 15 — Psalm 56

TRUST

MEMORY VERSE: *What time I am afraid, I will trust in thee* (Psalm 56:3).

David was no stranger to fear. He had been pursued by Saul who intended to kill him. Often, enemies had sought his life. Finally, rebellion racked his kingdom. He knew the twinge and tightening of fear. But he also knew what to do when fears came—*What time I am afraid, I will trust thee.*

Trust. What a good word!

Hudson Taylor was so feeble in the closing months of his life, that he wrote a friend, "I am so weak that I cannot work; I cannot read my Bible; I cannot even pray. I can only lie still in God's arms like a little child and trust." This great man of God came to a place of physical suffering and weakness where he could only lie still and trust. And that is all God asks in that hour. James McConkey gave this advice to those in the fierce fires of affliction: "Do not try to be strong. Just be still."

How wonderfully the Bible meets us where we are! Scores of times the Scriptures advise us not to fear. Isaiah wrote: *I will trust, and not be afraid* (Isaiah 12:2). Yet, knowing that some would experience fear in spite of all assurances, direction is given to those already afraid. The call is for a move from trembling to trust.

But how does one trust when immobilized by fear?

There is but one answer. Fill your mind and heart with the promises of the Bible. Read the old familiar chapters that you love. Sing the old hymns that are full of Bible truth. Let God assure you with His Word.

Trust will grow—even in a trembling heart!

June 16   Psalm 91

NIGHT AND DAY

MEMORY VERSE: *Thou shalt not be afraid for the terror by night; nor for the arrow that flieth by day* (Psalm 91:5).

While doing hospital visitation, I met an older lady and asked her if she spent any time reading the Bible.

"Yes," she answered, "I read the ninety-first Psalm every day."

While I was familiar with this great psalm, her statement sent me to it again for another reading. I concluded that if she thought it rich enough to read every day there must be a good reason. That hospital experience took place more than twenty years ago, but each time I read the ninety-first Psalm I remember the lady who read it every day. She is now in heaven, but her recommended reading has stayed with me.

The "terror by night" speaks of those unexpected things that come upon us without warning. Perhaps the psalmist referred to the adder that might slip into a tent while one was sleeping. His message is that we do not need to be afraid of being overtaken by unannounced tragedies. The Lord is with us at all times. The unexpected is known to Him.

The "arrow that flieth by day" refers to the common dangers during the working hours of life. For a soldier this might be an arrow aimed with death in mind. But there are many different kinds of arrows. Those propelled from vicious tongues may be the most dangerous of all!

Never mind. Day and night our Lord is watching over us.

He is our refuge and our fortress; our God. And we are safe in His care!

THE PROTECTOR

MEMORY VERSE: *The Lord is on my side; I will not fear: what can man do unto me?* (Psalm 118:6).

One with God is a majority.

The psalmist recognizes the sufficiency of God's protection and rejects all fears about being wronged or harmed by men. Paul echoed this truth in his letter to the Romans: *What shall we say then to these things? If God be for us, who can be against us?* (Romans 8:31).

But how can I know that the Lord is on my side?

He is on the side of those who receive Him as Saviour and Lord. And nothing shall cause Him to forsake them: *Who shall separate us from the love of Christ? shall tribulation, or distress, or persecution, or famine, or nakedness, or peril, or sword? Nay, in all these things we are more than conquerors through him that loved us. For I am persuaded, that neither death, nor life, nor angels, nor principalities, nor powers, nor things present, nor things to come, nor height, nor depth, nor any other creature, shall be able to separate us from the love of God, which is in Christ Jesus our Lord* (Romans 8:35,37-39).

So, we do not need to fear the attacks of others.

A young soldier, returned from battle, tried to avoid talking about his experiences in war by saying that nothing important had happened to him. His questioner was persistent, however, and said, "Something must have happened. Now tell me, of all your experiences, what was it that struck you most?"

"Well," said the soldier, "the thing that struck me most was the number of bullets that missed me."

We may also be struck by the number of dangers that have threatened us, only to be diverted by God's protecting hand!

NOT ALONE

MEMORY VERSE: *Fear thou not: for I am with thee: be not dismayed; for I am thy God: I will strengthen thee; yea, I will help thee; yea, I will uphold thee with the right hand of my righteousness* (Isaiah 41:10).

God anticipates our needs before we experience them.

Knowing there would be times we would feel alone, He said, *I am with thee.*

Understanding that sometimes we would not understand, He counseled assuringly, *Be not dismayed.*

Having compassion upon us in our fainting spells, He announced, *I will strengthen thee.*

Foreseeing times that our human strength would fall short of our needs, He promised, *I will help thee.*

Life teaches us of the weakness of man...our own weakness. There are problems too complicated for us to solve, burdens too heavy for us to bear, work too difficult for us to do. But God is able. Everything is within His power. And He wants to trade His strength for our weakness, His fellowship for our loneliness, His wisdom for our lack of understanding.

His method of meeting our needs is not the introduction of some "How To" program. Instead, it is the promise that He will be with us, directing us in His perfect will.

Are you at the end of yourself?

Have you arrived at "wits end corner"?

Is the race too long, the battle too fierce, or the struggle too great?

Are you afraid?

Fear not. He will be with you and will compensate your weakness with His strength, your disability with His ability. He will not fail!

HELP

MEMORY VERSE: *For I the LORD thy God will hold thy right hand, saying unto thee, Fear not; I will help thee* (Isaiah 41:13).

The Scotch preacher, John McNeill, related the following experience from his youth:

He had been to town and was late in starting the tramp of six or seven miles through the lonely glen on his way home. The night was very dark and the road had a reputation for danger. "In the densest of the darkness," said McNeill, "there suddenly rang out a great, strong, cheery voice: 'Is that you, Johnny?' It was my father—the bravest, strongest man I ever knew."

Then the famous preacher added: "Many a time since, when things have been getting very black and gloomy about me, I have heard a voice greater than any earthly father cry: 'Fear not: for I am with thee'"

A friendly voice in darkness is welcome.

But a friendly hand is more comforting.

God's promise to His fearful child is that He will take his hand.

What could be more comforting in a crisis than to have God take your right hand to lead you safely through? Like a father helping a little one down a difficult path, the Heavenly Father helps us in life's struggles by taking a trembling hand in His to lead the frightened one to safety.

Troubles may surround you to the point that you cannot even remember how you became involved in this situation. You're tired of struggling and wonder if life is worth the effort. You don't even know how to explain your problems to a counselor.

Then Isaiah's promise is for you. Just cry, "Help!"

You'll hear His answer: *Fear not; I will help thee* (Isaiah 41:13).

THE REDEEMED

MEMORY VERSE: *But now thus saith the LORD that created thee, O Jacob, and he that formed thee, O Israel, Fear not: for I have redeemed thee, I have called thee by thy name; thou art mine* (Isaiah 43:1).

The old hymn says, "Redeemed, how I loved to proclaim it!" And our redemption is worth proclaiming. The definition of *redeem* is "to regain possession of by paying a price." The price of our redemption was the blood of Christ: *Forasmuch as ye know that ye were not redeemed with corruptible things, as silver and gold, from your vain conversation received by tradition from your fathers; But with the precious blood of Christ, as of a lamb without blemish and without spot* (1 Peter 1:18,19).

To be redeemed is to belong to the Redeemer.

Since our Redeemer is Christ, we belong to Him.

This privileged position brings security. The Good Shepherd is our Redeemer and we are His sheep. Expose your fears to these promises: *I am the good shepherd: the good shepherd giveth his life for the sheep. I am the good shepherd, and know my sheep, and am known of mine. As the Father knoweth me, even so know I the Father: and I lay down my life for the sheep. My sheep hear my voice, and I know them, and they follow me: And I give unto them eternal life; and they shall never perish, neither shall any man pluck them out of my hand. My Father, which gave them me, is greater than all; and no man is able to pluck them out of my Father's hand. I and my Father are one* (John 10:11,14,15,27-30).

If you have been born again, you are one of the redeemed— one of His sheep. You belong to the Good Shepherd.

And here you are, afraid!

SECURITY

MEMORY VERSE: *Hearken unto me, ye that know righteous-ness, the people in whose heart is my law; fear ye not the reproach of men, neither be ye afraid of their revilings* (Isaiah 51:7).

The promises of God are given to a particular people, those who have received His Son as Saviour and Lord. Some mistakenly try to claim the promises without receiving the Saviour.

One may quote the beautiful Twenty-third Psalm and enjoy its description of green pastures and still waters, but it is vital to remember that the overflowing cup of the psalmist was based upon the first sentence of his expression of praise for provision: "The Lord is my shepherd."

Perhaps you have been reading the Bible to find peace and still your fears remain. Could it be that you have never been saved? My wife, Rexella, had a similar experience in her youth. Let her tell it:

"Following my solo in a church service—when I was sixteen—the moment of truth came. I left the service weeping and went to my parents' car to be alone. Concerned, my father followed me and asked what was wrong. 'Oh, Dad,' I sobbed, 'I've deceived my own heart. I've deceived our pastor and you and the whole church. I have known about the Lord all my life, but I don't really know Him.' Resisting the temptation to soothe my feelings, my father said: 'Be sure, Rexella.'

"A few days later, my older brother learned of my soul's distress when he heard me crying in my room. With genuine compassion and understanding, he led me through God's plan of salvation."

Tell the Lord of your doubts and uncertainty. Take Christ as your Saviour without delay. Trust Him to take away all your fears!

NOT ASHAMED

MEMORY VERSE: *Fear not; for thou shalt not be ashamed: neither be thou confounded; for thou shalt not be put to shame: for thou shalt forget the shame of thy youth, and shalt not remember the reproach of thy widowhood any more* (Isaiah 54:4).

The fear of failure holds many back from worthwhile accomplishments. Projects are abandoned before they are launched. Church building plans are scrapped. Business opportunities are lost. Witnessing responsibilities are neglected. Marriages are postponed. Missionary vision is squelched. Needed new ministries are aborted. And all because failure or embarrassment is a possibility.

You may stand at the very brink of success or blessing but are afraid to make the decisive move that is required to begin the journey to your brightest hour. There is a possibility of failure and you fear what others will say if you do not succeed. Having listed all the negatives to be sure that your decision is sound, you are dwelling on them and are paralyzed by their power.

What if you do not succeed? What if others laugh? What if the community is witness to your blunder? What if you're humiliated?

But there are other questions to ask.

What if you could have succeeded but didn't try? What might have been the results of an all-out effort? What might the community have thought of a step of faith that brought evident blessing? How many might have been won to Christ had you not been afraid to launch out?

Between these scary alternatives lies the will of God. Find it.

When you do—move ahead in faith. *Fear not; for thou shalt not be ashamed.* His blessing will attend your way!

OUR HERITAGE

MEMORY VERSE: *No weapon that is formed against thee shall prosper; and every tongue that shall rise against thee in judgment thou shalt condemn. This is the heritage of the servants of the LORD, and their righteousness is of me, saith the LORD* (Isaiah 54:17).

Imagine not having to protect yourself.

This is the position of a servant of Christ, living in God's will.

Our journey through this world may not be easy. "God has not promised skies always blue or flower-strewn pathways all our lives through." Annie Johnson Flint said it well. But God has promised to protect His servants.

No weapon that is formed against thee shall prosper, Isaiah revealed. Evidently weapons will be used against those who serve the Lord. Sometimes they will be but popguns unable to reach their mark, but there may be times when the devil levels his big guns against you. The sounds of battle may be frightening. Defeat may seem likely.

Don't ever accept it.

You will come through victorious. Shells may drop all around you but God will not allow you to be defeated...unless you insist on fighting in your own strength.

Tongues may rise against you. Jesus warned: *Woe unto you, when all men shall speak well of you! for so did their fathers to the false prophets* (Luke 6:26). Nevertheless, if you rest in the Lord and do not defend yourself, your consistency of life will condemn the slanderers. Your good testimony will cause their words to be crooked arrows, falling harmlessly to the ground...missing the mark.

You do not have to argue for your righteous position. Let your Heavenly Father take care of the critics.

This is the heritage of the servants of the Lord. Depend on it!

NEW EVERY MORNING

MEMORY VERSE: *It is of the LORD'S mercies that we are not consumed, because his compassions fail not. They are new every morning: great is thy faithfulness* (Lamentations 3:22,23).

In a book of tears, here is a shout of triumph. The Pulpit Commentary says of this text, "...even here there is a break, and the brightest sunlight streams through, all the more cheering for the darkness that precedes it. This is a remarkable testimony to the breadth and force of Divine grace. No scene is so terrible as to absolutely exclude all vision of it. Its penetrating rays find their way through chinks and crannies of the deepest dungeon. Were our eyes but open to see it, every one of us would have to confess to indications of its presence. Surely it is a great consolation for the desponding that even the exceptional sufferer of the Lamentations sees the unceasing mercies of God!"

This may be one of your down days.

God has brought you through these times before but you almost feel embarrassed to come seeking help again. You wonder if God may be tired of you and your bent to depression. How many times can one expect God to lift him from despair? Especially when he keeps falling back into the same rut?

Here is good news: God's mercies are new every morning.

Did you think you exhausted God's grace yesterday? Last week? There is a fresh supply available today.

God is faithful.

Bring Him today's burdens: And you will find help for today.

Your heart will echo the great old song, "Great Is Thy Faithfulness."

His mercies are new every morning!

THY WORDS WERE HEARD

MEMORY VERSE: *Then said he unto me, Fear not, Daniel: for from the first day that thou didst set tine heart to understand, and to chasten thyself before thy God, thy words were heard, and I am come for thy words* (Daniel 10:12).

You've been praying about something very important and the answer has not come. You wonder if you're getting through. Sometimes it seems you're writing your words on the ceiling. You're afraid God doesn't hear your prayers.

Fear not.

The Prophet Daniel evidently had a similar experience. The answer to his prayer was delayed for 21 days. He must have wondered why God did not answer. Finally the heavenly messenger let him know that his prayer had been heard and that all the time Daniel had been waiting and wondering, the answer had been on its way.

We need never doubt that God hears the prayers of His children. Though there may be delays, we can depend on His faithfulness. Often the answer is on the way but the timing of God demands patience. God is always on time.

The outstanding characteristics of the great New England preacher Phillip Brooks were poise and imperturbability. His close friends, however, knew that, at times, he suffered from impatience and irritability. One day a friend saw him pacing the floor like a caged lion. "What is the trouble, Dr. Brooks?" asked the friend. "The trouble," said Brooks, "is that I'm in a hurry and God isn't."

Take your burdens to the Lord and don't be afraid anymore. He hears and He will answer...*right on time!*

VALUABLE

MEMORY VERSE: *Fear ye not therefore, ye are of more value than many sparrows* (Matthew 10:31).

We are bird-watchers. Beginning in the early fall, we stock our backyard bird feeder and watch the feathered drama there through the cold winter months. The beauty and temperament of God's flying creatures amaze and amuse us. The action there is a scene we wouldn't miss.

Jesus drew lessons from the birds and they play other prominent roles in the Bible. Noah dispatched birds to see if the flood had ended sufficiently to embark from the ark. Elijah was fed by the ravens during the long drought that had come upon his land. The battle of Armageddon will provide a feast for birds of prey. Interestingly, the number of that kind of bird is increasing in the Middle East where the battle of Armageddon will take place.

God's care of the birds is revealed in the statement of Jesus that not one sparrow can fall to the ground without the Father's notice. Hence the song, "His Eye Is on the Sparrow." Nothing escapes the Father's view and all His creatures are objects of His concern and care.

But people are of more value than birds. Truth about the care of God for animals and birds should increase our confidence in the care of God for people. Every flying bird should remind us that God loves us and that He is concerned with our welfare and safety.

Martin Luther was once rebuked for being depressed by hearing a bird singing outside his window. A humorous sign says, "Cheer up! Birds have bills and they keep singing."

Put your fears to the sparrow test.

Know that He cares for you!

CATCHING MEN

MEMORY VERSE: *Fear not; from henceforth thou shalt catch men* (Luke 5:10).

Peter and his partners had toiled all night and had come back from fishing empty-handed. At the command of the Saviour, however, they let down the net one more time. Their act was only partial obedience, since the Lord had told them to let down their nets. When the net broke because of the size of the catch, Peter knew this was no ordinary fishing trip. He fell at Jesus' knees and admitted that he was a sinful man.

Awareness of sin in the presence of the Lord has been characteristic of people God has used. Abraham, Job, Isaiah, and others join Peter in this type of reaction to the holiness of God.

The experience that day was especially frightening because it looked as if the ships were going to sink. Peter's business seemed in jeopardy. His capital investment in equipment appeared to be headed for the bottom of the lake. No wonder the big fisherman asked the Lord to leave.

Fear not, the Saviour said, *from henceforth thou shalt catch men.*

Peter was going to enter a new field. His work would be changed from catching fish to catching men. His interest would move from sole to souls. History would feel the impact of this former fisherman and his friends. His rewards would be measured on the scales of eternity.

Simon Peter is not the only man called to full-time service when his business began to sink. Many have had to lose in order to gain.

Perhaps your means of livelihood is in danger. Have you considered the call of God? The Lord's word to Peter may be His call to you: *Fear not; from henceforth thou shalt catch men.*

BELIEVE ONLY

MEMORY VERSE: *But when Jesus heard it, he answered him, saying, Fear not: believe only, and she shall be made whole* (Luke 8:50).

Nothing strikes fear to the heart of a parent as much as the news of danger to one of his children. When the daughter of Jairus became ill, her father went to Jesus with the problem. What a good lesson for us all!

As the Saviour journeyed to the home of Jairus to minister to his daughter, this disheartening news arrived: *Thy daughter is dead; trouble not the Master* (vs. 49).

That bulletin would seem to have closed the matter. What use to travel on to the house when the girl had died? Still, Jesus instructed the troubled father to replace his fears with faith. *Believe only,* He said, *and she shall be made whole.*

Your problem may seem so desperate that there seems no reason to pray any more. It seems that all the reports are in and you are the loser. Hope is gone.

Remember Jairus and Jesus. "Believe only," Jesus said. And when they arrived at the house the Lord restored life to the believing father's twelve-year-old daughter.

Faith and prayer have often made the difference when word from the experts left little or no hope. Many are alive today who were given up by doctors. Businesses are thriving now that attorneys pronounced ripe for bankruptcy. Children walk with God who once were wayward. Husbands are good fathers and providers who were once thought but grist for divorce mills. Men and women are sober and good citizens who once were alcoholics despairing of worthwhile lives.

It's not too late. Only believe!

BOLD BELIEVERS

MEMORY VERSE: *So that we may boldly say, The Lord is my helper, and I will not fear what man shall do unto me* (Hebrews 13:6).

Eliminating the fear of people is a major victory. Wise Solomon wrote: *The fear of man bringeth a snare: but whoso putteth his trust in the LORD shall be safe* (Proverbs 29:25).

Since God is our helper, we should be bold in the face of all dangers. When fear is conquered, we have stopped the major energy drain of life. And most of this energy is wasted on fears that are unreal. Spurgeon wrote: "The unseen is indeed the most terrible to our feeble minds. We look through the telescope of apprehension, breathe on the glass, and then think we see clouds, when indeed it is only our anxious breath."

What would you do for God today if you were not afraid? And why are you afraid?

Do you fear the criticism of others? Do you fear the loss of friends? Do you fear embarrassment? Ridicule?

Whom do you really want to please in life? Who is your closest friend? Is this one closer than Jesus? Are you addicted to the praise of others? Are you ruled by the love of money?

Perhaps you are controlled by fear because you are not fully surrendered to the Lord. Early Christians were characterized by courage. Living in hostile times, they risked their lives to carry the gospel to the world. The secret of their boldness? Prayer and surrender to the Lord: *And when they had prayed, the place was shaken where they were assembled together; and they were all filled with the Holy Ghost, and they spake the word of God with boldness* (Acts 4:31).

Our Helper makes us unafraid! (See 2 Timothy 1:7.)

THE LIVING ONE

MEMORY VERSE: *And when I saw him, I fell at his feet as dead. And he laid his right hand upon me, saying unto me, Fear not; I am the first and the last* (Revelation 1:17).

There is really only one question about life and death: *Did Jesus Christ rise from the grave?* And careful investigation allows only one answer: *He arose.* He lives!

Since Christ lives, those who trust in Him do not need to fear life's end. No one is more miserable than the person who lives in fear of some illness or accident that will bring death. An old epitaph says:

> Here lies a man who lived to age,
> Yet still from death was flying;
> Who, though not sick, was never well,
> And died for fear of dying.

Neither does a Christian need to fear life. Some are brave in death and cowards in life. Bible Christianity embraces all of life and faces the issues of death, preparing the believer for both. Paul said it well: *For to me to live is Christ, and to die is gain* (Philippians 1:21).

How can you prepare to live and die?

By receiving Jesus Christ as your Saviour by faith. Accept this invitation: *If thou shalt confess with thy mouth the Lord Jesus, and shalt believe in thine heart that God hath raised him from the dead, thou shalt be saved* (Romans 10:9).

When you take this step of faith, expect changes: *Therefore if any man be in Christ, he is a new creature: old things are passed away; behold, all things are become new* (2 Corinthians 5:17).

Wouldn't you like to be free from fear?

Trust the Living One today!

July

THIS MONTH'S STUDY

Rejoicing and Praise

Days 1,4,10,13,23,27, and 30 contain quotes from "Three Thousand Illustrations for Christian Service," "Knight's Master Book of Illustrations," and "Knight's Treasury of Illustrations," all by Walter B. Knight, published by Wm. B. Eerdmans Publishing Company, Grand Rapids, Michigan. Used by permission.

FAMILY REJOICING

MEMORY VERSE: *And Jethro rejoiced for all the goodness which the LORD had done to Israel, whom he had delivered out of the hand of the Egyptians* (Exodus 18:9).

A family had gathered in their mother's room for what they feared would be her last night of life. The pastor came and as he was about to read the Bible, he turned to the aged saint and asked her what selection of Scripture he should read. She said: "Make your own selection, but let it be of praise." The weakness of old age was on her, and the pain of sickness, but there was no gloom. For her, it was light at eventide. God had been faithful to her during her life and she saw no reason to doubt His goodness at the end. Her heart was filled with praise.

Moses' father-in-law, Jethro, rejoiced at all that the Lord had done for Israel. And what great things God had done! The plagues had fallen upon Egypt, the Red Sea had opened before them, manna had fallen from heaven when they were hungry, and water had gushed from a rock to quench their thirst. God's faithfulness was the basis of Jethro's rejoicing.

Family members rejoicing in the goodness of God—what a sight! Heaven must react to that scene with singing. Here man's highest purpose is fulfilled. In seeing God's hand in every area of life, we get a taste of heaven.

Christians in America are especially blessed. We know little of persecution and hardship. The Lord has sheltered us from experiences that many in other places and other days have endured. Of all people, we ought to rejoice in the goodness of God!

TIME TO REJOICE

MEMORY VERSE: *And thou shalt rejoice in every good thing which the LORD thy God hath given unto thee, and unto thine house* (Deuteronomy 26:11).

The Children of Israel were promised many blessings in their new land. Here are a few of them:

Blessed shalt thou be in the city, and blessed shalt thou be in the field. Blessed shall be the fruit of thy body, and the fruit of thy ground, and the fruit of thy cattle, the increase of thy kine, and the flocks of thy sheep. Blessed shall be thy basket and thy store. Blessed shalt thou be when thou comest in, and blessed shalt thou be when thou goest out (Deuteronomy 28:3-6).

These promises of blessing were conditional. The condition was obedience. If they did not obey, great trouble would come to them. Hear the warnings of God:

Thou shalt have olive trees throughout all thy coasts, but thou shalt not anoint thyself with the oil; for thine olive shall cast his fruit. Thou shalt beget sons and daughters, but thou shalt not enjoy them; for they shall go into captivity. All thy trees and fruit of thy land shall the locust consume (Deuteronomy 28:40-42).

Among the verses describing Israel's coming trouble, this key verse appears: *Because thou servedst not the LORD thy God with joyfulness, and with gladness of heart, for the abundance of all things...*(Deuteronomy 28:47). They had been told to rejoice over daily blessings. Their first step in backsliding was their neglect of thanksgiving, joy and praise—rejoicing.

In the Christian life we are either rejoicing or retreating!

GLADNESS

MEMORY VERSE: *Thou hast put gladness in my heart, more than in the time that their corn and their wine increased* (Psalm 4:7).

The world is searching for gladness. Most, however, try to find it through outward sources: money, popularity, property, lust, or mood changers (booze—drugs).

Genuine gladness must be planted within. If not, it will be temporary and affected by circumstances. David, the psalmist, had experienced God's blessings in times of trouble: *Thou hast enlarged me when I was in distress* (Psalm 4:1). He knew then that the gladness of God would endure in difficult times.

Depression and despair are often the companions of trouble. Some have been so shaken by life's tragedies that they have refused to face the future, secluding themselves from society or even ending life. We must understand that God is faithful and that nothing separates us from His love: *For I am persuaded, that neither death, nor life, nor angels, nor principalities, nor powers, nor things present, nor things to come, nor height, nor depth, nor any other creature, shall be able to separate us from the love of God, which is in Christ Jesus our Lord* (Romans 8:38,39).

The dictionary defines *gladness* as "having a feeling of joy; pleasure, contentment, gratification." Do you have that? Why not?

In the Book of Esther, the Jews were the planned victims of an evil man named Haman. God used Esther to deliver them from this wicked person. As a result of their deliverance, they experienced *light, and gladness, and joy, and honour* (Esther 8:16). They were spared and their hearts were filled with gladness.

Through Christ, we are spared the penalty of sin. This should fill out hearts with the gladness of God!

TRUSTING

MEMORY VERSE: *But let all those that put their trust in thee rejoice: let them ever shout for joy, because thou defendest them: let them also that love thy name be joyful in thee* (Psalm 5:11).

History records how George Washington found rest and relief in prayer during the trying times he and his soldiers passed through at Valley Forge. With all the cares and anxieties of that time upon him, he used to have recourse to prayer.

One day a farmer approaching the camp heard an earnest voice. On coming nearer, he saw George Washington on his knees, his cheeks wet with tears, praying. The farmer returned home and said to his wife: "George Washington will succeed!"

"What makes you think so, Isaac?" asked his wife.

The farmer replied: "I heard him pray, Hannah; you may rest assured he will."

One night during the Civil War, a guest in the White House reported that he had heard Lincoln praying in the next room. He said the President prayed: "Thou God, who heard Solomon in the night when he prayed and cried for wisdom, hear me! I cannot guide the affairs of this nation without Thy help. I am poor and weak and sinful. O God, save this nation."

We have a great heritage. Without question, God has defended America in the past. We ought to rejoice in our independence. But we must never forget that this freedom is a gift from God. The moment we stop trusting Him, liberty is in jeopardy.

Christians who serve God and rejoice in Him are America's most valuable asset. What will YOU do for your country?

SALVATION

MEMORY VERSE: *But I have trusted in thy mercy; my heart shall rejoice in thy salvation* (Psalm 13:5).

The joy of the Lord begins with salvation. The moment of new birth gives cause for rejoicing. Heaven rejoices: *Likewise, I say unto you, there is joy in the presence of the angels of God over one sinner that repenteth* (Luke 15:10). The new-born Christian can also be glad for many reasons.

We can rejoice in salvation because we have a home in heaven. Earthly homes are temporary. Fire or foreclosure may take away your home on this earth. Not so your heavenly home. The things that are seen are temporal but the things that are not seen are eternal. Each Christian has a title deed to a home in heaven that is indestructible.

We can rejoice in salvation because we have become heirs of God and joint-heirs with Christ (see Romans 8:17). During your earthly journey, you may never inherit anything valuable, but if you have been saved, you will share the inheritance of the saints. Praise the Lord!

We can rejoice in salvation because our names are written in heaven. Jesus said: *Notwithstanding in this rejoice not, that the spirits are subject unto you; but rather rejoice, because your names are written in heaven* (Luke 10:20). Many people do not know your name. You are probably not on a first-name basis with world leaders. But, if you have been born again, your name is known in heaven.

Rejoice in God's salvation!

ISRAEL REJOICING

MEMORY VERSE: *Oh that the salvation of Israel were come out of Zion! when the LORD bringeth back the captivity of his people, Jacob shall rejoice, and Israel shall be glad* (Psalm 14:7).

Through the centuries, the Jewish people have endured untold persecutions. Moses wrote of their coming sorrows long ago. Read this heart-rending description of Israel's sufferings as prophesied by Moses: *And among these nations shalt thou find no ease, neither shall the sole of thy foot have rest: but the LORD shall give thee there a trembling heart, and failing of eyes, and sorrow of mind: And thy life shall hang in doubt before thee; and thou shalt fear day and night, and shalt have none assurance of thy life: In the morning thou shalt say, Would God it were even! and at even thou shalt say, Would God it were morning! for the fear of thine heart wherewith thou shalt fear, and for the sight of thine eyes which thou shalt see* (Deuteronomy 28:65-67).

There is a day of gladness and rejoicing coming for Israel. Before that times arrives, Jews will endure continued trouble that will reach its zenith during the great Tribulation, a time known as the day of Jacob's Trouble. Rejoicing will come for Israel when the Jews finally receive the Lord Jesus as Saviour. That day is coming. The Bible guarantees it.

The signs of the times that point to the salvation of Israel and the establishment of the kingdom of Christ also herald the return of Christ for the Church. The prospect of His return should bring rejoicing to every heart. No burden is so heavy that it cannot be lightened by the realization that Christ may come today!

Order my book *Israel's Final Holocaust.*

HELPED

MEMORY VERSE: *The LORD is my strength and my shield; my heart trusted in him, and I am helped: therefore my heart greatly rejoiceth; and with my song will I praise him* (Psalm 28:7).

A Christian in Central Russia wrote the following: "After our commune was closed, I spent some time in the place where God's servants have to stay...(in prison). And yet, I assure you, that during that time in my heart it was as though I were living in the Garden of Eden... Scarcely a single night passed when I did not rise from my bed and thank God. And what was that which moved me to praise Him? Why, the consciousness of His wonderful presence. The only thing for me to do was to get upon my knees and praise God for His faithful and unfailing presence."

The world has a saying: "The Lord helps those who help themselves." Some mistakenly think that this statement is in the Bible. The truth is—the Lord helps those who cannot help themselves. He meets us where we are in our deepest needs.

Paul was helped when buffeted by a messenger from Satan, a thorn in the flesh. Though the physical problem was not removed, grace was promised for that particular test: *My grace is sufficient for thee: for my strength is made perfect in weakness* (2 Corinthians 12:9).

How have you been helped? Have prayers been answered? Has money been supplied for a special need? Have you recovered from a serious illness? Has a loved one been saved? Were you protected from an accident? Were you given strength for a difficult task?

Are you rejoicing over the help granted to you? Praise God for His goodness and rejoice in His help.

IN THE LORD

MEMORY VERSE: *Rejoice in the LORD, O ye righteous: for praise is comely for the upright* (Psalm 33:1).

Rejoice in the Lord is a command given in both the Old and New Testaments. Paul admonished the Christians at Philippi: *Rejoice in the Lord alway: and again I say, Rejoice* (Philippians 4:4).

But how can one rejoice when all his castles are tumbling and everything seems to go wrong? Can we rejoice over unpaid bills? Poor health? A divided family? The loss of a job? Jangled nerves?

Perhaps not.

But we can rejoice in the Lord!

When everything seems to be coming apart, He is unchanged. Though others forsake us, He remains faithful. If financial reverses come, He provides for our needs. When earthly gain turns to loss, He offers permanent treasure in the bank of heaven. If death seems imminent, He has given eternal life. Though the love of those nearest us cool, His love is constant.

The rejoicing of the psalmist had to find expression. He played the harp, the psaltry, and an instrument of ten strings. He sang songs of praise. It was impossible to hold in his joy. Some may have thought him too emotional. Perhaps they preferred dead-pan religion. Nevertheless, the psalmist rejoiced in the Lord and announced his joy to others. His praise was public and he was not ashamed.

Regardless of the circumstances, we can rejoice in the Lord. Christians should never be "under the circumstances." Our Lord is above all. Today's problems have not taken Him by surprise. Praise the Lord!

AFTER BACKSLIDING

MEMORY VERSE: *Make me to hear joy and gladness; that the bones which thou hast broken may rejoice* (Psalm 51:8).

No load is heavier than the burden of backsliding. David had learned that lesson the hard way. After sin, the chastening of God had fallen upon him and he was tormented with conviction of his wrong doing.

At first he decided to ignore God's voice that called him to confession of sin. Listen to his description of that awful time: *When I kept silence, my bones waxed old through my roaring all the day long. For day and night thy hand was heavy upon me: my moisture is turned into the drought of summer* (Psalm 32:3,4).

Finally, tired of his backsliding, he made the right decision: *I acknowledged my sin unto thee, and mine iniquity have I not hid. I said, I will confess my transgressions unto the LORD; and thou forgavest the iniquity of my sin* (Psalm 32:5).

Psalm 51 is David's prayer of confession of sin. See his openness with God. Nothing is hidden. He calls for cleansing, forgiveness, a right attitude, and the joy of salvation. He fully intends to become an effective witness even though he has failed so badly: *Then will I teach transgressors thy ways; and sinners shall be converted unto thee* (Psalm 51:13).

How good it feels to be right with God! There is rejoicing in heaven over the return of the prodigal, but the prodigal also rejoices. Home is a wonderful word. And the Christian who returns to His Lord after backsliding has come home.

Come home. And rejoice!

PROSPERITY

MEMORY VERSE: *They drop upon the pastures of the wilderness: and the little hills rejoice on every side* (Psalm 65:12).

Sometimes those who prosper rejoice less than the poor. They hold earth's trinkets so tightly that the fear of losing them is ever with them. Often they have become slaves to the prosperity that has been their goal in life.

A few wealthy and prosperous people are free from the bondage of their possessions. A Christian doctor was asked what he had done during the past week. He replied, "On Monday, I preached the gospel in Brazil. Tuesday, I ministered among the Mexican people in southwest Texas. Wednesday, I operated on patients in a hospital in Africa. Thursday, I taught in a mission school in Japan. Friday, I helped establish a new church in California. Saturday, I taught classes in our seminaries. Sunday, I distributed Bibles in Korea."

The astonished questioner asked, "How could you be in so many places, doing so many different things?"

"I wasn't," said the doctor with a twinkle in his eye, "for I have been busy with my patients every day. But, you see, I hold the dollars God has enabled me to earn in trust for God, and some of them have been channeled into the places of need I have mentioned."

Walter Brown Knight wrote: "There are two ways to be rich—one is to have all you want, and the other is to be satisfied with what you have."

The real secret of joy in prosperity is the ability of rejoicing in the One who gives the power to get wealth. Rejoice in Him! All we have is from His hand.

DELIVERANCE

MEMORY VERSE: *He turned the sea into dry land: they went through the flood on foot: there did we rejoice in him* (Psalm 66:6).

While headed down an ice-covered hill on a country road, my car went out of control. When my lights illumined the road at the bottom of the hill, I saw that it was covered with water. In those few moments, as the swerving, sliding automobile skidded toward the water, I resigned myself to the coming crash, expecting the impact of the sliding wheels hitting the water to cause the car to overturn. But the accident didn't happen. My fears were never realized. Just before arriving at the flooded section of road, the car righted itself and we went safely on our way.

A friend braced himself for a collision when another driver pulled out of a side street directly in front of him. The coming accident seemed so inevitable that he froze at the wheel, unable to move. He says that at that moment the wheel turned in his hands and by the next breath the two cars had miraculously passed one another.

The Children of Israel had fled from slavery in Egypt and had arrived at the Red Sea. The army of their former taskmasters was approaching and there seemed no place to go. But God opened the sea for them and they walked through on dry land. Writing of it later, the psalmist said, *There did we rejoice in him* (Psalm 66:6).

But there are many times of deliverance when we forget to rejoice. Undoubtedly, our lives have been spared scores of times when we have been unaware of any danger. Being alive at this moment calls for rejoicing and praise to God for His goodness in sparing and protecting us another day!

THE RIGHTEOUS

MEMORY VERSE: *But let the righteous be glad; let them rejoice before God: yea, let them exceedingly rejoice* (Psalm 68:3).

Righteousness is rewarded.

Sometimes it doesn't seem that way.

Knowing there would be times when it appeared the wicked were coming out winners, the psalmist wrote: *Fret not thyself because of evildoers, neither be thou envious against the workers of iniquity. For they shall soon be cut down like the grass, and wither as the green herb* (Psalm 37:1,2).

Things are seldom what they seem. Outward success is meaningless unless the heart is right. Sin detracts from delight. The so-called "beautiful people" are often among the world's most unhappy.

Only the righteous can truly rejoice.

But it is sad when the righteous do not rejoice. Those who have every reason to be glad sometimes spend their days groaning about trivial matters. Equipped for daily victory they are continually defeated. Having become citizens of heaven they live like hopeless earthlings. Though heirs of God and joint-heirs with Christ, they have allowed themselves to take on the mental attitudes of spiritual paupers. They are more often found pouting than praising, fault-finding is their specialty and nothing escapes their criticism. They are part of the body of Christ and have great potential for service, but they spend their time murmuring and complaining instead of rejoicing and reaching out to the lost.

Let the righteous rejoice! This is the will of God for each one of His children.

OLD AGE

MEMORY VERSE: *My lips shall greatly rejoice when I sing unto thee; and my soul, which thou hast redeemed* (Psalm 71:23).

"Let it be our unceasing prayer that as we grow older we may not grow colder in the ways of God," said good George Muller.

Muller lived up into the late nineties—always bright, full of interest, hopeful, joyful. In his last years, he would often stop in the midst of his conversation to exclaim, "Oh, I am so happy!" And it was not a mannerism, nor was it feigned.

"As we advance in years," he had written long before, "let us not decline in spiritual power; but let us see to it that an increase of spiritual vigor and energy be found in us, that our last days may be our best days...Let the remaining days of our pilgrimage be spent in an ever-increasing, earnest consecration to God."

"The devil has no happy old people," it has been said. And that is understandable. How sad to have lived only for these few passing years and the thrills or compensations of them! In that case, old age is like a solemn countdown to the end. Treasures must be left behind. Moments must be drained of all good, for nothing good is expected beyond the grave.

In contrast, the Christian can rejoice in old age. He is still young in the light of eternity and every beat of his heart moves him closer to glory. He is not leaving his treasures but going to them. The end of life is but the end of his limitations. He savors every moment as another opportunity to serve his Lord and to be with loved ones, but he knows that better things are ahead and that a great reunion is coming in heaven.

Whether in church, his home, or in heaven, he can say, *My lips shall greatly rejoice when I sing unto thee.*

GOD REIGNS

MEMORY VERSE: *The LORD reigneth; let the earth rejoice; let the multitude of isles be glad thereof* (Psalm 97:1).

God reigns.

Have you ever thought how sad the plight of planet earth would be if that were not true?

We would all be on a hopeless voyage through space with no destination.

Every grave would be a place of despair and total separation.

Life would be without purpose.

The universe would be like a giant clock winding down until the end.

No prayer would ever be heard or answered.

Man would always walk the dark valley of death alone.

All of life's horizons would be limited by time.

The trinkets and thrills of this life span would be the only things of value.

But God reigns.

Therefore the earth can rejoice.

We are the recipients of the love of God and the beneficiaries of His boundless grace.

We do not walk through life alone if we have been born again.

The dark valley has been changed to the valley of the shadow of death—and He—the Light of the World—walks there with us.

Heaven is a real place for a prepared people. Treasures can be sent on ahead for enjoying forever.

In every perplexing situation in life, we know that He is in charge.

God reigns! Rejoice!

PRAISE

MEMORY VERSE: *Make a joyful noise unto the LORD, all the earth: make a loud noise, and rejoice, and sing praise* (Psalm 98:4).

Praise is powerful.

When we are occupied with praising God, our minds are turned from earthly problems. We are able to concentrate on but one thing at a time. Therefore, time given to praising God rests our emotions and soothes our nerves by giving them relief from the tensions of life.

Praise builds faith. Focusing on reasons for praise reminds us of the greatness of God, His love, and His power. If our relationship with God is only that of asking, we may forget the attributes of our Heavenly Father that make it worthwhile to pray. We ask because He is able to answer and because He cares. Praise Him for His compassion, His goodness, and His grace.

Praise God enthusiastically. Faint praise is no praise at all. The psalmist urges heartfelt adoration. Pay no attention to those who criticize your dedication and worry about your fervent faith. Their concern is a commentary on their understanding of the greatness of God.

Praise God publicly. There are times for walking through quiet fields and forests while silently lifting your heart to God in thankfulness for His beauty and blessings. But this should never be to the exclusion of public worship: *Not forsaking the assembling of ourselves together, as the manner of some is; but exhorting one another: and so much the more, as ye see the day approaching* (Hebrews 10:25). Join your heart and voice with others in hymns and songs of praise.

Praise the Lord!

THE DAY

MEMORY VERSE: *This is the day which the LORD hath made; we will rejoice and be glad in it* (Psalm 118:24).

Today comes only once in a lifetime. What a tragedy to waste 24 hours of life complaining about the weather or looking for the faults in people. This precious segment of time is given to use and enjoy. It will never return. Once spent it cannot be bought back at any price.

A dying queen once cried, "Millions in money for an inch of time." She would have gladly traded places with paupers in her kingdom who had time to live. But time cannot be bartered. It is here today and gone tomorrow.

Most of us have found ourselves saying "I'll be glad when…" We may think we'll be glad when we're older, when the mortgage is paid, when summer arrives, when the children are grown, or when we retire. The truth is when that time arrives, we may not be glad at all. Factors may have entered our lives by that time that make it far more difficult to be glad than it is today.

Today is the only day of which we can be sure. James wrote: *Go to now, ye that say, To day or to morrow we will go into such a city, and continue there a year, and buy and sell, and get gain: Whereas ye know not what shall be on the morrow* (James 4:13,14).

So, today is the day to live. It is the day to give, to serve, to worship, to pray, to work, to succeed, to rejoice. Do not let it escape misused or abused. It is the day to care, to be reconciled, to forgive, to trust, to love, to speak kindly, to forget old wrongs, to share the gospel, to obey the Bible, to appreciate loved ones, and to be glad.

This is the day which the LORD hath made—be glad in it!

THE BIBLE

MEMORY VERSE: *I rejoice at thy word, as one that findeth great spoil* (Psalm 119:162).

In our youth, most of us have fancied finding buried treasure. As adults, millions buy lottery tickets or gamble in other ways in the hope of receiving great treasure. The psalmist valued God's Word far more than any earthly bonanza.

If you have difficulty rejoicing today, praise God for the Bible. Think about its worth. Dwell on its riches. Apart from this divine revelation, we would know little of the personality of God. We might conclude that He is powerful and the Creator, for *the heavens declare the glory of God; and the firmament sheweth his handywork* (Psalm 19:1), but we could never understand His love and would therefore miss life's greatest blessing.

The Bible reveals God's plan of the ages. We do not have to stumble through life ever questioning the direction of history and fearing the future. God has explained His plan. History is His story. We do not fear what the future holds because we know the One who holds the future. And it has been revealed to us in the Bible.

The earth has some traumatic days ahead. Christ is coming. The dead will be raised. Christians will be raptured. Tribulation will overtake the earth. Political and religious chaos is sure to come. But none of these things will take God by surprise, and students of the Bible have been given a preview of these events.

Christians who read God's Word are "in the know." They are better informed than the world's most able news analysts.

What a book! Rejoice in it. Praise God for it. Let its message rule your life today!

HUSBANDS AND WIVES

MEMORY VERSE: *Let thy fountain be blessed: and rejoice with the wife of thy youth* (Proverbs 5:18).

Here is a good test for married couples. Estimate the number of years you have left together. Figure the number of hours that totals. Divide the number by three and subtract the answer from the total to find the number of waking hours together. Now divide the remaining amount by two to arrive at the approximate time apart because of work. How do you intend to spend the hours that remain?

How many hours do you intend to spend arguing? In hand-to-hand combat? Pouting? Administering the "silent treatment"? Grumbling? Finding fault? Putting one another down? Criticizing one another before friends? Being apart unnecessarily? Now that you've removed the clutter, what will you do with the time that is left to invest?

How many hours have you reserved for expressing your love for each other? Holding one another? Complimenting? Walking together? Laughing? Sharing projects of mutual enjoyment? Relaxing together? Planning new adventures? Enjoying your children or grandchildren? Praying together? Studying the Bible? Attending church services? Telling others of God's blessings?

Generally, we do not think about how quickly life escapes. The Bible speaks about the importance of "redeeming the time." Unless priority is given to rejoicing together, as God intends, couples may waste most of their lives in unpleasant tasks or sour attitudes, thereby missing God's will for their lives.

Rejoice with the wife of thy youth. And enjoy your husband while he's with you. It's the Bible way to live!

A MERRY HEART

MEMORY VERSE: *A merry heart doeth good like a medicine: but a broken spirit drieth the bones* (Proverbs 17:22).

Some are happy in the most difficult of circumstances. Others complain in affluence. Some rejoice at the smallest favor. Like Elijah who saw rain in a cloud the size of a man's hand, they need little encouragement to make faith soar. Others despair when surrounded with plenty. They difference lies in the heart. *A merry heart doeth good like a medicine.* Happy is the person who finds joy in daily duty.

After viewing a TV program dealing with work, a young lady wrote to the station saying: "I work in a gas station and I don't always feel like getting up at 5 a.m. 'cause it's still dark outside, but once I get some cereal in my stomach and get going I'm OK. I may not have the most beautiful job in the world but I'm doing a service for other people for the glory of God. If I would go to work with a crummy attitude and be mean and crabby to all the customers, they would go to their jobs and families and be crabby, too. Just think of all the people this would affect. There would be one bad chain reaction, but I pray that each day I will give good service and a friendly smile to all my customers." She had learned the value of a merry heart.

A rejoicing heart is normal for the child of God. The Holy Spirit produces joy within. When Christian joy is not present it is because we are quenching the Spirit. While the Holy Spirit provides the resource of joy in all situations, we can block that blessing by focusing on life's problems.

Let the joy of the Lord rule in your heart. Quench not the Spirit!

RIGHTEOUS LEADERS

MEMORY VERSE: *When the righteous are in authority, the people rejoice: but when the wicked beareth rule, the people mourn* (Proverbs 29:2).

The decisions of our nation's leaders have a great bearing on our lives. The quality of leadership in America depends a great deal upon our carrying out Christian responsibilities as citizens of this good land.

One of our greatest responsibilities toward the government is that of prayer for our nation's leaders: *I exhort therefore, that, first of all, supplications, prayers, intercessions, and giving of thanks, be made for all men; For kings, and for all that are in authority; that we may lead a quiet and peaceable life in all godliness and honesty. For this is good and acceptable in the sight of God our Saviour; Who will have all men to be saved, and to come unto the knowledge of the truth* (1 Timothy 2:1-4).

Listen to any conversation about politics and you will soon detect an attitude of complaining and criticism. Thankfully, in America, we can speak out against wrongs in government without fear of imprisonment or fines. Nevertheless, as Christians, our task is one of prayer. If we are not faithfully interceding for the nation's leaders, we have no Christian right to criticize them.

Praying Christians are the nation's greatest asset. Earnest prayer can place the right men in office and give them direction for all decisions. This is a perilous time for our land. It is time for God's people to be on their knees for the leaders of America.

Prayer can produce righteous leaders—and the people can rejoice!

THE DESERT

MEMORY VERSE: *The wilderness and the solitary place shall be glad for them; and the desert shall rejoice, and blossom as the rose* (Isaiah 35:1).

It is difficult for us to think of a rejoicing desert. Can land rejoice? Can soil enjoy? What does this unusual verse mean?

Isaiah is writing about the coming kingdom. Christ will come and rule for a thousand years. We call that period of time the "Millennium," meaning one thousand years. At that time, there will be great changes in nature. The earth will cease its struggle with man that was announced to Adam at the fall. Modern farming miracles that come from know-how and super chemicals will not compare with those that appear during the reign of Christ.

Those who have traveled in desert regions know the value of water in producing vegetation. A river winding through a desert leads a train of life through the barren wasteland. But in that day, God will give the deserts rain in season and they will blossom with roses and other beautiful flowers, as well as crops of food.

The blossoming desert pictures a life that has been transformed by the wonderful power of Christ. Though barren and unfruitful, your life can come into its own when you are born again. Like the rain in its season, the Holy Spirit brings life within. An unproductive life takes on new meaning. *Old things are passed away; behold, all things are become new* (2 Corinthians 5:17).

Do you want to see a rejoicing desert? Take the gospel of Christ to some lost person and observe the miracle of life. In a spiritual sense, when he believes, the desert will blossom as a rose!

JOHN THE BAPTIST

MEMORY VERSE: *And thou shalt have joy and gladness; and many shall rejoice at his birth* (Luke 1:14).

Zacharias and Elizabeth had waited long for a child. Their prayer for a son had been heard, though the waiting must have been discouraging. The coming birth of John was announced to Zacharias as he performed his work in the Temple. When praying, it is best to continue our daily responsibilities in faith that God will answer in His time.

When the child was born, his parents were filled with joy. The promise of the angel who announced his birth had been that many others would also rejoice at his birth and in his life. That promise was confirmed when John the Baptist began his powerful ministry. The words of the Prophet Isaiah were fulfilled, and the voice was crying in the wilderness to prepare the way of the Lord.

God always keeps His Word and He is always on time. You may have been praying long for a special need or desire and it has not yet come. Your faith is faltering. You wonder if there is any use in praying. You are about to surrender in defeat.

Do not give up. Any prayer in the will of God will be answered: *And this is the confidence that we have in him, that, if we ask anything according to his will, he heareth us: And if we know that he hear us, whatsoever we ask, we know that we have the petitions that we desired of him* (1 John 5:14,15).

The parents of John the Baptist rejoiced at his birth. But the answer was sure long before the actual birth took place and they could have rejoiced in the fulfillment of God's promise even then.

Do you dare to rejoice in God's answer—before it arrives?

PERSECUTION

MEMORY VERSE: *Blessed are ye, when men shall hate you, and when they shall separate you from their company, and shall reproach you, and cast out your name as evil, for the Son of man's sake* (Luke 6:22).

Pastor J. H. Crowell, when about sixteen, shipped on a sailing vessel where he was the only Christian in a crew of twelve. Before leaving his mother he promised to meet her three times a day at the throne of grace, and so he regularly went below and prayed knowing that his mother was praying at the same time at home beside her bed.

The other crew members were furious over his praying and persecuted him severely. They threw wood at him and poured buckets of water over him, but they could not put out the fire in his soul.

Finally, they tied him to the mast and laid thirty-nine stripes on his back. Still he prayed on. At last, they tied a rope around him and threw him overboard. He swam as best he could, and when he took hold of the side of the ship, they pushed him off with a pole. When his strength gave way and he thought he would die, he called out: "Send my body to my mother and tell her I died for Jesus."

The wrath of the angry sailors seemed finally to be exhausted and they pulled the young Christian up on the deck and left him there unconscious. Shortly after he revived, conviction began to seize his companions on the ship. Before night, two of them were saved. Within a week, everyone on board, including the captain, had been born again.

The persecution was difficult, but J. H. Crowell met it as a Christian, counting it joy to suffer for Christ. The Lord rewarded him with the conversion of his persecutors.

Can you rejoice in opportunities to suffer for the Lord? (See 2 Timothy 3:12.)

NAMES IN HEAVEN

MEMORY VERSE: *Notwithstanding in this rejoice not, that the spirits are subject unto you; but rather rejoice, because your names are written in heaven* (Luke 10:20).

What thrilling days those must have been for the disciples! Called from their nets and other tasks to be fishers of men, they were sent forth in the power of God and with the message of His kingdom. Returning, they said: *Lord, even the devils are subject unto us through thy name* (Luke 10:17). At that, Jesus gave them a greater reason to rejoice. He said: *Your names are written in heaven.*

We have this great privilege in common with the disciples and all other Christians—our names are written in heaven. When a person's name is recorded in some earthly hall of fame, it makes news, though it often takes place after death. How much better to have our names in God's book, guaranteeing eternal life.

Perhaps this has been a difficult week. Your plans have fallen through. You missed the promotion. The children have been sick. The car didn't start and you were late for an appointment. The mortgage payment is overdue. And to top it all, the pastor spoke yesterday on rejoicing in tribulation.

What is there to rejoice about?

You can rejoice that your name is written in heaven. That is true if you have received the Lord Jesus Christ as your personal Lord and Saviour.

All earthly troubles are temporary. His salvation lasts forever!

THE LOST FOUND

MEMORY VERSE: *And when he hath found it, he layeth it on his shoulders, rejoicing* (Luke 15:5).

What makes the heart of God rejoice?

Lost people being found.

We should not be surprised to find that the salvation of a soul delights the heart of God. The message of the Bible is that of God's love for lost people: *The Lord is not slack concerning his promise, as some men count slackness; but is longsuffering to us-ward, not willing that any should perish, but that all should come to repentance* (2 Peter 3:9). Therefore, if we long to bless the heart of our Lord, we ought to take the gospel to people and lead as many as possible to salvation.

Every biblical means of evangelism should be employed. Church visitation programs ought to be supported. Tract distribution should become a regular habit. We must go to people in their times of need to let them know of the love of Christ. Hospital visitation and calling on shut-ins need not be left to pastors alone. Every member of the body of Christ can go with the gospel. Radio and television are powerful tools of outreach, penetrating national borders and gleaning souls in lands where open preaching is forbidden.

The reaching of lost people will also bring rejoicing at the coming of the Lord. *For what is our hope, or joy, or crown of rejoicing? Are not even ye in the presence of our Lord Jesus Christ at his coming? For ye are our glory and joy* (1 Thessalonians 2:19,20).

Soulwinners and the Saviour rejoice in the winning of the lost: *He that goeth forth and weepeth, bearing precious seed, shall doubtless come again with rejoicing, bringing his sheaves with him* (Psalm 126:6). Join the joyous harvest!

REJOICING IN HEAVEN

MEMORY VERSE: *Likewise, I say unto you, there is joy in the presence of the angels of God over one sinner that repenteth* (Luke 15:10).

The man who knelt beside me was the son of a preacher of the gospel. His father had gone to heaven long ago. Now the son, a grandfather, was asking the Lord Jesus to save him. When he had finished his prayer of faith, I rejoiced with him in his salvation and then said, "Your father knows that you have been born again."

"I hope so," he sighed.

"I guarantee it," I said reassuringly. Then I shared our memory verse with him.

There is no doubt about it. Those in heaven know when any person on earth is saved and it brings great rejoicing there. The angels are glad and joy breaks out among the saints. Another soul will share heaven with them.

I would like to have been there when that former circuit-riding preacher was notified of the salvation of his son, Bill. I'm sure he had led many to Christ in days gone by and had rejoiced to see them saved, but always there had been that longing over his son. Through life he had prayed for him, expecting his conversion year after year but never seeing it happen. Perhaps he had experienced times of doubting that his prayer would ever be answered. Preachers are human enough to go through valleys of doubt and depression. Sometimes he may have felt like giving up—but always he went back to his knees. It was all he could do. Then, finally, his earthly sojourn ended and he went to heaven without his prayer answered. It may have been the only touch of sadness that he felt in arriving there. But now the victory had come.

Heaven rejoiced!

THE HARVEST

MEMORY VERSE: *And he that reapeth receiveth wages, and gathereth fruit unto life eternal: that both he that soweth and he that reapeth may rejoice together* (John 4:36).

Early one morning, William Gladstone was at his desk at No. 10 Downing Street, London. A timid knock on the door called him from preparing an important speech he was to deliver that day in Parliament.

Standing at the door was a little boy whose friendship Gladstone had won by little deeds of kindness. The boy said, "My brother is dying. Won't you please come and show him the way to heaven?"

Leaving his important work for the most important work any Christian can do, Gladstone went to the bedside of the dying boy. In a matter of moments, the boy was rejoicing in his newly found Saviour!

Returning to his office, Gladstone wrote at the bottom of the speech he had been preparing: "I am the happiest man in London today!" He had been the human instrument in the hands of God, to lead a boy to the Saviour.

Gladstone was there in the hour of reaping and rejoiced. Some, however, miss the moment of reaping, yet share in the winning of lost people. They are the sowers.

Sowers may have difficulty finding courage or words for the moment of decision in soulwining, but they faithfully witness and give out the gospel. Some sowers mail scores of letters with enclosed tracts. Other sowers live consistent Christian lives and show compassion to those in need.

In the harvest, the sowers and reapers rejoice together! (See John 4:37,38.)

LOVE REJOICING

MEMORY VERSE: *Rejoiceth not in iniquity, but rejoiceth in the truth* (1 Corinthians 13:6).

We learn a lot about people when we discover what causes them to rejoice. There is something wrong in the heart of the person who rejoices in iniquity or injustices. The life that is directed by the love of Christ deplores injustice in any form. It is inconceivable that those who love and trust the God of justice should rejoice in iniquity.

Love rejoices in the truth. Even when it hurts. Love chooses truth regardless of the cost personally. Christians who walk in the light discard dishonesty in all its forms for in following Christ, truth is the only way.

But there is a deeper truth here.

The world is steeped in iniquity. Sin is rampant. It permeates every human society affecting everything from commerce to comedy. The Christian, then, will not build his life around these passing things. He will not rejoice in them because they are tainted with sin and will cause him to be shallow or carnal.

Where, then, can he find the truth in which to rejoice?

Christ is truth personified. He said: *I am the way, the truth, and the life: no man cometh unto the Father, but by me* (John 14:6).

So the Christian who serves and loves His Lord, stops rejoicing in iniquity and rejoices in Jesus—the Truth.

In what do you rejoice?

IN CHRIST JESUS

MEMORY VERSE: *For we are the circumcision, which worship God in the spirit, and rejoice in Christ Jesus, and have no confidence in the flesh* (Philippians 3:3).

In his book, *When Iron Gates Yield*, Geoffrey Bull speaks of the joy which came to him when he was released from solitary confinement in a Chinese Communist prison where he was kept for months and deprived of all possessions, including his Bible. One day he heard a prisoner in a cell below sing, "Onward Christian Soldiers!" How thrilled he was to hear the name of Jesus. Exultantly, he exclaimed, "Praise the Lord! That's the sweetest sound I've heard during my months of imprisonment."

Paul combines his statement about rejoicing in Christ with a declaration that he has no confidence in the flesh. In that verse, he gave the story of his life—his testimony. Paul's former pride of ancestry is evident in his writings: *...though I might also have confidence in the flesh. If any other man thinketh that he hath whereof he might trust in the flesh, I more: Circumcised the eighth day, of the stock of Israel, of the tribe of Benjamin, and Hebrew of the Hebrews; as touching the law, a Pharisee; Concerning zeal, persecuting the church; touching the righteousness which is in the law, blameless* (Philippians 3:4-6).

Once he had rejoiced in his lineage, now he rejoiced in His Lord.

Once he had rejoiced in his race, now he rejoiced in his Redeemer.

Once he had rejoiced in the Law, now he rejoiced in the Lord Jesus.

Once he had rejoiced in his works, now he rejoiced in his wonderful Saviour.

Rejoice in Jesus!

IN TROUBLE

MEMORY VERSE: *Wherein ye greatly rejoice, though now for a season, if need be, ye are in heaviness through manifold temptations* (1 Peter 1:6).

Though Christians will not pass through the Tribulation, in this world we have tribulation. This is not strange. Salvation transforms sinners into citizens of heaven but it does not deliver them from earthly trials.

Some seem to have more than their share. Perhaps you feel you are one of them.

Still, God is faithful and has promised that He will not allow us to be tempted above what we are able. Henry Ward Beecher wrote: "No physician ever weighed out medicine to his patients with half so much care and exactness as God weighs out to us every trial. Not one grain too much does He ever permit to be put in the scale.

So, the Bible says we can rejoice in our trials.

Does this seem contradictory?

Not at all! These trials are designed to try our faith. And through them all we are kept by the power of God (see 1 Peter 1:5).

Like Peter, who began to sink when he looked at the wind and the waves while walking on the sea to Jesus, we may waver at times. But He never wavers. Our faith may sometimes be weak. But the object of our faith—Jesus—is strong.

No wonder we can rejoice in our temporary troubles. We have everlasting life! And we are in the care of our Eternal God.

PARTAKERS

MEMORY VERSE: *But rejoice, inasmuch as ye are partakers of Christ's sufferings; that, when his glory shall be revealed, ye may be glad also with exceeding joy* (1 Peter 4:13).

Christians are on a collision course with the world. They have staked their eternal destiny on Jesus and have publicly identified themselves with Him. That means trouble. Jesus said so. *If the world hate you, ye know that it hated me before it hated you. If ye were of the world, the world would love his own: but because ye are not of the world, but I have chosen you out of the world, therefore the world hateth you. Remember the word that I said unto you, The servant is not greater than his lord. If they have persecuted me, they will also persecute you; if they have kept my saying, they will keep yours also* (John 15:18-20).

Through the centuries, Christians have endured untold suffering for their faith in Christ. Millions have been put to death or have been imprisoned for the simple crime of trusting the Saviour and living for Him. It is estimated that our century has produced more martyrs than any other because of the cruelty of Communist nations. It costs to be a Christian.

To a lesser degree, it costs to be a Christian in America. The Christian heritage of our land makes it more hospitable up to this date. Suffering is possible, however, and yours is real to you. You may be hurting because of your testimony for Christ.

Praise the Lord! It will be worth it all when we see Jesus. We'll share in His glory and be glad again on that great day (see Matthew 5:10-12).

August

THIS MONTH'S STUDY

Roaming Through Romans

Days 1,4,5,16,19,21,24, and 30 contain quotes or information from "Three Thousand Illustrations for Christian Service," "Knight's Master Book of New Illustrations," and "Knight's Treasury of Illustrations," all by Walter B. Knight, published by Wm. B. Eerdmans Publishing Company, Grand Rapids, Michigan. Used by permission. Days 6,8,14,27, and 28 from "Let's Communicate," by Roger F. Campbell, published by Christian Literature Crusade, Fort Washington, Pa. Day 9 from "Lectures on Romans," by H. A. Ironside, published by Loizeaux Brothers, Neptune, N.J. Days 11,23, and 29 from "Romans in the Greek New Testament," by Kenneth Wuest, published by Wm. B. Eerdmans Publishing Company, Grand Rapids, Michigan. Day 20 from "Weight! A Better Way to Lose," by Roger F. Campbell, published by Victor Books, Wheaton, Illinois. Day 25 from "Spurgeon's Proverbs and Sayings With Notes," by C. H. Spurgeon, published by Baker Book House, Grand Rapids, Michigan.

THE GUARANTEE

MEMORY VERSE: *And declared to be the Son of God with power, according to the spirit of holiness, by the resurrection from the dead* (Romans 1:4).

The resurrection of Christ guarantees His deity.

Some years ago, Dr. Will Houghton, then president of the Moody Bible Institute, was in the Holy Land during the Easter season. With great interest he watched a large crowd of people march along a street. In front of the procession was a life-size wax figure of Christ—dead!

Mothers held up their little children and said, "Kiss the Christ!"

Dr. Houghton became sick at heart at the hollow mockery. He thought, "It is a lie—a base lie! He is not dead! The cross and the tomb are past! He is alive forevermore!"

Paul's Epistle to the Romans is a book of deep doctrinal truth and practical help. And it begins with a declaration that Jesus is the Son of God...this fact being demonstrated by His resurrection.

Nearly two thousand years after the writing of Paul's letter, the world has yet to discover any power that compares to resurrection power. With the passing of the centuries, man has learned to destroy more effectively, to halt some of the old plagues, and to make life's daily tasks easier, but resurrection power still eludes the most brilliant scientists. Man cannot engineer life.

Life resides in Christ.

And He imparts resurrection power to those who trust Him, not to the raising of the dead (though that will take place at His return) but so that we can have daily victory over sin and peace in the midst of life's storms. His mighty power is sufficient for all our needs.

It's guaranteed.

NOT ASHAMED

MEMORY VERSE: *For I am not ashamed of the gospel of Christ: for it is the power of God unto salvation to every one that believeth; to the Jew first, and also to the Greek* (Romans 1:16).

What is the gospel?

"Good news," someone answers.

True, but what is this good news?

Let Paul answer: *Moreover, brethren, I declare unto you the gospel which I preached unto you, which also ye have received, and wherein ye stand...how that Christ died for our sins according to the scriptures; And that he was buried, and that he rose again the third day according to the scriptures* (1 Corinthians 15:1,3,4).

Isn't it strange that there are so many divisions over this simple and wonderful message? Why do cults rise with far-out formulas for salvation?

Blindness.

Christ died for you and me. He was buried and rose again according to the Scriptures. That message produces the new birth. All who go to heaven arrive there because of this message. God has made His way of eternal life understandable. How sad that man makes it complicated.

To believe the gospel is to receive Christ by faith.

So, we do not follow the theological concoctions of some self-styled religious charlatan. Our faith rests in the everlasting gospel. And that is good news worth sharing.

Let the whole world know.

Don't be ashamed of the gospel of Christ. It's the power of God unto salvation...needed by all. Cut through meaningless conversation. Speak up for Christ today.

THE GOODNESS OF GOD

MEMORY VERSE: *Or despisest thou the riches of his goodness and forbearance and longsuffering; not knowing that the goodness of God leadeth thee to repentance?* (Romans 2:4).

Repentance is misunderstood. Some think of it as a time of deep sorrow for sin and long crying. Sorrow and tears may be a part of repentance but one may shed buckets of tears and never repent. To repent is to make an about-face. Repentance is a change of direction...a change of mind about sin and about the Saviour.

Many repent during difficult times or after experiencing some great loss, but others turn to Christ because He has been so good to them. "The goodness of God" leads them to repentance.

And God has been good to us all.

The eloquent DeWitt Talmage wrote: "It is high time you began to thank God for present blessing. Thank Him for your children, happy, buoyant, and bounding. Praise Him for fresh, cool water, bubbling from the rock, leaping in the cascade, soaring in the mist, falling in the shower, dashing against the rock, and clapping its hands in the tempest. Love Him for the grass that cushions the earth, and the clouds that curtain the sky, and the foliage that waves in the forest. Thank Him for the Bible to read, and a cross to gaze upon, and a Saviour to deliver."

Talmage had a way with words. But your silent song of thanksgiving rising to God from a grateful heart may outdo the great orator and preacher if you give thought to all of God's wondrous blessings.

Has God been good to you?

Isn't it time you became serious about repentance?

HYPOCRISY

MEMORY VERSE: *Thou therefore which teachest another, teachest thou not thyself? thou that preachest a man should not steal, dost thou steal?* (Romans 2:21).

There are many words which cause Bible translators difficulty when translating them into the languages of tribes and nations. There is one word, however, which presents no difficulty to the translators, and that word is hypocrisy.

Hypocrisy is a universal sin.

The hypocrite is found everywhere.

The Indian tribes in Latin American have various ways to denote the hypocrite. They designate him as "a man with two faces," "a man with two hearts," "a man with two kinds of talk," "a two-headed man," "a forked tongue person," "a two-sided man," and "a man with a straight mouth and a crooked heart!"

The only way to conquer hypocrisy is to be genuine through and through. Walter Brown Knight said: "Unless piety stems from inward righteousness it will degenerate into an outward form of religion, worn only on the sleeve for effect, with long-facedness being an ever-attendant characteristic."

Spurgeon observed: "I do not know of anything more dreadful than to be fattened without and to be starved within; to have everything that the heart could wish for, and yet not to have the best thing that the heart ought to wish for. May God save us from the appearance of prosperity which is only a veiled desolation!"

Is your life impressive outwardly?

How about your heart?

Are you as good as others think?

GOD FORBID

MEMORY VERSE: *For what if some did not believe? shall their unbelief make the faith of God without effect?* (Romans 3:3).

A minister proclaimed the gospel in an open-air meeting in Glasgow, Scotland. At the conclusion of his message, an unbeliever stepped from the crowd and said: "I don't believe what the minister said. I don't believe in heaven or hell. I don't believe in God or Christ. I haven't seen them."

Then a man, wearing dark glasses, came forward and said: "You say there is a river near this place—the River Clyde. There is no such thing. You say there are people standing here, but it cannot be true. I haven't seen them—I was born blind! Only a blind man could say what I have said. Likewise you are spiritually blind and cannot see. The Bible says of you, *But the natural man receiveth not the things of the Spirit of God: for they are foolishness unto him: neither can he know them, because they are spiritually discerned* (1 Corinthians 2:14).

Christians often are shaken over the arguments of atheists. That is a mistake. Their unbelief does not change the truth of God. What if atheists finally outnumbered believers? Would unbelief by the majority make the Bible less dependable?

God forbid.

What if all the scientists in the world determined that God does not exist? Would their unbelief eliminate the Almighty?

God forbid.

And what if some should doubt that God will take you safely through your present crisis? Will their unbelief cancel the promises of God?

Nor for a moment. God forbid.

You're safe in His care.

SINS GONE

MEMORY VERSE: *Being justified freely by his grace through the redemption that is in Christ Jesus...* (Romans 3:24).

Wava Campbell's poem, "Where Will You Go," expresses the anxiety of conviction and the relief of forgiveness. Apply its truth to your heart.

> Where will you go to hide from God
> If you don't forsake that sin?
> If you cherish that wrong
> Until it's so strong
> That it has you conquered within?
> Where will you go to hide from God
> When His Spirit convicts you so?
> And where will you run from the Holy One?
> Backslider, where will you go?
> Where will you go to hide from God
> When life becomes empty and drear?
> When your heart seems to shout
> That you can't live without
> The God whose correction you fear?
> Where can you go except to God,
> Confessing your sin and shame?
> In humble prayer just meet Him there.
> And call on His holy name.
> Then peace like a river will flood your heart,
> And gratitude will flow,
> So quickly run to the Holy One,
> There's just no place else to go.
>
> ...Wava Campbell

SPIRITUAL PROSPERITY

MEMORY VERSE: *Blessed is the man to whom the Lord will not impute sin* (Romans 4:8).

Forgiveness comes through faith.

Abraham believed God and it was counted to him for righteousness.

Here's good news: through faith the record is made clean. What could not be accomplished through law keeping or religious ceremony has become a reality through faith. In his book, *Romans in the Greek New Testament,* Kenneth Wuest translates Romans 4:6-8 as follows: "Even as David also declares the spiritual prosperity of the man to whose account God puts righteousness apart from works, spiritually prosperous are those whose lawlessnesses were put away and whose sins were covered. Spiritually prosperous is the man to whose account the Lord does not put sin."

Faith is the account settler.

And that is hard for man to grasp.

Hundreds of cults exist because of the human demand to do something more than faith to be right with God. Any teaching that adds anything to faith as a requirement for salvation is cultic. To add to the gospel is to detract from its saving message.

Have you received the Lord Jesus Christ by faith?

If so, the old account is settled. And your faith is counted for righteousness. You are spiritually prosperous. God has cleared your record...completely.

Millions in earthly holdings cannot compare to the value of a clear account with God. Monetary prosperity rises and falls with the condition of the nation's economy. Those who trust in Christ are spiritually prosperous forever.

What blessing! Thank God for it.

HE STAGGERED NOT

MEMORY VERSE: *He staggered not at the promise of God through unbelief; but was strong in faith, giving glory to God* (Romans 4:20).

Abraham is called the father of the faithful because he believed God. His faith was translated into action. When called to do so, he stepped out on faith, completely committed to the will of God.

Faith adds adventure to drab living. See if your experience has matched that of the following poem:

TO WALK BY FAITH
To walk by faith is such a great adventure;
It thrills the spirit every passing day
To see God's hand, and know whatever happens,
He understands, and He will lead the way.
To walk by sight is something very tragic;
It makes the spirit droop, the heart grow cold.
It makes the Christian plan, and fume, and fumble;
It makes his body feel so tired and old.
Just how to walk life's road is our decision.
God leaves the choice with us, and us alone.
But if we choose to walk by sight, we'll see not;
By faith His will is seen, and felt, and known.
...Wava Campbell

Many miss life's best because they stagger when called upon to act in faith. James calls it being "double minded." Staggering at God's promises is an affliction brought on by meditating on all the negative possibilities in any given situation. Trust God. Expect the most from His hand.

Stop staggering.

TRIBULATION WORKETH PATIENCE

MEMORY VERSE: *And not only so, but we glory in tribulation also: knowing that tribulation worketh patience* (Romans 5:3).

Most want patience.

Few want tribulation.

But tribulation produces patience.

Commenting on this text, Dr. H. A. Ironside has written: "But ere we reach the glory we must tread the sands of the wilderness. This is the place of testing. Here we learn the infinite resources of our wonderful God. So we are enabled to glory in tribulations, contrary though these may be to all that the natural man rejoices in. Tribulation is the divinely appointed flail to separate the wheat from the chaff. In suffering and sorrow we learn our own nothingness and the greatness of the power that has undertaken to carry us through. These are lessons we could never learn in heaven...Thus 'tribulation worketh patience' if we accept it from our loving Lord himself, knowing it is for our blessing. Out of patient endurance springs fragrant Christian experience, as the soul learns how wonderfully Christ can sustain in every circumstance. And experience blossoms into hope, weaning the heart from the things of earth and occupying them with the heavenly scene to which we are hastening."

There is a design in our difficulties.

Like a potter forming a valuable vase, our Heavenly Father works on His children with the wheel of circumstance, always tempering each move with love and forming us according to His perfect will.

Your troubles have a purpose...even those that hurt just now.

Tomorrow you will be better because of trials faced today.

REIGNING

MEMORY VERSE: *For if by one man's offence death reigned by one; much more they which receive abundance of grace and of the gift of righteousness shall reign in life by one, Jesus Christ* (Romans 5:17).

On a tombstone in St. Andrews churchyard in Scotland, marking the resting place of four infants, the following epitaph appears:

"Bold infidelity, turn pale and die.
Beneath this stone four sleeping infants lie;
Say, are they lost or saved?
If death's by sin, they sinned, for they are here.
If by heaven's by works, in heaven they can't appear,
Reason, ah, how depraved!
Turn to the Bible's sacred page, the knot's untied:
They died, for Adam sinned; they live,
for Jesus died." (See Romans 5:18.)

All men die.
Death rules.
Grace overrules.

There is no argument about the fact that death comes upon all men and therefore death has reigned over men. But those who receive Christ are to reign (rule) as kings in life. Every cemetery should remind the believer that death's dominion is temporary and that at the moment he received Christ he was given the gift of righteousness and grace for every experience in life.

Christians should not be defeated.
Fears should not conquer them.
Kings don't cower.

While in this temple we reign through Christ. In eternity we shall reign with Christ. Talk about showers of blessing...we're reigning.

SERVANTS OF SIN

MEMORY VERSE: *Know ye not, that to whom ye yield your-selves servants to obey, his servants ye are to whom ye obey; whether of sin unto death, or of obedience unto righteous-ness?* (Romans 6:16).

Sin enslaves. Promising freedom, it brings bondage.

Paul's references to sin in this chapter have to do with the sinful nature of man. Kenneth Wuest says of Paul's opening question: "Shall we continue habitually to sustain the same relationship to the sinful nature that we sustained before we were saved, a relationship which was most cordial, a relation-ship in which we were fully yielded to and dependent upon that sinful nature, and all this as a habit of life?"

He continues: "The Christian has the same power over the evil nature that he has over his radio. When a program sud-denly comes over the air unfit for Christian ears, he can shut the radio off with a 'There, you cannot bring that smut into my life.' Before salvation, the evil nature had absolute domin-ion over the sinner. Since salvation has wrought its benefi-cent work in his inner being, he has absolute dominion over it. Believe this, child of God, and act upon it. The evil nature is a dethroned monarch. Paul personifies it as a king reigning (Romans 5:21, *as sin hath reigned* as king). The Holy Spirit at the time of the sinner's salvation, enthroned the Lord Jesus in the throne room of the believer's heart. He stays on the throne so long as the believer keeps yielded to the Spirit and rejects the behests of the evil nature."

Christians have been emancipated...set free.

Reject temptation.

Avoid further slavery.

Keep Christ on the throne of your heart.

SERVANTS OF RIGHTEOUSNESS

MEMORY VERSE: *Being then made free from sin, ye became the servants of righteousness* (Romans 6:18).

We are all servants...either of sin or of righteousness.

To serve sin is to experience temporary gratification that leads to frustration, guilt, and emptiness of life. To serve righteousness is to know lasting satisfaction leading to permanent rewards.

Christians have been set free from the power of sin. Not one child of God is obligated to be ruled by the old nature. Defeat in the Christian life is never necessary...always the result of self-indulgence. Even temptation confronting those who have been born again is limited to what they can overcome: *There hath no temptation taken you but such as is common to man: but God is faithful, who will not suffer you to be tempted above that ye are able; but will with the temptation also make a way to escape, that ye may be able to bear it* (1 Corinthians 10:13).

The Christian life is enriched by total surrender. When we plunge into life, seizing each opportunity for the glory of God, we become happy servants of righteousness... busy about our Master's business.

Are you less enthusiastic about serving Christ than you once were in sinful pursuits?

Remember—the blessings that come from Christian service are eternal: *But now being made free from sin, and become servants to God, ye have your fruit unto holiness, and the end everlasting life* (Romans 6:22).

If being a servant of righteousness becomes difficult at times, think of the coming reward. His "well done" will make it all worthwhile.

NEWNESS OF SPIRIT

MEMORY VERSE: *But now we are delivered from the law, that being dead wherein we were held; that we should serve in newness of spirit, and not in the oldness of the letter* (Romans 7:6).

Here is one of the key texts of the New Testament.

Keeping the "letter of the Law" cannot compare to the "higher ground" reached through yielding to the Holy Spirit. The Spirit-filled person goes beyond the letter to the very heart of the law...fulfilling the precepts on which it is based. The life resulting from this new relationship is described in Galatians 5:22,23: *But the fruit of the Spirit is love, joy, peace, longsuffering, gentleness, goodness, faith, meekness, temperance: against such there is no law.*

Matthew Henry says: "The day of our believing, is the day of being united to the Lord Jesus. We enter upon a life of dependence on Him, and duty to Him. Good works are from union with Christ; as the fruitfulness of the vine is the product of its being united to its roots: there is no fruit to God, till we are united to Christ. The law, and the greatest efforts of one under the law, still in the flesh, under the power of corrupt principles, cannot set the heart right with regard to the love of God, overcome worldly lusts, or give truth and sincerity in the inward parts, or any thing that comes by the special sanctifying influences of the Holy Spirit. Nothing more than a formal obedience to the outward letter of any precept, can be performed by us, without the renewing, new-creating grace of the new covenant."

What does all this have to do with today's problems and temptations? It means we are equipped to be all that we ought to be and that in daily yielding to the Holy Spirit we live above the "letter of the Law."

THE BATTLE

MEMORY VERSE: *I find then a law, that, when I would do good, evil is present with me* (Romans 7:21).

Each one of us is born with a nature that is given to sin. That nature never improves. Even after conversion it struggles against the work of the Holy Spirit.

The battle rages.

Discouraging?

Not at all! We have been made partakers of the divine nature and through Christ can have victory. He sets us free.

FREE INDEED

Fear not, O broken sinful heart,
And tremble ye no more;
For Jesus died on Calvary,
His mercy to outpour.

Though strongly held by Satan's power
Your wretched soul may be,
Just cast yourself on Jesus Christ,
And He will set you free.

So when temptations plague your soul,
You need not pay them heed,
For Jesus Christ has made you free,
And you are free indeed.

...Wava Campbell

We must always remember that success in the Christian life does not depend on improving the "old man." God is not in the redecorating business. The Holy Spirit within makes all things new.

AGAIN TO FEAR

MEMORY VERSE: *For ye have not received the spirit of bondage again to fear; but ye have received the Spirit of adoption, whereby we cry, Abba, Father* (Romans 8:15).

When Dr. William McCarrell wrote a book on this wonderful chapter he titled it, *Eternal Treasures in Romans Eight.* This chapter of victory is a well from which one can drink again and again. It is so deep that it defies a single reading and yet so understandable that millions have turned to it for strength in times of trouble.

In our text, we are called upon to remember that we have not received the spirit of bondage that holds its victims in fear. By faith in Christ we have become the children of God. His Spirit is within us. We do not have to be afraid.

Because we belong to the Lord, we can cry out to our Heavenly Father in times of danger. Martin Luther says that *Abba, Father,* means "Dear Father." Other authorities say that *Abba* is a Syrian word meaning "father." Paul may be saying that when we are afraid we can just cry, "Father, Father," or "Daddy, Daddy." This is our right as children of God.

Christians are loved by their dear Father. To be afraid after becoming one of His children is to forget His love: *There is no fear in love; but perfect love casteth out fear: because fear hath torment. He that feareth is not made perfect in love* (1 John 4:18).

What did you fear before you became a Christian?

Has that fear returned?

Don't entertain old fears.

Call out to your dear Father.

You're the object of His love.

ALL THINGS

MEMORY VERSE: *And we know that all things work together for good to them that love God, to them who are the called according to his purpose* (Romans 8:28).

There are some wonderful "alls" in the Bible.

Christ died for ALL sinners: *All we like sheep have gone astray; we have turned every one to his own way; and the LORD hath laid on him the iniquity of us all* (Isaiah 53:6).

We can do ALL things through Christ. Paul said: *I can do all things through Christ which strengtheneth me* (Philippians 4:13).

The blood of Christ cleanses from ALL sin: *But if we walk in the light, as he is in the light, we have fellowship one with another, and the blood of Jesus Christ his Son cleanseth us from all sin* (1 John 1:7).

And then there is our text. This wonderful promise assures us that everything in the universe revolves around God's children. He is arranging the events of our lives so that good will somehow come from every experience of the day. What a mind-boggling thought! What love!

Many years ago, missionaries in Peking, China, were astounded when an old man rose and said: "I am glad I am a leper! For if I had not been a leper, I would never have come to this mission hospital; if I had not come to this hospital, I never would have learned to know Jesus. And I had rather be a leper with Christ than to be free from leprosy without Him."

Undoubtedly there have been experiences in your life that at the time they were happening, seemed to be severe trials. You may have even questioned God. Now you can see how He has worked things out for your good. Thank Him. And remember He's still in control today.

CONCERN

MEMORY VERSE: *For I could wish that myself were accursed from Christ for my brethren, my kinsmen according to the flesh* (Romans 9:3).

Paul had a consuming passion for the salvation of his fellow Jews. He states it in the strongest words, declaring that he would be willing to be lost if by this his brethren according to the flesh would be saved.

Few care for souls.

Why?

The answer is evident: other things have priority.

Would you rather have a new car or win your neighbor to Christ? Which are you systematically working toward?

Would you rather retire comfortably or become a soulwinner? In which goal are you investing?

Would you rather be the top in your profession or receive eternal rewards for reaching the lost? Which thought thrills you the most?

If you are like most Christians, you are far more likely to get a new car, make the top place in your profession, and retire comfortably than you are to become a soulwinner. Don't you think it's time to take another look at your priorities?

Now, of course, there is nothing wrong with setting goals or working hard to meet the needs of your family. The Bible demands diligence in daily labor and says that one who does not care for those of his own household has denied the faith and is worse than an infidel. Nevertheless, not many give adequate concern or time to reaching others with the gospel message. And this is what life is all about.

Trying to decide what to do with your life?

Care enough to become a soulwinner.

THE STUMBLINGSTONE

MEMORY VERSE: *As it is written, Behold, I lay in Sion a stumblingstone and rock of offence: and whosoever believeth on him shall not be ashamed* (Romans 9:33).

Salvation through faith alone seemed too easy to Israel. They held to their legalism and rejected Christ. The way of life was so simple that they stumbled over it. Note again Paul's description of their error: *But Israel, which followed after the law of righteousness, hath not attained to the law of righteousness. Wherefore? Because they sought it not by faith, but as it were by the works of the law. For they stumbled at that stumblingstone* (Romans 9:31,32).

Men are still stumbling. All who add anything to faith as a requirement for salvation are stumbling.

All cults have stumbled at the message that Jesus saves through faith alone: hence the many complicated systems of religion demanding ceremony and sacraments, works and submission to leaders, for salvation.

The "Stone of Stumbling" (see Acts 4:11) will someday fall upon the kingdoms of this world, ending man's efforts to find peace and thwarting the plans of the final world dictator, the Antichrist. By that time, repentant Israel will recognize Christ as their Messiah and Lord and will see Him as the chief cornerstone. The Rapture of the Church will precede this event by seven years and can take place at any moment.

See the good news in the text for believers: *Whosoever believeth on him shall not be ashamed* [confounded]. The world is confused, but Christians see the world drama unfolding and know that their Heavenly Father is but working out His plan.

Aren't you glad you know Christ as your own?

NO DIFFERENCE

MEMORY VERSE: *For there is no difference between the Jew and the Greek: for the same Lord over all is rich unto all that call upon him* (Romans 10:12).

The *Pacific Garden Mission News* carried the following article: "Remember, the man on Skid Row is not different IN KIND from the rest of us. He is merely worse in degree. On Skid Row we see fallen man at his dismal worst. In the better neighborhoods we see him at his polished best, but he is the same man for all his disguise. In the gutter we find him chained by dope and drink and dirt. On the Avenue we find him bound by pride and greed and lust. To God there is no difference. He sees beyond appearances and He knows what is in every man. His remedy for every man is the same, a new birth and the impartation of a new kind of life. (See John 3:5,7.)

"The Gospel is the power of God operating toward the moral and spiritual transformation of man. And it works! Thousands will testify that it does. No man who wants to climb up out of his past and find a new and better life should overlook the Gospel. It is God's way out, and there is no other."

The gospel meets men where they are; all men. And they are all found in the same need. The ground is level at the cross. All need to be saved and all can be saved.

But do we see all people the same?

Are we as likely to witness to the poor as to the rich? Are we as eager to reach those who have little and therefore can give little? Does our concern go out equally to people of all races? Do we long to share heaven with all people? Even those who are not kind to us?

In the sight of God there is no difference (see Romans 2:11).

Let us see all those we meet today as people in need of the Saviour.

BUILDING FAITH

MEMORY VERSE: *So then faith cometh by hearing, and hearing by the word of God* (Romans 10:17).

Many long to have great faith.

Few are willing to pay the price required to build great faith.

Faith is developed by exposure to the Bible. It cannot be pumped up; it cannot be faked. Its source is the Scriptures.

God's promises encourage faith. As you take time to study the Bible you will find guarantees of strength, peace, courage, salvation, power, victory, and answered prayer. The exploits of others who have conquered through faith will build your own. As you identify with these promises and personal triumphs, your faith will increase. Depression will depart. Expectation will emerge. You will know that you can become what you want to be, in the will of God.

Like most things, faith grows through exercise. David was able to face Goliath because he had already conquered wild beasts that attacked his father's sheep. By the time Moses lifted his rod and parted the Red Sea, he had witnessed the power of God in bringing the plagues on Egypt. The falling of the walls of Jericho came after Joshua had led his people through the river Jordan.

If you want to increase your faith you must start using the faith you now have. Do something that demands faith. Trust God. Flex your spiritual muscles. Expect God to answer prayer. Spurgeon once said: "A little faith will bring your soul to heaven, but great faith will bring heaven to your soul."

Remember the textbook of the school of faith is the Bible. Feed upon its truth daily and faith will grow.

Desire great faith...devour God's Word and you shall have it.

NO MORE GRACE

MEMORY VERSE: *And if by grace, then is it no more of works: otherwise grace is no more grace. But if it be of works, then is it no more grace: otherwise work is no more work* (Romans 11:6).

During his last hours John Knox woke from a slumber sighing, and told his friends that he had just been tempted to believe that he had "merited Heaven and eternal blessedness, by the faithful discharge of his ministry. But blessed be God who enabled me to beat down and quench the fiery dart, by suggesting to me such passages of Scripture as these: *What has thou that thou didst not receive? By the grace of God I am what I am...Not I, but the grace of God which was with me.*"

There are two great errors concerning the Jews often adopted by Gentiles: the first is the foolish notion that God has cast away His people and that there is no hope for Jews either nationally or as individuals. The second is the belief that Jews have some merit before God apart from Christ because they are God's chosen people. The truth is that Jews and Gentiles are alike lost because of sin and there is no difference between them: *For there is no difference: For all have sinned, and come short of the glory of God* (Romans 3:22,23). The only hope for either Jews or Gentiles is the grace of God (His unmerited favor).

The continuing human mistake is to attempt to gain more favor with God through works. The Bible is clear. Favor with God is ALL of grace. If works could enhance our standing with Him our relationship would be no more grace (see Ephesians 2:8,9).

The miracle of grace is that there is enough for me.

PAST FINDING OUT

MEMORY VERSE: *O the depth of the riches both of the wisdom and knowledge of God! how unsearchable are his judgments, and his ways past finding out!* (Romans 11:33).

The final four verses of this chapter comprise a doxology. Think of singing them...shouting them. Paul's heart seems so full of praise that he cannot find words to express his feelings. In effect, he is saying, "HOW GREAT THOU ART!"

Matthew Henry's comment here is excellent. He writes: "The apostle Paul knew the mysteries of the kingdom of God as well as any man: yet he confesses himself at a loss; and despairing to find the bottom, he humbly sits down at the brink, and adores the depth. Those who know most in this imperfect state, feel their own weakness most. There is not only depth in the Divine counsels, but riches; abundance of that which is precious and valuable. The Divine counsels are complete; they have not only depth and height, but breadth and length (see Ephesians 3:18), and that passing knowledge. There is that vast distance and disproportion between God and man, between the Creator and the creature, which for ever shuts us out from knowledge of His ways. What man shall teach God how to govern the world? The apostle adores the sovereignty of the Divine counsels. All things in heaven and earth, especially those which relate to our salvation, that belong to our peace, are all of Him by way of creation, through Him by way of providence, that they may be to Him in their end...Whatever begins, let God's glory be the end: especially let us adore Him when we talk of the Divine counsels and actings. The saints in heaven never dispute, but always praise."

Join in the doxology.

Let your heart express its highest praise.

A LIVING SACRIFICE

MEMORY VERSE: *I beseech you therefore, brethren, by the mercies of God, that ye present your bodies a living sacrifice, holy, acceptable unto God, which is your reasonable service* (Romans 12:1).

Christians are to be forever on the altar.

After finishing the doctrinal and dispensational sections of his epistle, Paul opens the practical concluding chapters with a call to consecration. "A living sacrifice" must be understood to embody the complete giving over to God of all that is called for in the Old Testament animal sacrifices. The sacrifice was to be the best of the flock. And we are to give our best to Christ.

The apostle begs his Christian brothers to present their bodies to the Lord. He is asking them to put their bodies at God's disposal. Chrysostom wrote: "How can the body become a sacrifice? Let the eye look on no evil, and it is a sacrifice. Let the tongue utter nothing base, and it is an offering. Let the hand work no sin and it is a holocaust (Webster gives as a definition of *holocaust*, 'a sacrifice wholly consumed by fire'). But more, this suffices not, but besides we must actively exert ourselves for good; the hand giving alms, the mouth blessing them that curse us, the ear ever at leisure for listening to God."

Wuest says: "...the physical body of the believer, put at the disposal of God, presented to Him, is holy, both in the sense of being set apart for His use, and holy in the sense of being used for pure and righteous purposes, and thus, free from sinful practices."

Concluding his call to consecration, Paul says such a surrender is "your reasonable service." Serving Christ with all your heart is the intelligent thing to do.

August 24

Romans 12:10-21

THE SAME MIND

MEMORY VERSE: *Be of the same mind one toward another. Mind not high things, but condescend to men of low estate. Be not wise in your own conceits* (Romans 12:16).

Divisions among Christians are usually the result of pride. Of the disciples on the Day of Pentecost, it was said: *They were all with one accord in one place* (Acts 2:1). The power that flowed through that united minority shook all Jerusalem and ultimately the world. Bickering and fighting in local churches holds back the blessing of God and presents a sorry spectacle to any community. The time has come for believers to be of the same mind.

Humility is the way to harmony. When pride departs, people stop demanding their own way. Andrew Murray wrote: "Here is the path to the higher life: Down, lower down! This was what Jesus taught His disciples when they were thinking of being great in the kingdom. Do not seek or ask for exaltation—that is God's work. Let us take no place before God or man but that of a servant."

Kindness flows naturally from a humble heart. Submission is difficult for the proud but easy for the humble. The lowly will not feel out of place in submitting to others. And submission would heal most of the rifts that exist between the children of God.

Have you been demanding your own way?

Are you at the heart of controversy in your church?

Surprise the antagonists. Choose the way of humility and submission.

Be lowly of heart and serve as a peacemaker.

Be of the same mind. The world needs shaking again.

Such power will cost you your pride. But the reverse is also true. And you have been powerless long enough.

LOVE IN ACTION

MEMORY VERSE: *Love worketh no ill to his neighbour: therefore love is the fulfilling of the law* (Romans 13:10).

Jesus said it first: *Thou shalt love the Lord thy God with all thy heart, and with all thy soul, and with all thy mind. This is the first and great commandment. And the second is like unto it, Thou shalt love thy neighbour as thyself. On these two commandments hang all the law and the prophets* (Matthew 22:37-40).

Long ago, C. H. Spurgeon quoted Wither's moving poem on love. And it bears quoting again:

> No outward mark we have to know,
> Who thine, O Christ, may be,
> Until his Christian love doth show
> Who appertains to thee:
> For knowledge may be reached unto,
> And formal justice gained,
> But till each other love we do,
> Both faith and works are feigned.

Every commandment is based on love. The person who loves God will have no other gods. The person who loves God will not use His name in vain. The person who loves God will take time to worship Him. The person who loves his neighbor will not steal from him nor defraud him in any way.

The Law was fulfilled in Christ by His WORK OF LOVE for us on the cross, paying for our sins. No wonder those who belong to Him are to be identified by their love: *By this shall all men know that ye are my disciples, if ye have love one to another* (John 13:35).

The degree of our dedication to Christ can be told by our love.

What is your spiritual temperature?

ALMOST DAWN

MEMORY VERSE: *The night is far spent, the day is at hand: let us therefore cast off the works of darkness, and let us put on the armour of light* (Romans 13:12).

Each passing day in this dark world brings us nearer to the time when Christ, the Light of the World, shall appear. The works of darkness may be prevalent now but a better day is coming...the day of our Lord's return.

The night is far spent. If that was true in Paul's day, how much more in ours. The works of darkness surround us and are the topic of nearly every daily paper: crime, war, greed, and lust. Since the night of sin's reign is nearly over, we must cast off the works of darkness. Children of light do not always live up to their name. Compromise with the world and its degrading practices is on the increase.

But this is no time for compromise.

It is almost dawn.

How quickly the darkness flees at the first light of the morning. Christians must separate from the works of darkness because their Lord may soon appear, the "Dayspring from on high." Upon His return we must all stand before the Judgment Seat of Christ. It is time to get right with God (see 2 Corinthians 5:10).

Honesty of heart is needed.

Drunkenness, envy, and strife must be put away and all else that grieves our Lord. Instead of these dark pastimes, we ought to occupy ourselves with the Lord Jesus.

Christ may return today.

Are you walking in the light?

OUR MOST IMPORTANT ENGAGEMENT

MEMORY VERSE: *So then every one of us shall give account of himself to God* (Romans 14:12).

It is a sobering thought that every Christian must one day stand before the One who has saved him to have his service reviewed. We are all accountable to Jesus for our stewardship of time and talents. The Judgment Seat of Christ will be examination day for the saints.

God has not left us on this planet to waste our lives in useless chatter and earthbound projects. We are to be carrying the gospel to our world. We have been commissioned to occupy until He comes. We are to be as lights in a dark place. Our earthly vocations should be but the means of support that make it possible for us to be witnesses in our communities.

If all that seems too great a load to bear, remember that one day it will be worth it all. Paul's life was filled with hardship and suffering, yet at the end of the road he eagerly anticipated his departure, and looked forward to the Judgment Seat of Christ. He spoke of it as "that day." He expected to receive eternal rewards that would outweigh any trial he had experienced along the way.

The judgment of the children of God will take place at the Lord's return for His Church. Jesus said, *And, behold, I come quickly; and my reward is with me, to give every man according as his work shall be* (Revelation 22:12).

The Judgment Seat of Christ is your most important coming engagement. It will be a revealing day: *For we must all appear before the judgment seat of Christ; that every one may receive the things done in his body, according to that he hath done, whether it be good or bad* (2 Corinthians 5:10).

What on earth are you doing for heaven's sake?

EDIFYING OTHERS

MEMORY VERSE: *Let us therefore follow after the things which make for peace, and things wherewith one may edify another* (Romans 14:19).

To edify is to build up another.

Christians are to be builders. Too many belong to wrecking crews. In her poem, "A Prayer of Thanksgiving," Wava Campbell expresses her appreciation for the "builders" she has met along the way.

A PRAYER OF THANKSGIVING
Lord, thanks for those dear Christians
Who seemed to understand
Each time I tripped or stumbled,
And lent a helping hand.
Oh, thank You for their patience,
And love, and may it be
That some dear Christian somewhere
Is giving thanks for me.
Lord, thanks for those dear Christians
You've placed along my way;
How blessed I've been to know them,
And that is why I pray
That I may be the Christian
That You would have me be,
For then I know that others
Will offer thanks for me.

...Wava Campbell

How many builders do you know?

Wouldn't this be a good time to call at least one of them to express your thanks for the positive influence of this friend upon your life?

HELPING THE WEAK

MEMORY VERSE: *We then that are strong ought to bear the infirmities of the weak, and not to please ourselves* (Romans 15:1).

The strong must be selfless.

In a family the big brother or older sister may be expected to come to the aid of younger children. In the family of God, those who have matured in the faith must bear the burdens of the weak. They must have no feelings to be hurt. They must be willing to forego activities that might offend the weaker ones.

When a weaker brother or sister is overtaken in sin, the stronger must work to restore the one who has stumbled: *Brethren, if a man be overtaken in a fault, ye which are spiritual, restore such an one in the spirit of meekness; considering thyself, lest thou also be tempted* (Galatians 6:1).

Wuest says of this text: "The STRONG here are believers whose understanding of the Word frees them from religious scruples. The WEAKER are believers whose understanding of the Word is so limited, that they consider some things which are right in themselves, to be wrong. These false notions are included in the infirmities here spoken of...

"The pleasing one's neighbor in this context refers to the act of the believer foregoing a legitimate act because that weaker Christian thinks it to be wrong. It pleases him because it removes a source of temptation to him to do that thing, and makes his attempt to live a life pleasing to God easier. But the stronger Christian is to do this only in the instance where the weaker Christian would be edified or built up in the Christian life."

Remember—Christ pleased not himself.

THE PIONEER MISSIONARY

MEMORY VERSE: *Yea, so have I strived to preach the gospel, not where Christ was named, lest I should build upon another man's foundation* (Romans 15:20).

Some wish to serve Christ where all the trail blazing has been done for them. They want plush working conditions and plenty of pay.

Not Paul. He wanted to break new ground.

Paul's desire to be a pioneer came from his love for souls. The adventures in faith of this man of God were the result of his passion to reach the lost and tell them of Christ. Nothing deterred him.

Is the salvation of the lost your consuming desire and the motive of all your Christian service or do you just like to be known as a Christian worker, a Sunday school teacher, or a member of the church board? Do you take part in missionary ventures because you care for souls or do you just like the thought of being involved in your church?

David Brainerd prayed: "Oh, that I were a flame of fire in my Master's cause!" He had such intense compassion for souls, and was so earnest for their salvation that he said, "I cared not where or how I lived, or what hardships I went through, so that I could but gain souls to Christ. While I was asleep, I dreamed of these things, and when I awoke the first thing I thought of was this great work. All my desire was for the conversion of the heathen, and all my hope was in God."

Have you been shrinking from Christian service because the conditions are poor?

Consider the thrill of serving God in a difficult place.

Is God calling you to be a pioneer?

TROUBLEMAKERS

MEMORY VERSE: *Now I beseech you, brethren, mark them which cause divisions and offences contrary to the doctrine which ye have learned; and avoid them* (Romans 16:17).

The final chapter of Paul's letter to the Romans contains an honor roll of faithful men and women. Phebe had ministered to Paul's needs and to the needs of others. Priscilla and Aquila had been helpers of Paul in his service for Christ. Mary had labored to aid Paul and other Christians. The list goes on.

While many were faithful, a few were troublemakers; dividers of the brethren. These deceivers were eloquent and were able to sway some with their "fair speeches" but Paul made it clear that their effect was limited by the Christian character of those who stood true.

Many churches are described here in miniature. Most of the members are faithful, dedicated Christians. A few are troublemakers.

Do you have troublemakers in your church?

Do you head a brigade of busybodies?

Is your pastor's ministry hindered by your critical attitude?

Are you dividing the flock?

Recognize the seriousness of your sinful course. Confess your sins to the Lord and forsake them. Stop looking for faults and develop a compassion for souls. Pray for unity among the believers in your fellowship. Then extend this prayer for unity towards all members of Christ's Body.

And about the other troublemakers; what shall you do about them?

Avoid them.

Get busy in the work of Christ. You'll be too busy to be a busybody.

September

THIS MONTH'S STUDY

Old Testament Character Studies

Days 3,9, and 22 contain quotes from "Meet Yourself in the Bible," by Roy Laurin, published by Van Kampen Press, Wheaton, Illinois. Day 14 contains a quote from "All the Women of the Bible," by Edith Deen, published by Harper & Row, New York. Day 15 contains a quote from "Knight's Master Book of New Illustrations," published by Wm. B. Eerdman's Publishing Company, Grand Rapids, Michigan. Used by permission. Day 20 contains a quote from "Pepper N' Salt," by Vance Havner, published by Fleming Revell Company, Old Tappan, New Jersey. Days 21 and 24 contain poems from "Let's Communicate," by Roger F. Campbell, published by Christian Literature Crusade, Fort Washington, Pennsylvania. Day 28 contains a quote from "Daniel the Prophet," by H. A. Ironside, published by Loizeaux Brothers, Neptune, New Jersey. Day 30 contains a quote from "Jonah—Fact or Fiction?" by Dr. M. R. DeHaan, published by Zondervan Publishing Company, Grand Rapids, Michigan.

ADAM AND EVE

MEMORY VERSE: *And Adam said, This is now bone of my bones, and flesh of my flesh; she shall be called Woman, because she was taken out of Man* (Genesis 2:23).

Eve was made, "not from Adam's head to be over him; nor from his feet to be trampled by him; but from his side to be next to him; from under his arm to be protected by him; and near to his heart to be loved by him."

God has established the home, not the herd.

No earthly bond is so close and wonderful as that special relationship existing between a man and a woman who have been joined in marriage.

Adam must have been the most handsome of men and Eve the most beautiful of all women. They lived in a world untouched by sin. Grief and tears were unknown until after the fall. We struggle to understand such ideal conditions. Nevertheless, Christian marriage can be a taste of heaven. When two people are in love and express their affection continually while living in an atmosphere of faith in Christ and dedication to His will, they experience something of the blessing shared by Adam and Eve in the Garden of Eden.

Adam said that Eve was bone of his bone and flesh of his flesh. Paul said the same is true of Christ and the Church. *For we are members of his body, of his flesh, and of his bones. This is a great mystery: but I speak concerning Christ and the church* (Ephesians 5:30,32).

Grasping this truth makes living the Christian life an adventure in faith. F. J. Huegel has written: "What is impossible to me as in imitator of Christ becomes perfectly natural as a participant of Christ."

Now don't you feel close to Jesus?

ENOCH

MEMORY VERSE: *And Enoch walked with God: and he was not; for God took him* (Genesis 5:24).

Enoch must have been a remarkable man. He was one of only two chosen to escape death. The New Testament names him as a man of faith and says that his life pleased God: *By faith Enoch was translated that he should not see death; and was not found, because God had translated him: for before his translation he had this testimony, that he pleased God* (Hebrews 11:5).

This man of faith was taken to heaven before the flood came and is a type (picture) of the Church and its coming rapture before the Tribulation. Many expect Enoch to return to the earth as one of the two "witnesses" spoken of in Revelation 11:3-12. These two will announce the coming of Christ in power and great glory to set up His kingdom. Their ministry will come during earth's most difficult time. The Antichrist will be furious and attempt to destroy these Tribulation prophets but God will protect them until their mission is fulfilled.

Should Enoch be one of these "olive trees," he will be able to declare the same message that he heralded before the flood: *And Enoch also, the seventh from Adam, prophesied of these, saying, Behold, the Lord cometh with ten thousands of his saints, to execute judgment upon all, and to convince all that are ungodly among them of all their ungodly deeds which they have ungodly committed, and of all their hard speeches which ungodly sinners have spoken against him* (Jude 14,15).

How interesting that God let Enoch in on scenes of the endtime!

It pays to walk with God.

And only those who walk with Him below will walk with Him above.

NOAH

MEMORY VERSE: *And the LORD said, My spirit shall not always strive with man, for that he also is flesh: yet his days shall be an hundred and twenty years* (Genesis 6:3).

We can identify with Noah.

Our day is much like his: *And as it was in the days of Noe, so shall it be also in the days of the Son of man. They did eat, they drank, they married wives, they were given in marriage, until the day that Noe entered into the ark, and the flood came, and destroyed them all* (Luke 17:26,27).

In his book, *Meet Yourself in the Bible,* Roy Laurin has written of Noah: "In the midst of this general corruption and violence stood one man. He did not stand with it but against it. He grieved over it. He protested against it. He plead with the people to turn from their wickedness. Let any man stand up and out against the sins and derelictions of his generation and he will be branded as a crank. No one can stand against the world and yet stand in the world."

Peter calls Noah a "preacher of righteousness." No wonder he wasn't popular.

But God has not called His people to win popularity contests. We are to be ambassadors for Christ. And that calls for righteous living.

Noah also lived in a time of shrinking opportunity. God had declared that the flood would come in 120 years. During that time Noah must build the ark and preach. While each day saw the ark nearer completion, it also saw the period remaining before the coming flood grow shorter. Deliverance was nearer but so was destruction.

Like Noah, we must stand for righteousness. And make good use of the shrinking time that remains until our Lord returns.

NOAH

MEMORY VERSE: *Now the LORD had said unto Abram, Get thee out of thy country, and from thy kindred, and from thy father's house, unto a land that I will shew thee* (Genesis 12:1).

In responding to God's call, Abraham gained the title, "the father of the faithful." He is known as the friend of God.

Of God's call to Abraham, F. B. Meyer observed: "God's commands are always linked with promises. Count the six *shalls* and the *wills* of this promise. God does not always give His reasons; but He is generous of His promises. The one cry of Scripture is for separation, to which we are graciously allured. The keynote of Abram's life was separation; not all at once, but step by step: until country, kindred, Lot, worldly alliances, fleshly expedients—were one after another cast aside; and he stood alone with God."

Abraham obeyed and his obedience gave evidence of his faith. As a result, he has become a symbol of great faith even today. God's faithfulness to Abraham went well beyond his expectations. Thousands of years after his act of faith and the completion of his life of faith, people who walk with God carry a book (the Bible) that contains Abraham's name. God made his name great as was promised.

Paul pointed to Abraham as an example of justification by faith: *What shall we say then that Abraham our father, as pertaining to the flesh, hath found? For if Abraham were justified by works, he hath whereof to glory; but not before God. For what saith the scripture? Abraham believed God, and it was counted unto him for righteousness* (Romans 4:1-3).

Believe God.

His faithfulness will be greater than your faith.

SARAH

MEMORY VERSE: *Is any thing too hard for the LORD? At the time appointed I will return unto thee, according to the time of life, and Sarah shall have a son* (Genesis 18:14).

All Christians are either problem conscious or power conscious.

Sarah looked at the problems concerning giving birth to Abraham's child and they seemed insurmountable. Her husband was just entering his second century and she was ninety years old. When the word came from God that she would bear a son, she laughed.

Her faith was small...the mustard seed variety.

But God was better than Sarah's faith. And Sarah learned that nothing is too hard for the Lord.

Interesting, in the New Testament record of this encounter with Sarah, there is no mention of her laughter. Though her faith was small, God honored it and Sarah is listed in the great faith chapter of the New Testament as follows: *Through faith also Sara herself received strength to conceive seed, and was delivered of a child when she was past age, because she judged him faithful who had promised* (Hebrews 11:11).

Sarah's trembling faith made her part of a miracle. Her first reaction to God's promise did not make her unfit to be the vessel He would use. After thinking about the promise, Sarah concluded that although her faith was weak, God was strong and faithful. Once that was settled, her laughter of unbelief ended.

Why?

Simply because she turned her thoughts from the problems to the power of God. Sarah needed that question: "Is any thing too hard for the Lord?" And you may need it, too!

Stop focusing on your problems. Consider His power.

LOT

MEMORY VERSE: *And while he lingered, the men laid hold upon his hand, and upon the hand of his wife, and upon the hand of his two daughters; the LORD being merciful unto him: and they brought him forth, and set him without the city* (Genesis 19:16).

Lot lingered in Sodom when judgment was imminent.

His investments were there.

Had Peter not revealed that Lot was a righteous man (see 2 Peter 2:8), we might have concluded he was a bad man, a lost man. But the Scriptures declare him righteous. Peter says Lot was uncomfortable in Sodom, vexing his righteous soul from day to day with the sinful acts of the citizens there. Nevertheless, he stayed. And his staying cost him dearly.

Writing of Lot's misery, J. C. Ryle says: "Make a wrong choice in life—an unscriptural choice—and settle yourself down unnecessarily in the midst of worldly people, and I know no surer way to damage your own spirituality, and to go backward in your eternal concerns. This is the way to make the pulse of your soul beat feebly and languidly. This is the way to make the edge of your feeling about sin become blunt and dull. This is the way to dim the eyes of your spiritual discernment, till you can scarcely distinguish good from evil, and stumble as you walk. This is the way to bring a moral palsy on your feet and limbs, and make you go tottering and trembling along the road to Zion, as if the grasshopper was a burden. This is the way to...give the devil vantage-ground in the battle...to tie your arms in fighting...to fetter your legs in running...to dry up the sources of your strength."

Facing an important decision today?

Make it prayerfully and carefully. And don't compromise!

LOT'S WIFE

MEMORY VERSE: *Remember Lot's wife* (Luke 17:32).

In the setting of His second coming, Jesus said, *Remember Lot's wife*. Mrs. Lot is then a beacon for our day.

What a strange choice!

One would think the Lord would have chosen a woman who was known for her faith. Instead, the woman we are to remember is Lot's wife.

Remember her privileges. She had a righteous husband. She had lived in the company of godly Abraham and his family. She had known faithful Sarah and had probably gathered with the family of the friend of God for times of worship and praise. She had been the object of Abraham's prayers. Yet, surrounded by spiritual opportunities, she remained aloof and spiritually cold. Today, more tools for getting out the gospel are being used than ever before. Especially in America, the average person is offered the gospel time and again. Ours is a day of religious privilege. Still, many ignore God's message of love.

Remember her possessions. Lot was a successful man. His wife evidently had no lack of this world's goods. Sadly, she failed to see that all earth's toys are temporal. Like many today, she was caught up in the merry-go-round of getting. Affluence is often the enemy of spirituality. And in the abundance of things, many are missing the abundant life made so available in these last days.

Remember her perishing. When warned of the coming destruction of Sodom and given instructions for safety, she looked back and became a pillar of salt. Ignoring the clear direction for deliverance, she died.

Week after week, the message of Christ's return goes out from the pulpits and over radio and television. Don't reject God's offer of salvation. Turn to Christ while there is time.

Remember Lot's wife.

JACOB

MEMORY VERSE: *Then Jacob was greatly afraid and distressed: and he divided the people that was with him, and the flocks, and herds, and the camels, into two bands* (Geneses 32:7).

Jacob was on his way home. And he was a troubled man. Fear ruled his heart. More than twenty years earlier he had left his home after cheating his brother, Esau. Now every mile brought him closer to an encounter with the man he had feared for all this time.

Jacob's fear of Esau affected his spiritual life, making him doubt the promises of God. This journey homeward was in obedience to God's command and had been accompanied with a wonderful promise: *Return unto thy country, and to thy kindred, and I will deal well with thee* (Genesis 32:9). In spite of this divine assurance, Jacob was distressed.

Jacob's fear affected his handling of his finances. To appease Esau, he sent an expensive gift. How like Jacob we are! Fear often prevents us from being good stewards of what God has given us. Far more has been lost by those who have allowed fear to rule their financial transactions than by those who have dared to give or invest by faith.

Jacob's fear caused him to play favorites with his family. As he approached the meeting with Esau, Jacob placed his favorites the farthest from danger. This act of unbelief must have grieved the members of his family that were exposed to the first attack. The danger never developed but Jacob's true feelings would never be forgotten.

Jacob was afraid and suffered distress of mind and heart for nothing. His fears were groundless. Esau's anger had long been put away. When they met, Esau embraced Jacob and wept. Jacob's worrying had been useless. He could have trusted God and enjoyed his journey home.

JOSEPH

MEMORY VERSE: *So now it was not you that sent me hither, but God: and he hath made me a father to Pharaoh, and lord of all his house, and a ruler throughout all the land of Egypt* (Genesis 45:8).

Joseph's life is a living example of the truth of Romans 8:28: *And we know that all things work together for good to them that love God, to them who are the called according to his purpose.*

Roy Laurin has written: "It seems that all through Joseph's life he was followed by the plotters of evil. It began in his own family at an early age. Here his brothers, growing jealous of their father's favorite son, planned to dispose of him so they could have their own evil way.

The excuse for this was their father's favoritism, but the reason for it was their own wickedness. It seems that early in life, Joseph took a stand for righteousness and refused to join his brothers in doing things which they knew their father would condemn. This, of course, angered the brothers and turned them against Joseph. Naturally it made it difficult for him as it will today for anyone who will live for principle. Joseph might have appeased his brothers and remained quiet, but he was a man of high principle. The deeds his brothers designed for evil, God purposed for good. God permitted them to carry out these evil things but used them to bring Joseph to the place of mighty power. Let us believe that if we do what Joseph did, God will do for us what He did for Joseph."

It is seldom popular to stand for righteousness. The sinless life of Jesus angered the hypocrites of His day and they rejected Him. Paul promised persecution to all who live godly in Christ Jesus (see 2 Timothy 3:12), and many have found his warning true.

But God is still on the throne. Remember Joseph.

September 10   Exodus 2:1-10

JOCHEBED

MEMORY VERSE: *By faith Moses, when he was born, was hid three months of his parents, because they saw he was a proper child; and they were not afraid of the king's commandment* (Hebrews 11:23).

The mother of Moses is mentioned by name only three times in the Bible but her impact on the history of Israel was immense. Faced with the order of Pharaoh to destroy all male children born to those of her race, this godly woman devised a plan that was to spare the deliverer of her people.

Giving birth is always a painful experience, but imagine the emotional anguish when faced with an execution order in the event of the birth of a son. Jochebed was not willing to settle for death. This child was a gift from God and she was willing to risk the king's wrath because she believed her Lord would make a way for her son to live.

The ingenious plan of Jochebed not only saved Moses' life; it also allowed her to act as his nurse during those important childhood years. Without doubt, it was the faith and instruction of Jochebed that made Moses a man of courage and faith. See the good work of this faithful woman in the life of her son as is set forth in the following verses: *By faith Moses, when he was come to years, refused to be called the son of Pharaoh's daughter; Choosing rather to suffer affliction with the people of God, than to enjoy the pleasures of sin for a season; Esteeming the reproach of Christ greater riches than the treasures in Egypt: for he had respect unto the recompence of the reward. By faith he forsook Egypt, not fearing the wrath of the king: for he endured, as seeing him who is invisible* (Hebrews 11:24-27).

Jochebed's teaching and example brought out the potential of a man destined to be used by God.

God, give us mothers like Jochebed.

MOSES

MEMORY VERSE: *And it came to pass, when Moses came down from Mount Sinai with the two tables of testimony in Moses' hand, when he came down from the mount, that Moses wist not that the skin of his face shone while he talked with him* (Exodus 34:29).

Moses had traveled many miles since his experience at the burning bush. Egypt would never forget him. Nor would the world. He was God's man for his hour and his impact on history is permanent. John's vision of heaven includes a scene where the martyrs of the Tribulation sing a song of Moses, the servant of God, and the song of the Lamb (see Revelation 15:3).

His service for his Lord had taken him to the courts of Pharaoh. Many have entered the service of Christ and have been amazed at the doors opened to them by their Master. He is the One who opens and no man can shut. There is no earthly occupation so adventurous as being in the service of the King.

Now Moses has returned to Mount Sinai. The cloud has enveloped him and he has communed with God. When he returns to the people, his face is shining but he doesn't know it. Others can see that he has been in the presence of the Lord, though Moses is ignorant of the heavenly glow.

F. B. Meyer says it well: "True Christian excellence is as unconscious of its beauty as Moses was; whenever it becomes self-conscious it loses it charm. Beware of the man who talks about his graces. There is such a thing as being proud of humility, and making capital out of nothingness. The man who boasts of a shining face is a counterfeit and a cheat. The possessor of the genuine article never talks about it, never thinks about it; and would almost be overwhelmed to hear of any such thing ascribed to him."

Spend time with God but don't boast about it. The glow will show.

CALEB

MEMORY VERSE: *And Caleb stilled the people before Moses, and said, Let us go up at once, and possess it; for we are well able to overcome it* (Numbers 13:30).

Chosen by Moses to look over the Promised Land, he responded with courage and faith. And he found the land to be all that God had promised.

When the spies returned, Caleb and Joshua turned in a minority report. Caleb was the spokesman. All the other spies admitted the land had great potential, but they feared the inhabitants and urged the people not to attempt to enter its borders in spite of the bountiful harvest they had found. That didn't make sense to Caleb. God had been faithful thus far. Why should they doubt Him now? Why this complaining?

Others saw the giants; Caleb saw the Lord.

Others saw the problems; Caleb saw the possibilities.

Others saw the obstacles; Caleb saw the hand of his omnipotent God.

And God rewarded him.

Because of their unbelief, all of that generation of the Children of Israel died during the next forty years of wilderness wandering except Caleb and Joshua. Note the reward of faith: *But my servant Caleb, because he had another spirit with him, and hath followed me fully, him will I bring into the land whereinto he went; and his seed shall possess it. Your carcases shall fall in this wilderness; and all that were numbered of you, according to your whole number, from twenty years old and upward, which have murmured against me. Doubtless ye shall not come into the land, concerning which I sware to make you dwell therein, save Caleb the son of Jephunneh, and Joshua the son of Nun* (Numbers 14:24,29,30).

Are you a complainer or a Caleb?

JOSHUA

MEMORY VERSE: *Have not I commanded thee? Be strong and of a good courage; be not afraid, neither be thou dismayed: for the LORD thy God is with thee whithersoever thou goest* (Joshua 1:9).

The death of Moses did not mean the end of the march to the Promised Land. Some panic at the death of leaders as if omnipotence was in the hand of man. God will always raise up His leaders to complete His program. Matthew Henry observes: "God will change hands to show that whatever instrument He uses, He is not tied to any."

Joshua became Israel's leader.

What a task! Enough to make one tremble!

Yet this immense assignment was accompanied with a promise of success: *Every place that the sole of your foot shall tread upon, that have I given unto you, as I said unto Moses* (Joshua 1:3). Joshua had then but one question to face: "How big are my feet?"

Conquering Canaan would be difficult. There would be days of discouragement and fierce battles, even some defeats. And before the campaign could begin the flooded Jordan must be crossed, beyond which lay Jericho, that great walled city.

Never mind.

This company will move under the direction of God himself. Joshua will be successful for he will not serve in his own strength nor rely on human wisdom. Faith will make the difference, even in conquering mighty Jericho. Especially then: *By faith the walls of Jericho fell down, after they were compassed about seven days* (Hebrews 11:30).

Like Joshua, we all have territory to conquer, some walled cities to overcome...some Jordans to cross. Some struggles await. But success all comes down to this matter of faith in our unfailing God.

HANNAH

MEMORY VERSE: *For this child I prayed: and the LORD hath given me my petition which I asked of him* (1 Samuel 1:27).

Hannah was childless and the fourth woman whose grief over her inability to bear a child is recorded in the Bible. Among the four, she stands out as the most fervent in prayer.

In her book, *All the Women of the Bible*, Edith Deen says of Hannah: "Hannah's environment was not conducive to prayer, for the people of Israel had lapsed from the high standards of morality and spirituality set up by Moses. She had to break away from the old traditions and find a new path. Her home environment was not conducive to great dreams either. Her husband, Elkanah, was a good but easygoing, undistinguished priest; and in these polygamous times he and his other wife, Peninnah, had children, while Hannah had none.

"But she believed with all her heart that God was the Creator of children and that only God could convert a woman into a mother."

Hannah's trial has become our blessing. Had she not at first been childless, we would have been deprived of her story and her moving prayer. Her statement of dedication concerning her son Samuel has become the test for nearly every child dedication: *Therefore also I have lent him to the LORD; as long as he liveth he shall be lent to the LORD. And he worshipped the LORD there* (1 Samuel 1:28).

And here lies a lesson for us all. Our trials are often for the blessing of others. In difficult places, faith grows and as we share our experiences with others they are helped.

In reading of her faith and of Hannah's fervent prayer, others have dared to trust God when all seemed hopeless.

Coming through a difficult time? Don't despair...look to God in prayer. And when God answers, spread the word.

SAMUEL

MEMORY VERSE: *And the LORD came, and stood, and called as at other times, Samuel, Samuel. Then Samuel answered, Speak; for thy servant heareth* (1 Samuel 3:10).

Samuel was the first great prophet after Moses and the last of the judges. His important position brought him into contact with the first two kings of Israel. It was he who anointed David while the singer of sweet songs was still a boy tending sheep. The son of Hannah, he was dedicated to the service of the Lord while a child. His answer to the call of God would be a fitting response for every Christian: *Speak; for thy servant heareth.*

H. C. Mason tells of a man who in a prayer meeting prayed earnestly that God would with His finger touch a certain man. Suddenly he stopped praying. When asked why, he replied, "Because God said to me, 'You are My finger.' So now I must go and touch the man for God."

Samuel's response would change many prayer meetings. Though prayer for others is vital, many prayers would be answered by the concerned person actually going to the object of his concern with the gospel message or with a word of comfort or encouragement.

Complete obedience would change some occupations. Many toy with the thought of full-time Christian service. They dream of serving the Lord on some mission field but never go beyond dreaming. They are visionaries who ought to be missionaries. An obedient heart could change intention to action.

Samuel's prayer would change lives from dreary sameness to adventure. Imagine being just where God wants you to be, saying just what He wants you to say at all times. It can happen. Samuel's response is all that is needed.

Speak; for thy servant heareth.

DAVID

MEMORY VERSE: *Then went David in, and sat before the LORD, and he said, Who am I, O Lord, GOD? and what is my house, that thou hast brought me hitherto?* (2 Samuel 7:18).

David had come from the sheepfold to the throne. His flock became the entire nation of Israel. Serving under this great responsibility, his moods ran from ecstasy to despair and as a result his Psalms provide help to people in all situations.

Do you have enemies? So did David: *LORD, how are they increased that trouble me! many are they that rise up against me. Many there be which say of my soul, There is no help for him in God. Selah. But thou, O LORD, art a shield for me; my glory, and the lifter up of mine head* (Psalm 3:1-3).

Are you surrounded by complainers? Identify with David: *There be many that say, Who will shew us any good? LORD, lift thou up the light of thy countenance upon us. Thou hast put gladness in my heart, more than in the time that their corn and their wine increased* (Psalm 4:6-7).

Do you fear chastening? You're not alone: *O LORD, rebuke me not in thine anger, neither chasten me in thy hot displeasure. Have mercy upon me, O LORD; for I am weak: O LORD, heal me; for my bones are vexed* (Psalm 6:1,2).

Do you feel like you stand alone? It's not a new development: *Help, LORD; for the godly man ceaseth; for the faithful fail from among the children of men* (Psalm 12:1).

Are you backslidden? Pray David's prayer: *Have mercy upon me, O God, according to thy lovingkindness: according unto the multitude of thy tender mercies blot out my transgressions* (Psalm 51:1).

Are you worried? Try David's antidote: *The LORD is my shepherd; I shall not want* (Psalm 23:1).

MEPHIBOSHETH

MEMORY VERSE: *So Mephibosheth dwelt in Jerusalem; for he did eat continually at the king's table; and was lame on both his feet* (2 Samuel 9:13).

Mephibosheth was the son of Jonathan. He had been injured from a fall when he was a child and was lame in both feet. He had been in hiding since David had been king, and David's restoring of property and place to this descendent of Saul is a wonderful Old Testament picture of salvation by grace.

We all suffer from the fall. We cannot walk as we ought.

Mephibosheth feared a contact from the king. He was in hiding in Lo-debar, meaning "the place of no pasture." All lost people fear contact with Christ and as a result dwell where there is no pasture.

David sent for Jonathan's son for the following reasons:

...to show the kindness of God (vs. 3).

...to get to know him on a first name basis (vs. 6).

...to take away his fears (vs. 7).

...to bless him for the sake of another (vs. 7).

...to restore what he had lost (vs. 7).

...to provide for his daily needs (vs. 7).

...to treat him as a son (vs. 11).

The chapter ends with the lame man sitting at the king's table. David has restored his lost possessions and has arranged for him to profit from them. Mephibosheth is still lame in both his feet but he now can keep his lame feet under the king's table out of sight. Thus God also does away with sins when one comes to Christ (see Micah 7:19).

SOLOMON

MEMORY VERSE: *Behold, I have done according to thy words: lo, I have given thee a wise and an understanding heart; so that there was none like thee before thee, neither after thee shall any arise like unto thee* (1 Kings 3:12).

Solomon's choice of wisdom in order to rule his people well brought him both wisdom and riches. Matthew Henry concludes: "Solomon had wisdom because he asked for it, and wealth because he did not."

The Books of Proverbs and Ecclesiastes, place some of Solomon's wisdom within our reach. In studying Ecclesiastes, it is important to note that the key phrase is "under the sun." In other words, it presents man's reasoning about life.

Containing 31 chapters, Proverbs makes an excellent book to read daily for one month. One can start on any day of the month reading the chapter numbered for that day. The next month on that day the book will have been completed.

Try applying the wisdom of Solomon.

Are you lazy? *Go to the ant, thou sluggard; consider her ways, and be wise* (Proverbs 6:6).

Are you afraid to give? *There is that scattereth, and yet increaseth; and there is that withholdeth more than is meet, but it tendeth to poverty* (Proverbs 11:24).

Having trouble with your temper? *He that is slow to anger is better than the mighty; and he that ruleth his spirit than he that taketh a city* (Proverbs 16:32).

Do you give up easily? *If thou faint in the day of adversity, thy strength is small* (Proverbs 24:10).

Do you bend to public opinion? *The fear of man bringeth a snare: but whoso putteth his trust in the LORD shall be safe* (Proverbs 29:25).

ELIJAH

MEMORY VERSE: *For thus saith the LORD God of Israel, The barrel of meal shall not waste, neither shall the cruse of oil fail, until the day that the LORD sendeth rain upon the earth* (1 Kings 17:14).

Elijah was a powerful prophet. He announced a drought because of the sins of his people and there was neither dew nor rain for three and one half years. James reveals that Elijah prayed for the drought to come: *Elias* [Elijah] *was a man subject to like passions as we are, and he prayed earnestly that it might not rain: and it rained not on the earth by the space of three years and six months. And he prayed again, and the heaven gave rain, and the earth brought forth her fruit* (James 5:17,18).

During the drought, God took care of Elijah and others who were faithful. God is as able to provide our needs in times of famine or depression as in times of prosperity. Christians ought not waste time worrying about the state of the economy or the outcome of international politics. God's plan is unfolding and our responsibility is to be faithful in witnessing for Christ while there is time.

On one occasion, God used a widow to feed His servant. The widow had but a handful of meal and a little oil but God would stretch those meager provisions and make them last until rain came. The widow's act of faith in providing for Elijah has caused her to be remembered to this day.

Finally, Elijah called for a contest to prove how foolish it was to worship the false god, Baal. In his call, he challenged the people to get off the fence and worship the Lord. *How long halt ye between two opinions? if the LORD be God, follow him* (1 Kings 18:21).

Take Elijah's advice and give your all to Jesus.

ELISHA

MEMORY VERSE: *And he took the mantle of Elijah that fell from him, and smote the waters, and said, Where is the LORD God of Elijah? and when he also had smitten the waters, they parted hither and thither: and Elisha went over* (2 Kings 2:14).

Elisha was a prophet with a passion for power. Most of us would have settled for ten percent of the power of Elijah, but not Elisha. He demanded a double portion...twice the power of that great prophet. And God gave him his desire.

Too many start out well in the Christian life, longing for a closer walk with Christ each day and seeking His power, only to finally settle down in a Christian routine that is neither hot nor cold. Vance Havner has written: "I have often been reminded of the wild duck that came down on migration into a barnyard and liked it so well that he stayed there. In the fall his erstwhile companions passed overhead and his first impulse was to rise and join them, but he had fed too well and could rise no higher than the eaves of the barn. The day came when his old fellow travelers could pass overhead without his even hearing their call. I have seen men and women who once mounted up with wings like eagles but are now content to live in the barnyard of this world. Sometimes, in a good old-fashioned meeting under powerful preaching they may have a momentary impulse to sing the song of saints on higher ground.

> "My heart has no desire to stay
> Where doubts arise and fears dismay.

"But they have fed too well down here and the day comes when they no longer respond to the call from on high. It is a tragic thing to settle in the barnyard of this world."

JABEZ

MEMORY VERSE: *And Jabez called on the God of Israel, saying, Oh that thou wouldest bless me indeed, and enlarge my coast, and that thine hand might be with me, and that thou wouldest keep me from evil, that it may not grieve me! And God granted him that which he requested* (1 Chronicles 4:10).

Some, in reading through the Bible, skip over this chapter. What a mistake!

This life-changing text caught hold of the missionary known as Praying Hyde and transformed his life and ministry. It contains a prayer for prosperity (*Oh that thou wouldest bless me indeed, and enlarge my coast*), for the power of God (*and that thine hand might be with me*), and for purity (*and that thou wouldest keep me from evil, that it might not grieve me*). Wava Campbell has explained it in a church setting:

AFTERGLOW

No wayward soul had come to Christ.
A few believers stayed;
They wiped away each other's tears
And prayed as Jabez prayed.
"Oh, bless us, Lord, indeed!" they cried,
"Enlarge our work for You!"
"I surely will," the Lord replied.
"If you stay pure and true."
They pledged themselves to serve the Lord;
They took a solemn oath;
They prayed for loving unity—
But most of all for growth.
May all God's people everywhere
Put self and sin away;
May Christians seek revival now
And really start to pray.

...Wava Campbell

NEHEMIAH

MEMORY VERSE: *Then answered I them, and said unto them, The God of heaven, he will prosper us; therefore we his servants will arise and build: but ye have no portion, nor right, nor memorial, in Jerusalem* (Nehemiah 2:20).

Nehemiah led a company of his people back from captivity to Jerusalem to rebuild the city. It was an ambitious building program under difficult working conditions. Enemies attempted to halt construction of the walls and Nehemiah and his workmen had to keep weapons handy while doing their work. In spite of the opposition, however, they were successful. The key to their success is revealed in Nehemiah 4:6: *So built we the wall; and all the wall was joined together unto the half thereof: for the people had a mind to work.*

When God's people have a mind to work, they overcome all difficulties. And their accomplishments glorify God. At the completion of the walls of Jerusalem, Nehemiah reported the results: *So the wall was finished in the twenty and fifth day of the month Elul, in fifty and two days. And it came to pass, that when all our enemies heard thereof, and all the heathen that were about us saw such things, they were much cast down in their own eyes: for they perceived that this work was wrought of our God* (Nehemiah 6:15,16).

Roy Laurin wrote: "Nehemiah finished what he started. He succeeded in what he set out to accomplish. This will always be the crowning accomplishment of his life. He will be remembered as a stedfast man who obeyed God and persevered in his work. His life should be a great incentive to all who regard it."

Most churches could use some of Nehemiah's crew.

Do you have a "mind to work"?

ESTHER

MEMORY VERSE: *And who knoweth whether thou art come to the kingdom for such a time as this?* (Esther 4:14).

God is always on time.

In the darkest day, God makes a way. The Jews were faced with extinction because of the evil plan of a Jew hater named Haman. He was not the first nor the last to attempt to destroy the Jews. History's graveyards are filled with those who hoped to do away with the Children of Israel.

Esther was the queen but had never revealed her racial identity to the king. Now Mordecai, her relative who had raised her, came to ask her to intercede on behalf of her people. It was a risky request, placing Esther's life in danger.

God uses a woman or a man to fulfill His plan. Throughout history, God has raised up people to carry out His will. Moses' mother defied Pharaoh's law and spared the life of her son, who was destined to deliver his people. David arrived at the camp of Israel when Goliath had intimidated the armies of Saul. John Wesley was converted and his heart was set afire for Christ in time to save England from revolution. John Knox was there when Scotland needed him. Esther must face the challenge of rescuing her people.

Esther's cry was to do or die. She laid her life on the line. Read again her response to the call of duty: *Go, gather together all the Jews that are present in Shushan, and fast ye for me, and neither eat nor drink for three days, night or day: I also and my maidens will fast likewise; and so will I go in unto the king, which is not according to the law: and if I perish, I perish* (Esther 4:16).

Esther rose to the occasion and saved her people.

Who knoweth whether thou art come to the kingdom for such a time as this? (See Acts 1:8).

JOB

MEMORY VERSE: *For I know that my redeemer liveth, and that he shall stand at the latter day upon the earth* (Job 19:25).

Job came through his trials victorious because of his faith in his living Redeemer. With property, family, and health gone, he could still rejoice in his Redeemer. Job had real property amid absolute poverty. He had possessions that could not be touched by Satan's power. And every Christian can join Wava Campbell in saying:

AMEN, JOB, AMEN!
If I should lie, some future day
As I've seen others do,
Unable then to move or speak,
And pain-racked through and through—
If you should see and pity me,
Just look at me once more,
And say, Her heart is singing
As it always did before.
It matters not that flesh may rot—
The song will be the same:
A song of glad thanksgiving,
To my precious Saviour's name.
For He, by grace, prepared a place
Where someday I shall dwell
In this same body, glorified,
And truly strong and well.
In view of this expected bliss,
All aches and pains grow dim;
For though this body be destroyed,
I shall, in flesh, see Him.

...Wava Campbell

Your Redeemer lives. Rejoice!

JOB'S WIFE

MEMORY VERSE: *But he said unto her, Thou speakest as one of the foolish women speaketh. What? shall we receive good at the hand of God, and shall we not receive evil? In all this did not Job sin with his lips* (Job 2:10).

Job's wife may be the most maligned woman in the Bible. It's not fair.

What she said was bad, but one must remember when she said it. Her children had just lost their lives. She and her husband had lost all their property. And now the man she loved had lost his health. Under such conditions many would have said foolish things. Depression often causes words to drop from our lips that would never be uttered under normal circumstances.

We must be careful not to judge the man by the moment. Or the woman.

Job understood his wife's state of mind and spoke to her tenderly. He didn't call her a fool. He knew her too well for that...and loved her. He simply told her that she was talking like one of the foolish women. He reminded her that she was out of character. This was not like her. There is not a touch of bitterness in his word of correction. This patient and good man knew the load of grief being carried by his deprived wife and he had compassion on her.

And now a good word for Mrs. Job. It is said that whenever a man reaches the top a good woman is holding the ladder. And Job had become a prosperous and respected man. Mrs. Job had evidently been a loyal and helpful companion through the years, a good homemaker and mother. She doesn't deserve the criticism heaped on her for her single lapse of judgment during a time of deep depression.

To attack others when they are down is to act like the foolish ones. *Husbands, love your wives* (Ephesians 5:25).

ISAIAH

MEMORY VERSE: *Also I heard the voice of the Lord, saying, Whom shall I send, and who will go for us? Then said I, Here am I; send me* (Isaiah 6:8).

Isaiah was given a vision of the Lord and he never got over it.

His reaction to the vision was characteristic of other great men in the Bible. He was convicted of his own sins: *Woe is me! for I am undone; because I am a man of unclean lips, and I dwell in the midst of a people of unclean lips: for mine eyes have seen the King, the LORD of hosts* (Isaiah 6:5).

Notice that Isaiah was concerned about his own sins...then the sins of his people. Too often recognition of wrong doing runs in the other direction. Many are burdened about the moral condition of America but aren't really all that bothered about their own sins. They see the faults of public officials and the general moral slide of the nation but somehow overlook their own spiritual coldness. They would take to the streets to get prayer back in public schools but don't take time to pray fervently themselves. And to them, prayer meeting at the church is a forgotten gathering. Isaiah had lip trouble and he confessed that sin immediately. He ought to have a lot of company.

Thankfully, in Isaiah's case, forgiveness followed confession: *Lo, this hath touched thy lips; and thine iniquity is taken away, and thy sin purged* (Isaiah 6:7). That is still true. *If we confess our sins, he is faithful and just to forgive us our sins, and to cleanse us from all unrighteousness* (1 John 1:9).

Isaiah surrendered to the will of God. His "Here am I, send me," gave God total control of his life.

Make Isaiah's prayer your own.

JEREMIAH

MEMORY VERSE: *Be not afraid of their faces: for I am with thee to deliver thee, saith the LORD* (Jeremiah 1:8).

Jeremiah is known as the weeping prophet. His task was difficult. He was called to tell the people of their sins and to warn them of a coming captivity as a result. His message made him unpopular and brought persecution.

Faced with the call of God, Jeremiah felt inadequate: *Then said I, Ah, Lord GOD! behold, I cannot speak: for I am a child* (Jeremiah 1:6). Matthew Henry says: "The Lord who formed us, knows for what particular services and purposes He intended us....But though a sense of our own weakness and insufficiency should make us go humbly about our work, it should not make us draw back when God calls us."

Jeremiah's expression of concern for his people speaks of a compassion needed today: *Oh that my head were waters, and mine eyes a fountain of tears, that I might weep day and night for the slain of the daughter of my people* (Jeremiah 9:1).

In a desperate day, Jeremiah recorded one of the greatest prayer promises in the Bible: *Call unto me, and I will answer thee, and shew thee great and mighty things, which thou knowest not* (Jeremiah 33:3).

Jeremiah's tears and plain preaching are needed now, as well as his message of God's mercy. In his book of tears, Lamentations, Jeremiah has given us this encouraging word: *It is of the LORD'S mercies that we are not consumed, because his compassions fail not. They are new every morning: great is thy faithfulness* (Lamentations 3:22,23). These verses became the inspiration for one of the most blessed songs in Christendom.

And Jeremiah's God is still faithful today.

DANIEL

MEMORY VERSE: *But Daniel purposed in his heart that he would not defile himself with the portion of the king's meat, nor with the wine which he drank: therefore he requested of the prince of the eunuchs that he might not defile himself* (Daniel 1:8).

Daniel was given a preview of the future. He troubles skeptics because his prophecy concerning the rise and fall of the major empires of history is absolutely accurate. But what kind of man received such inside information from God? And how can we best understand his prophecies of the endtime?

Dr. H. A. Ironside gives this important recommendation: "This little company, Daniel, Hananiah, Mishael, and Azariah, four devoted young men, set themselves against all the evil of the kingdom of Babylon. They said, 'We will not defile ourselves' and these were the men to whom God would communicate His mind. I believe it is important to dwell on this, because in our own day, alas, in many cases prophetic study has been taken up by very unspiritual persons. If we are going to get the mind of God in studying this book we must remember that it consists of revelations, deliverances, and visions given to a spiritually-minded man who was separated from the iniquity of his day; and if we are to understand it, we also need to be spiritually-minded, and to walk apart from all that is unholy, all that would hinder progress in divine things. We need ever to have before us the words, *Look to yourselves, that we lose not those things which we have wrought, but that we receive a full reward* (2 John 8).

So, if we are to understand Daniel's book, we must follow his example.

How is it with your heart? Have you purposed to be clean?

NEBUCHADNEZZAR

MEMORY VERSE: *Now I Nebuchadnezzar praise and extol and honour the King of heaven, all whose works are truth, and his ways judgment: and those that walk in pride he is able to abase* (Daniel 4:37).

Nebuchadnezzar was the king of the mighty Babylonian Empire. The city of Babylon itself covered an area of 200 square miles and was surrounded by walls that were wide enough at the top to have rows of small houses on either side with a space between them wide enough for the passage of chariots. There were 50 temples in the city as well as a huge complex of impressive buildings. The palace was built of blue enameled bricks and its construction carried the mark of master craftsmen, many of whom were probably captives who had been chosen for this special project because of their abilities.

Here too, Nebuchadnezzar built the famous hanging gardens as a special gift to his wife, a Median princess. They consisted of terraces, supported by massive masonry arches, on which carefully tended gardens had been laid out on different levels, containing a variety of Persian and Babylonian plants and trees. Vegetation transplanted from the queen's mountain home was intended to comfort her when she was homesick. The Greeks considered the hanging gardens one of the seven wonders of the world.

Nebuchadnezzar was extremely proud of his city and his position and felt no need of God. Then his reason was taken away. His frightening experience is heart rendering. When his senses returned to normal, the king's heart was changed. He saw his folly and pride and turned to the Lord. In this chapter, Nebuchadnezzar gives his testimony...a changed man.

Is pride keeping you from Christ? Be careful.

God loves you just as He loved Nebuchadnezzar. Don't wait until all is gone before you trust the Saviour.

JONAH

MEMORY VERSE: *Then were the men exceedingly afraid, and said unto him, Why hast thou done this? For the men knew that he fled from the presence of the LORD, because he had told them* (Jonah 1:10).

Dr. M. R. DeHaan opened his book, *Jonah—Fact or Fiction?* as follows: "The Book of Jonah is the story of a man, a prophet of the Lord, who had one of the strangest experiences in all of human history. The place from which he prophesied was the bottom of the sea. The pulpit from which he preached was the stomach of a fish. Yet striking as are the circumstances of his prophecy, still more striking was the prophecy itself, for Jonah preached the gospel of the Death and Resurrection of the Lord Jesus Christ, eight hundred years before Christ was born. The entire Old Testament contains no clearer type, no more definite picture of the Death and Resurrection of our Saviour than the Book of Jonah."

Jonah ended up inside the great fish because of his reluctance to obey the Lord's call to warn Ninevah of coming judgment. Fleeing from the Lord was futile and Jonah found himself in the midst of a severe storm at sea, being questioned by a group of anxious sailors. When the backslidden prophet related his story, his shipmates confronted him with a question that ought to be asked of all backsliders: "Why hast thou done this?"

Backsliding robs one of God's blessings. Why do it?

Backsliding hurts others. Why do it?

Backsliding brings the chastening of the Lord? Why do it?

If this final message finds you far from God, return today. Confess your sins to Him. Accept His forgiveness. Serve Him.

God's way is best.

October

THIS MONTH'S STUDY

God—The Trinity

Days 3,5,10,14,16, and 22 contain quotes or information from "Three Thousand Illustrations for Christian Service," "Knight's Master Book of New Illustration," and "Knight's Treasury of Illustrations" all by Walter B. Knight, published by Wm. B. Eerdmans Publishing Company, Grand Rapids, Michigan. Used by permission.

MEETING GOD

MEMORY VERSE: *In the beginning God created the heaven and the earth* (Genesis 1:1).

The first sentence in the Bible is a magnificent introduction to Almighty God. With one glance, we learn that there is one God, who is eternal, all powerful, and the Creator of the universe. Commenting on Genesis 1:1, F. B. Meyer said: "With the pen of unerring truth the Spirit of Inspiration writes God's name on all things."

Towering high above all the theories of man, the Bible presents the only rational answer to the beginning of things. All other explanations of the reason for being must either ask the question: "What came before that?" or settle for belief in an eternal impersonal universe. In contrast, the inspired writer simply takes us back beyond the beginning of all things and explains that God has always existed. Captivated by this tremendous truth, the psalmist wrote: *LORD, thou hast been our dwelling place in all generations. Before the mountains were brought forth, or ever thou hadst formed the earth and the world, even from everlasting to everlasting, thou art God* (Psalm 90:1,2).

Equally thrilling is the revelation that God is able to create by the power of His Word. "Let there be light," He said. And there was light. The rest of creation, apart from that of man, was simply spoken into existence.

The vastness of God's creation lets us know that He is a God of unlimited power. Its minuteness reveals that He cares. Keeping the planets in their courses will be His concern today, as will a single teardrop that falls from your eye.

THE TRINITY

MEMORY VERSE: *Go ye therefore, and teach all nations, baptizing them in the name of the Father, and of the Son, and of the Holy Spirit* (Matthew 28:19).

Cults often attack the Trinity. Yet, teaching about the Father, Son, and Holy Spirit is found throughout the Bible.

The first verse in the Bible contains the plural form of the word that is translated God, *elohim*. Plurality is also indicated in such statements as: *And God said, Let US make man in OUR image, after OUR likeness...* (Genesis 1:26). *And the Lord God said, Behold, the man is become as one of US* (3:22).

Still, the Bible insists that God is ONE: *Hear, O Israel: The LORD our God is one LORD* (Deuteronomy 6:4). In short, then, the Hebrew words used for God and to describe God call for a plurality in unity.

But who are the persons of this plurality?

One Person is the Father. *Doubtless thou art our father* (Isaiah 63:16).

One Person is the Son. *I will declare the decree: the LORD hath said unto me, Thou art my Son; this day have I begotten thee* (Psalm 2:7).

One Person is the Holy Spirit. *And the earth was without form and void; and darkness was upon the face of the deep. And the Spirit of God moved upon the face of the waters* (Genesis 1:2).

Paul's benediction at the end of his second letter to the Corinthians makes it clear: *The grace of the Lord Jesus Christ, and the love of God, and the communion of the Holy Ghost, be with you all. Amen* (2 Corinthians 13:14).

Who could ask for more?

THE GREAT CREATOR

MEMORY VERSE: *All things were made by him; and without him was not any thing made that was made* (John 1:3).

Napoleon said: "I marvel that whereas the ambitious dreams of myself, Caesar, and Alexander should have vanished into thin air, a Judean peasant—Jesus—should be able to stretch His hands across the centuries and control the destinies of men and nations." But the dismayed fallen leader had forgotten to take into consideration the fact that Jesus was far more than a Judean peasant.

Had Jesus been but a man, He could not have atoned for the sins of the world. It was the great Creator who came down in human form to redeem His creation. No wonder He spoke with authority. No wonder the wind and waves were subject to Him. No wonder death could not hold Him.

John explains that Christ is the source of light and life. Doubters used to attack the reliability of the Bible account of creation because light is said to have been created before the sun. Now we know that there are other sources of light in the universe. How foolish to suppose that the Creator would be dependent upon the sun for illumination. That fiery ball is but one of His deputies assigned to provide light and physical life to planet earth.

At the moment of new birth, the same creative power that called the universe into existence becomes active within the believer: *Therefore, if any man be in Christ, he is a new creature: old things are passed away; behold, all things are become new* (2 Corinthians 5:17).

GOD IS HOLY

MEMORY VERSE: *And one cried unto another, and said, Holy, holy, holy, is the LORD of hosts; the whole earth is full of his glory* (Isaiah 6:3).

A lady once prayed: "O Lord, forgive us. We do so many things now that we used to think were wrong." Her prayer is a commentary on many lives.

When Isaiah was given a vision of the Lord, he was most impressed with God's holiness. That is not surprising since, in his vision, the creatures about the throne were occupied day and night with that attribute of God.

The holiness of God is taught throughout the Bible. Sodom and Gomorrah could not be allowed to continue in their wickedness. The angels that left their first estate were not spared. The world in Noah's day had but one hundred twenty years to turn from wickedness before destruction. Ninevah had to repent in forty days in response to the preaching of Jonah or be overthrown.

The most powerful illustration of God's holiness is found in the death of Christ on the cross. Sin could not be excused. It had to be judged. There was but one way for God to be just and the justifier: The Innocent One had to atone for the guilty. Christ died for us, taking our place: *For he hath made him to be sin for us, who knew no sin; that we might be made the righteousness of God in him* (2 Corinthians 5:21).

Live carefully. The price of sin is high. And one day soon we must stand before our Holy God (see Romans 14:12).

GOD IS TRUE

MEMORY VERSE: *And they sing the song of Moses the servant of God, and the song of the Lamb, saying, Great and marvellous are thy works, Lord God Almighty; just and true are thy ways, thou King of saints* (Revelation 15:3).

Dr. Philpot once had the sad duty of going to tell a Christian woman that her husband had died in battle. After greeting her he said, "I am the bearer of sad tidings. Your dear husband has been slain in battle!" The woman fell to the floor and wept uncontrollably. The faithful pastor did all he could to bring comfort to her but the grief-stricken woman, seemingly deaf to his words, would only cry out, "Is it true after all?" Thinking that she doubted the sad news, he said: "Yes, my good woman, it is true. Your husband has given his life in the service of his country." "Oh, Pastor," she sobbed, "I know that my husband is gone, but is it really true that there is a God who cares?"

There are many difficult experiences in life and in some of them we may be tempted to doubt the goodness and wisdom of God. Castles tumble. Plans do not work out. Health flees. Everything seems to go wrong. What is the answer?

The answer lies in our inability to know all the details of any given situation as God knows them. Our information is incomplete. God, knowing the future and all the results of every possible set of events, brings about what is best for His own (see Romans 8:28).

When we meet Him, we'll join the heavenly chorus singing: *Great and marvellous are thy works, Lord God Almighty; just and true are thy ways, thou King of saints.*

GOD IS JUST

MEMORY VERSE: *To declare, I say, at this time his right-eousness: that he might be just, and the justifier of him which believeth in Jesus* (Romans 3:26).

Why does God allow war? Why do children die? Why do the evil prosper? Why all the crippling and killing diseases? Why does the devil exist?

These questions all have one thing in common. They ask if God is just. Though you may never have voiced the words, you have probably entertained questions that are similar to these. Can you count on God to always do the right thing?

Thankfully, we can depend on the justice of God. Many Bible verses guarantee this truth: *Wherefore now let the fear of the LORD be upon you; take heed and do it: for there is no iniquity with the LORD our God, nor respect of persons, nor taking of gifts* (2 Chronicles 19:7); *The fear of the LORD is clean, enduring for ever: the judgments of the LORD are true and righteous altogether* (Psalm 19:9); *Because he hath appointed a day, in the which he will judge the world in righteousness by that man whom he hath ordained; whereof he hath given assurance unto all men, in that he hath raised him from the dead* (Acts 17:31); *If we confess our sins, he is faithful and just to forgive us our sins, and to cleanse us from all unrighteousness* (1 John 1:9); *For Christ also hath once suffered for sins, the just for the unjust, that he might bring us to God, being put to death in the flesh, but quickened by the Spirit* (1 Peter 3:18).

So, we can expect God to do right. If we are to be like Him, we must be just in all our dealings with others.

GOD IS LOVE

MEMORY VERSE: *He that loveth not knoweth not God; for God is love* (1 John 4:8).

Many claim the name "Christian" who are not genuine. Some who profess Christ as Saviour are filled with bitterness, malice, selfishness, hatred, and envy. They are quick to gossip and they delight when others stumble along the way. Often these people are themselves deceived, and are of the opinion that their religious charade commends them to God.

Christians are people who have been born again through faith in the Lord Jesus Christ. This new birth is possible because of God's love for us. His love is seen in His many blessings and provisions but especially in the death of His Son on the cross: *But God commendeth his love toward us, in that, while we were yet sinners, Christ died for us* (Romans 5:8).

The love of God is placed in our hearts by the Holy Spirit: *And hope maketh not ashamed; because the love of God is shed abroad in our hearts by the Holy Ghost who is given unto us* (Romans 5:5).

It is totally inconsistent for one who has been saved to be filled with hate, bitterness, and malice. John wrote: *If a man say, I love God, and hateth his brother, he is a liar: for he that loveth not his brother whom he hath seen, how can he love God whom he hath not seen?* (1 John 4:20).

Since God loves us, let us communicate His love to others. John put it all together well: *Beloved, if God so loved us, we ought also to love one another* (1 John 4:11).

GOD IS OMNIPOTENT

MEMORY VERSE: *Behold, I am the LORD, the God of all flesh: is there any thing too hard for me?* (Jeremiah 32:27).

God is all powerful. Theologians call this attribute "omnipotence." To most of us that just means that God can do anything.

The first verse in the Bible guarantees God's limitless power: *In the beginning God created the heaven and the earth* (Genesis 1:1). Still, the mind of man has continually staggered at God's ability to perform many of the miracles recorded in His Word.

How inconsistent!

The God who formed the seas could easily open one of them for His people to cross dry-shod. The God who feeds the angels could easily drop enough from heaven's table to feed the Israelites in the wilderness. The God who called forth water from the first spring could easily open a new fountain in a rock so that thirsty people could drink. The God who filled the seas with life could easily prepare a great fish perfectly designed to swallow backslidden and disobedient Jonah. The God who laid the foundations of the earth could easily cause it to tremble beneath the walls of Jericho until the mighty fortress fell. The God who holds the wind in His hands could easily call for a calm on the Sea of Galilee when it was raging in a storm. The God who engineered the human body could easily give ability to the lame to walk and the blind to see. The God who gave life could easily return it to one from whom it had taken flight.

And the God who knows your tomorrows can easily carry you through the darkest day.

GOD IS OMNISCIENT

MEMORY VERSE: *Thou knowest my downsitting and mine uprising; thou understandest my thought afar off* (Psalm 139:2).

God knows all.

He knows all the past. While historians and archaeologists study and dig to solve the stubborn secrets of antiquity, God knows all about them. Questioning Job, the Lord said: *Where wast thou when I laid the foundations of the earth? declare, if thou hast understanding. Who hath laid the measures thereof, if thou knowest? or who hath stretched the line upon it?* (Job 38:4,5).

He knows all about the present. Philosophers puzzle over present problems. Politicians probe for answers. Stargazers try to discern the signs of the times in order to advise the public on their horoscopes. But God knows. Nothing takes Him by surprise. Everything is open before His gaze.

He knows all about the future. No crystal ball is needed for God to chart our tomorrows. He sees them more clearly than we remember yesterday. And He holds the future in His hands. All events still to come are written in His history book. The movements of the nations, the rise and fall of political leaders, and the personal triumphs and tragedies of us all are already in His mind.

Knowing Him, then, we can feel safe. We do not need to fear what the future holds for we know the One who holds the future. Even in times of trial, we can experience the confidence and assurance that carried Job through such great loss. In the darkest of hours, he declared: *But he knoweth the way that I take: when he hath tried me, I shall come forth as gold* (Job 23:10).

October 10 — Psalm 139:7-12

GOD IS OMNIPRESENT

MEMORY VERSE: *Whither shall I go from thy spirit? or whither shall I flee from thy presence?* (Psalm 139:7).

God is everywhere.

A celebrity attended the services of an old minister in a small church. The aged preacher spoke with his accustomed earnestness and seemed unshaken by the presence of the visitor. At the close of the service, some members of the congregation said, "Pastor, we had a distinguished visitor today, but you did not seem embarrassed." Their wise pastor replied: "I have been preaching in the presence of Almighty God for forty years, and do you think, with Him as one of my constant Hearers, any man can embarrass me by his presence?"

The ability of God to be everywhere is hard for us to grasp. Our minds struggle with such infinite information. Yet it is true. A number of Bible verses confirm it. Solomon wrote: *But will God indeed dwell on the earth? behold, the heaven and heaven of heavens cannot contain thee; how much less this house that I have builded* (1 Kings 8:27). The psalmist declared: *Nevertheless I am continually with thee; thou hast holden me by my right hand. Thou shalt guide me with thy counsel, and afterward receive me to glory. Whom have I in heaven but thee? and there is none upon earth that I desire beside thee. My flesh and my heart faileth: but God is the strength of my heart, and my portion for ever* (Psalm 73:23-26).

Though it is beyond our understanding, we can claim the promise of His presence. He will never leave us nor forsake us (see Hebrews 13:6). And so the child of God is never alone.

GOD IS UNCHANGING

MEMORY VERSE: *Every good gift and every perfect gift is from above, and cometh down from the Father of lights, with whom is no variableness, neither shadow of turning* (James 1:17).

God is the same today as He was yesterday. In all our tomorrows, He will be the same. Dr. Lewis Sperry Chafer wrote: "In no sphere or relationship is God subject to change. He could not be less than He is, and, since He filleth all things, He could not be more than He is. He could be removed from no place, nor is His knowledge or holiness subject to change."

The Bible says of God: *For I am the LORD, I change not; therefore ye sons of Jacob are not consumed* (Malachi 3:6); *Of old hast thou laid the foundation of the earth: and the heavens are the work of thy hands. They shall perish, but thou shalt endure: yea, all of them shall wax old like a garment; as a vesture shalt thou change them, and they shall be changed: But thou art the same, and thy years shall have no end* (Psalm 102:25-27).

In my youth, I would often kneel to pray in our humble home in Detroit. There I unloaded many burdens and asked for many blessings. Since that time, most things have changed. The community has changed. The neighbors have changed. I have changed. But God remains the same. He is as ready to bear the burdens of this preacher as He was to hear the prayer of that boy so long ago. Events of the day may change the course of our lives, but God is unchanging: *Jesus Christ the same yesterday, and to day, and for ever* (Hebrews 13:8).

GOD IS SOVEREIGN

MEMORY VERSE: *For of him, and through him, and to him, are all things: to whom be glory for ever. Amen* (Romans 11:36).

God is in charge.

The Creator is working out His plan and is not shaken by any event brought about by man. He knows the end from the beginning and though He allows man to run his course, control never slips from divine fingers.

In her prophetic prayer, Hannah observed: *The LORD killeth, and maketh alive: he bringeth down to the grave, and bringeth up. The LORD maketh poor, and maketh rich: he bringeth low, and lifteth up. He raiseth up the poor out of the dust, and lifteth up the beggar from the dunghill, to set them among princes, and to make them inherit the throne of glory: for the pillars of the earth are the LORD'S and he hath set the world upon them* (1 Samuel 2:6-8).

The person who understands that God's plan in the world is being developed will find peace in troubled times. This is especially important when world conditions are upsetting. We are fast moving toward that time when men's hearts will fail them for fear of the things coming upon the earth (see Luke 23:26). Modern means of communication are often less than helpful to the nervous system. There was a day when people were blissfully unaware of trouble on the other side of the world, but now unrest thousands of miles away can be distressing. The simple life is past. Man's inventions have him trapped in a complex web of hurry and worry.

How good it is to know that God is still on the throne.

GOD IS GOOD

MEMORY VERSE: *Thou art good, and doest good; teach me thy statutes* (Psalm 119:68).

Many know the child's prayer:

"God is great, God is good;
Let us thank Him for our food;
By His hand we all are fed;
Give us now our daily bread. Amen."

Have you thought how important it is that God is good? Imagine a universe with a bad god.

But God is good!

It is especially important to remember that His will for our lives is good: *And be not conformed to this world: but be ye transformed by the renewing of your mind, that ye may prove what is that good, and acceptable, and perfect, will of God* (Romans 12:2).

Yielding to the will of God will bring good to our lives. Jesus warned that saving one's life (resisting total surrender to Christ) would result in loss, while losing one's life for His sake would bring eternal gain. Spiritual giants have demonstrated this truth through the centuries.

It is disappointing to hear a speaker warning his hearers that the will of God will probably take them to the area or work that they dislike, as if it can be expected that God will give His dedicated servants earth's most unpleasant tasks. On the contrary, the will of God is good. His will may lead us to a difficult place, but that will always be the place of blessing. We can confidently place our lives and futures in His hands and at His disposal.

He is good. And His will is good for us.

THE GOD OF NATURE

MEMORY VERSE: *The heavens declare the glory of God; and the firmament sheweth his handywork* (Psalm 19:1).

A man sat in the heat of the day under a walnut tree looking at a pumpkin vine. He began to muse, "How foolish God is! Here He puts a great heavy pumpkin on a tiny vine without strength to do anything but lie on the ground. He puts tiny walnuts on a tree whose branches could hold the weight of a man. If I were God, I could do better than that!" Suddenly a breeze knocked a walnut from the tree. It fell on the man's head. He rubbed the bump, a sadder and wiser man. He remarked: "Suppose there had been a pumpkin up there instead of a walnut! Never again will I try to plan the world for God, I shall thank Him that He has done it so well!"

Everything in nature carries in it the mark of the Creator. The psalmist says that the entire earth is given witness to the glory of God through the beauty and action in the sky. Still men turn their eyes from the heights and scan the earth trying to find support for a theory that disregards the Creator and traces the history of man to a beginning other than that stated in the Bible.

With the testimony of nature so strong, one wonders why men reject the reality of God's existence. Desire must be father to their action. Some would rather not accept the truth of God for fear of being accountable to Him for their sins.

Their escape route is a deception. They are still accountable. As are we all.

GOD IS INFINITE

MEMORY VERSE: *For as the heavens are higher than the earth, so are my ways higher than your ways, and my thoughts than your thoughts* (Isaiah 55:9).

God has no boundaries. No limits. He has always existed and He will always exist. He cannot be bound by time or space for they are His creations. His knowledge is beyond us.

We have many limits. There are things we do not comprehend. So many things we cannot do. We are limited in knowledge, in strength, and in ability. Even the strongest have areas of weakness. It is the way of mankind. We are a fallen race, still suffering from the effects of that traumatic tumble. We are finite beings.

How wonderful that the infinite God loves us as we are! How interesting that He should desire to have fellowship with us! The thought seems too great to take in.

Yet it is true.

At first glance, the gap seems too wide to bridge—from God to man—from the Holy One to sinners. And that first evaluation would stand were it not for the cross. There on that rugged hill, reconciliation was made, the barrier to blessing broken down: *For through him we both have access by one Spirit unto the Father* (Ephesians 2:18).

Amazing grace? And then some! Reaching from the heights to the depths. Linking us to the Lord of heaven and earth, when we respond by faith. Making us partakers of the divine nature (see 2 Peter 1:4), children of the King (see John 1:12), joint-heirs with Christ (see Romans 8:17).

And that is infinitely more than we deserve.

WAITING

MEMORY VERSE: *But they that wait upon the LORD shall renew their strength; they shall mount up with wings as eagles; they shall run and not be weary; and they shall walk, and not faint* (Isaiah 40:31).

Phillips Brooks was well known for his poise and patience. His close friends, however, knew that at time he suffered moments of frustration and irritability. One day a friend saw him pacing the floor like a caged lion. "What is the trouble, Dr. Brooks?" asked the friend. Brooks answered: "The trouble is that I am in a hurry, but God isn't!"

Few enjoy waiting. Most of us pray like the psalmist, who said: "Make haste, O God!" We live in an age of hurry. Patience is a virtue hard to find. Still it is important to learn to wait.

Walter Brown Knight wrote: "Remember that the cogs of our lives are geared to the cogs of God's working. The gear teeth of God's plans are stronger than our own. When we speed up while God keeps His pace, we strip our gears. We wear out. We crack up nervously, mentally, and physically."

To be able to patiently wait upon God we must be convinced that He is in control and that He is working things out for our good (see Romans 8:28). That demands faith, as do most of God's blessings.

Patience is cultivated through trouble: *Tribulation worketh patience* (Romans 5:3). Problems, though unwelcome, produce patience. Sometimes that is the design in our difficulties. And the Designer does all His work in love.

October 17   Jeremiah 12:1-5

WHAT MADE YOU CROSS?

MEMORY VERSE: *If thou hast run with the footmen, and they have wearied thee, then how canst thou contend with horses? and if in the land of peace, wherein thou trustedst, they wearied thee, then how wilt thou do in the swelling of the Jordan?* (Jeremiah 12:5).

A long time ago I received a letter with a tract enclosed. I have forgotten the message of that leaflet, but the title "What Made You Cross?" has stayed with me. It is a good question. I suppose most of us are ashamed that trifles touch off our tempers and disturb our dispositions.

J. Hudson Taylor wrote: "It is not so much the greatness of our troubles, as the littleness of our spirit, which makes us complain."

It doesn't take a theologian to discover the characteristic joy of first century Christians. Under the toughest of circumstances they were triumphant. Even in prison, you find them singing praises to God. The disturbing dimension to this comparison is the thought that most present day Christians might really cave in if persecution came. If we are edgy in affluence, what would we do under oppression?

The need of dealing with this problem may be far more urgent than we realize. We do not know what the future holds. At any rate, there is sure to be great profit for hearts and homes if we stop exploding to gain our rights and start yielding to God in all things. It is only then that we will be able to *do all things without murmurings and disputings* (Philippians 2:14).

—R.F.C.

JESUS IS LORD

MEMORY VERSE: *Let this mind be in you, which was also in Christ Jesus: Who, being in the form of God, thought it not robbery to be equal with God* (Philippians 2:5,6).

A chapter in my book, *Great Salvation Themes*, asks these thought-provoking questions: "Did Christ exist before His descension to earth? Was He conceived through the instrumentality of the Holy Spirit? Was He truly God from all eternity?

These questions might be summarized in this one. Is Jesus God?

If you accept the Bible as your authority, you will conclude that Jesus is Lord. Here's proof: John the Baptist came to prepare the way for Jesus. Isaiah said of John: *The voice of him that crieth in the wilderness, Prepare ye the way of the LORD, make straight in the desert a highway for our God* (Isaiah 40:3). Christ was the Creator: *In the beginning was the Word, and the Word was with God, and the Word was God. The same was in the beginning with God. All things were made by him; and without him was not any thing made that was made* (John 1:1-3). The Lord of glory was crucified: *Which none of the princes of this world knew: for had they known it, they would not have crucified the Lord of glory* (1 Corinthians 2:8). When Christ returns to reign, all will admit that He is Lord: *And that every tongue should confess that Jesus Christ is Lord, to the glory of God the Father* (Philippians 2:11).

If you are born again, it is because you have received the LORD Jesus Christ. Be sure that He is the LORD of your life.

GM

MEMORY VERSE: *Call unto me, and I will answer thee, and shew thee great and mighty things, which thou knowest not* (Jeremiah 33:3).

David was a bright and outstanding Christian young man who had been a diabetic since early childhood. Now he was losing his sight. While preparing for total blindness, he enrolled in courses in a school in Detroit, Michigan. Across the street there was a large sign advertising General Motors products with the customary GM abbreviation for the world's largest corporation.

One day, while on vacation from school, David told me that God had given him a wonderful reminder of His promises through that General Motors sign. "Every day I look across the street at that GM sign and am reminded of the 'GREAT AND MIGHTY' promise in Jeremiah 33:3." To David, the great and mighty power of God far surpassed the value of all the expensive automobiles produced by the giant automaker.

We grow accustomed to the signs of power in business or politics and are sometimes awed by their seeming greatness. Actually, all the power of all the nations is but a drop in the bucket compared to the great and mighty power of God. That power is at our disposal through prayer. Yet, we are often blind to His promises. While David's physical sight was failing, his spiritual perception was clear.

Do you see signs of the great and mighty work of God in your life?

YOUR LIFE STORY

MEMORY VERSE: *For we are his workmanship, created in Christ Jesus unto good works, which God hath before ordained that we should walk in them* (Ephesians 2:10).

Dr. Ironside was once approached by a lady who offered to tell his fortune. He replied that he had a book in his pocket that told her past, present, and future. Surprised, she asked what book that might be. He immediately produced a New Testament.

Our text presents the life story of any Christian. We were all dead in trespasses and sins before being born again and at that time lived under bondage to the lusts of the flesh. As Paul puts it, we "were by nature the children of wrath, even as others." Had it not been for the entrance of the love and grace of God, we would have been without hope.

The grace of God flows out of His love and offers completely unmerited favor. We deserve hell, but through His grace we gain heaven. We deserve to be eternally separated from God, but through His grace we will be with Him forever.

As wonderful as the grace of God is, it would be frustrated apart from the death of Christ on the cross as our substitute. Even grace could not provide another way of salvation. The songwriter was correct: "Grace Is Flowing From Calvary."

Those saved by grace are the workmanship of God, ordained to walk in good works. The purpose of our good works is given in Matthew 5:16: *Let your light so shine before men, that they may see your good works, and glorify your Father which is in heaven.*

October 21   2 Corinthians 12:1-11

STRENGTH

MEMORY VERSE: *And he said unto me, My grace is sufficient for thee: for my strength is made perfect in weakness. Most gladly therefore will I rather glory in my infirmities, that the power of Christ may rest upon me* (2 Corinthians 12:9).

When we come to the end of human endurance, it is good to know that God has promised strength to His fainting children. The Christian who has exhausted his own resources has the privilege of trading in his weakness for the power of God. Remembering that God is all powerful (omnipotent), that is an exciting alternative.

Bible personalities have historically recognized that God's strength was available for their times of need. Consider these examples: *The LORD is my strength and song, and he is become my salvation* (Exodus 15:2); *I will love thee, O LORD, my strength* (Psalm 18:1); *GOD is our refuge and strength, a very present help in trouble* (Psalm 46:1); *In God is my salvation and my glory: the rock of my strength, and my refuge, is in God* (Psalm 62:7); *The LORD God is my strength, and he will make my feet like hinds' feet, and he will make me to walk upon mine high places* (Habakkuk 3:19).

Wava Campbell wrote:

> Oh Lord, today my strength is small
> I seem to have no strength at all,
> And yet the lost ones must be sought
> And many little children taught;
> I'll have to use Your strength today,
> It works out better anyway.

October 22　　　1 Corinthians 1:26-31

WEAK PEOPLE

MEMORY VERSE: *But God hath chosen the foolish things of the world to confound the wise; and God hath chosen the weak things of the world to confound the things which are mighty* (1 Corinthians 1:27).

Investigators of the work of Mary Slessor, missionary in Africa, were amazed when they saw that she, a weak woman, had been able to mold tribal chieftains to her will. One of the chiefs explained, "You have evidently forgotten to take into account the woman's God."

Most of the disciples were not noted for their abilities. Peter had trouble with his temper and was unstable at the crucifixion. Philip was always trying to figure a faithless way out of problems. Thomas at first doubted the Resurrection. Yet that small group of imperfect people rose to the occasion after the Resurrection and planted churches throughout the world.

The fact that Christianity exists today is evidence of their amazing accomplishments. The only explanation for their success in the face of such opposition and persecution is the power of God.

Few doubt that God is powerful. Even a layman's look at the wonders of the universe is overwhelming. Scientists who understand something about the atom have an immense appreciation for the power that is stored in the elements of God's creation. The destruction of an earthquake, a thunderstorm, or a tornado reminds us of the awesome power of God. The most moving example of God's power is the Resurrection.

But what makes that power available to us?

The answer is faith.

God imparts His power to those who trust Him.

KNOWING GOD THROUGH PRAYER

MEMORY VERSE: *That I may know him, and the power of his resurrection, and the fellowship of his sufferings, being made comformable unto his death* (Philippians 3:10).

Paul desired to know his Lord better. Though certainly saved, he longed to ever walk closer with the Saviour. Spiritual giants are never satisfied. They are always deepening their devotion and increasing in love for their Lord. One avenue of spiritual growth is earnest prayer.

Sir Isaac Newton once wrote: "I can take my telescope and look millions and millions of miles into space; but I can lay my telescope aside, go into my room and shut the door, get down on my knees in earnest prayer, and see more of heaven and get closer to God than I can when assisted by all the telescopes and material agencies on earth."

Martin Luther said: "I am so busy now that I find if I did not spend two or three hours each day in prayer, I could not get through the day. If I should neglect prayer but a single day, I should lose a great deal of the fire of faith."

Communication with God through prayer deepens spiritual life and sometimes it shows outwardly. When Moses returned from Mt. Sinai his face was shining, though he was not aware of it.

The closer we walk with the Lord, the more His personality will show through. The believer's body is God's temple and as we yield to Him, others see the evidence of God's work in our lives. We begin to show more love, treat people with more grace, and become more just in our dealings.

When Christ returns we shall be like Him. Until then, let His life be evident in yours.

WHO RAISED JESUS?

MEMORY VERSE: *Therefore doth my Father love me, because I lay down my life, that I might take it again* (John 10:17).

Those who doubt the truth of the Trinity must ignore the resurrection of Christ. A number of such groups reject the bodily resurrection and teach that Christ arose only in spirit. It is understandable that these two errors would be joined, since the Resurrection is one of the Bible's clearest demonstrations of the work of the Father, Son, and Holy Spirit.

Peter wrote about the work of the Father and the Holy Spirit: *Blessed be the God and Father of our Lord Jesus Christ, which according to his abundant mercy hath begotten us again unto a lively hope by the resurrection of Jesus Christ from the dead* (1 Peter 1:3); *For Christ also hath once suffered for sins, the just for the unjust, that he might bring us to God, being put to death in the flesh, but quickened by the Spirit* (1 Peter 3:18).

Jesus himself spoke about His part in the Resurrection. Perhaps His clearest declaration is found in John 2:19-21: *Jesus answered and said unto them, Destroy this temple, and in three days I will raise it up. Then said the Jews, Forty and six years was this temple in building, and wilt thou rear it up in three days? But he spake of the temple of his body.*

In this miracle, the Father, Son, and Holy Spirit brought hope to hopeless sinners and help for daily living. Because of the Resurrection, the Living One walks with us below and someday we shall walk with Him above.

WHO KEEPS US SAFE?

MEMORY VERSE: *My Father, which gave them me, is greater than all; and no man is able to pluck them out of my Father's hand* (John 10:29).

It is great to be saved. And wonderful to know it.

But how can we be sure that our salvation will last? Temptation is so strong and we are so weak. Are we not likely to someday be separated from God, even though we walk with Him now? May we not lose our grip on the Saviour's hand?

Thankfully, our safety is in better hands. It is guaranteed by each Person of the Trinity. Christ declared that no man can pluck His own out of His hand. Furthermore, He said that none can pluck the saved from the Father's hand. Paul emphasized this Father-Son protection as follows: *Who shall lay any thing to the charge of God's elect? It is God that justifieth. Who is he that condemneth? It is Christ that died, yea rather, that is risen again, who is even at the right hand of God, who also maketh intercession for us* (Romans 8:33,34).

But what about the Holy Spirit? Paul shares that good news with us also: *And grieve not the holy Spirit of God, whereby ye are sealed unto the day of redemption* (Ephesians 4:30).

Peter tied it all together: *Who are kept by the power of God through faith unto salvation ready to be revealed in the last time* (1 Peter 1:5).

The hymn says it well: "More secure is no one ever; Than the loved ones of the Saviour."

It's good to be saved—and safe!

OUR FATHER

MEMORY VERSE: *Jesus saith unto him, I am the way, the truth, and the life: no man cometh unto the Father, but by me* (John 14:6).

Some teach that God the Father is the spiritual father of all people and that we are all His children. This is known as the Universal Fatherhood of God. It is a false teaching.

Jesus shocked the religious leaders of His day by calling them the children of the devil: *Ye are of your father the devil, and the lusts of your father ye will do. He was a murderer from the beginning, and abode not in the truth, because there is no truth in him. When he speaketh a lie, he speaketh of his own: for he is a liar, and the father of it* (John 8:44).

We become the children of the Heavenly Father through faith in His Son, the Lord Jesus Christ: *But as many as received him, to them gave he power to become the sons of God, even to them that believe on his name* (John 1:12). The disciples were taught to pray: "Our Father which art in heaven, Hallowed be thy name."

As a result of the new birth, the Christian is a child of the Father. He has been born into the family of God. And all the family benefits belong to him.

Samuel Zwemer wrote: "I understand the loving fatherhood of God as Jesus taught it because I saw it in my own father." The tender and close relationship of a father to his child enables us to grasp something of the Heavenly Father's closeness to us.

I feel secure with my Father's hand in mine.

THE FATHER'S LOVE

MEMORY VERSE: *For the Father himself loveth you, because ye have loved me, and have believed that I came out from God* (John 16:27).

Billy Bray, who was known for his constant Christian joy, once had a very poor crop of potatoes. He said the devil came to taunt him about his small potatoes and to mock him for continually rejoicing in the Lord. But Billy was up to the confrontation, "There you go criticizing my Father again," said Billy. "Why, when I served you, I had not potatoes at all."

Billy had learned that discouraging experiences do not mean that our Heavenly Father loves us less. His love is unchanging. He loves with a Father's love. Paul wrote to his friends in Thessalonica about the comfort of knowing that the Father loves us: *Now our Lord Jesus Christ himself, and God, even our Father, which hath loved us, and given us everlasting consolation and good hope through grace, comfort your hearts, and stablish you in every good word and work* (2 Thessalonians 2:16,17).

If we should ever be tempted to doubt the Father's love, we can simply remember that He sent His Son to die for us. Every step of Jesus along the dusty roads of Palestine said: "The Father loves you!" Every lash of the cruel Roman whip in the scourging of Jesus said, "The Father loves you!" The shout of Jesus "It is finished!" as He completed His work of redemption on the cross was really a shout conveying that same wonderful message: "The Father loves you!"

Rest secure in the Father's love.

THE FATHER UNDERSTANDS

MEMORY VERSE: *For he knoweth our frame; he remembereth that we are dust* (Psalm 103:14).

An old song says:
"God understands your heartache,
He sees the falling tear;
And whispers I am with thee,
Then falter not nor fear."
The psalmist agrees and points out that God never forgets our human limitations. He remembers what we are made of dust.

We are not iron people and therefore burdens and responsibilities can get too heavy for us. Our emotional cords are sometimes strained to the breaking point. We become weary in the race. Panic, on occasion, grips our hearts. Even when we know better.

Never mind. God understands.

God knows our physical limitations. Sickness may drain our normal vitality, making it hard to do even the routine work of the day. Lack of sleep may rob us of our usual alertness and we may become depressed because we haven't had time to rest. Financial needs may be so pressing that our work hours are lengthened to keep food on the table. The pressure may seem unbearable. Still, God knows the limit of our endurance and offers to compensate for our weakness.

God knows about broken hearts. "Where was God when my son died?" demanded an angry father of his pastor. "The same place He was when His own Son died," said the wise man of God. Our Lord knows about grief and tears. He made the human body with the ability to release tension through weeping and designed our emotions to cooperate.

The old song ends: "Then let Him bear your burden; He understands and cares." What good news for needy people!

THE FATHER KNOWS OUR NEEDS

MEMORY VERSE: *Behold the fowls of the air: for they sow not, neither do they reap, nor gather into barns; yet your heavenly Father feedeth them. Are ye not much better than they?* (Matthew 6:26).

Here is the Saviour's prescription for curing anxiety: TRUST IN THE FATHER'S CARE. Jesus puts His finger on our most common concern—the supply of our daily needs—and reminds us that the Heavenly Father is well able to care for us.

It is interesting that those who have perfect peace about their eternal state because of their faith in Christ, often find themselves overcome with worry and fear about tomorrow's provision. Perhaps that is because we have come to think that God only cares for our spiritual needs. Actually, His care encompasses everything that concerns us.

Test your anxiety with these questions: Have you ever had this need before? Were you concerned about it then? Did it seem there was no way for the need to be met? How did you survive? Since you made it through your previous crisis, is it possible there will be a way out of this one? Was God faithful before? Do you think He loves you less now? Can you trust Him for the rest of the day? Do you expect Him to be alive tomorrow?

Remember: YOU HAVE PROVED THE SUFFICIENCY OF GOD ONLY WHEN YOU HAVE TRUSTED HIM FOR THE IMPOSSIBLE. And He is sufficient: *My God shall supply all your need according to his riches in glory by Christ Jesus* (Philippians 4:19).

THE FATHER GAVE HIS SON

MEMORY VERSE: *For God so loved the world, that he gave his only begotten Son, that whosoever believeth in him should not perish, but have everlasting life* (John 3:16).

You can give without loving, but you cannot love without giving. Since God loves more than any other, He gave more—His only begotten Son.

This familiar verse is the heart of the Bible message. We must be careful not to neglect it because it is so well known. There is a reason for favorite Bible verses becoming favorites. This one is rich with meaning and expresses earth's greatest message, the love of God.

Have you ever considered the consequences had the message of John 3:16 not been given? What if God had not loved the world? What if He had not given His Son? What if eternal life was offered on a basis other than faith? What if the perishing could not be rescued? What if everlasting life could not be attained?

But this wonderful message is ours to receive. Have you responded to it? Do you understand that God loves you? Do you believe He gave His Son for you? Is it clear that you must come to Him just as you are to receive Him as your personal Lord and Saviour?

Act immediately on the truth of John 3:16. Turn from your sins to Christ and receive Him by faith right now. Rejoice in the love of God and thank Him for His salvation.

You'll be born again.

HEIRS OF THE FATHER

MEMORY VERSE: *And if children, then heirs; heirs of God, and joint-heirs with Christ; if so be that we suffer with him, that we may be also glorified together* (Romans 8:17).

Occasionally newspapers carry stories of people who have been surprised to learn that they have inherited large sums of money. Others dream of being named in the will of a millionaire. Probably neither will happen to you.

Nevertheless, if you are a Christian you are an heir of the greatest Benefactor in the universe. A joint-heir with Jesus Christ of His Father's fortune. You will share in His unspeakable riches because you have become one of His children through faith in His Son.

And how large is your inheritance? Remembering that you are a joint-heir with Christ, try to comprehend all that's contained in these verses: *GOD who at sundry times and in divers manners spake in time past unto the fathers by the prophets, hath in these last days spoken unto us by his Son, whom he hath appointed heir of all things, by whom also he made the worlds* (Hebrews 1:1,2).

So, you're an heir of all things. Look about you. Everything you see belongs to the Lord. He is presently allowing men to use His property, but it all belongs to Him. When Christ comes to set up His kingdom on this earth, all believers will rule and reign with Him...possessing our inheritance at that wonderful time. Until then, the Holy Spirit living within is the guarantee of the promise being fulfilled.

Congratulations on your coming inheritance.

November

THIS MONTH'S STUDY

The Holy Spirit

Days 4,12,16,17, and 18 contain quotes from "Three Thousand Illustrations for Christian Service," "Knight's Master Book of New Illustrations," and "Knight's Treasury of Illustrations," by Walter B. Knight, published by William B. Eerdmans Publishing Co., used by permission. Days 11,13,14,15, and 27 contain quotes from "Weight! A Better Way to Lose," by Roger Campbell, published by Victor Books, used by permission.

MEET THE HOLY SPIRIT

MEMORY VERSE: *And the earth was without form, and void; and darkness was upon the face of the deep. And the Spirit of God moved upon the face of the waters* (Genesis 1:2).

There is no waiting to meet the Holy Spirit. The seeking student finds Him in the second verse of the Bible. When the earth was without form and void, the Spirit of God was there moving upon the face of the waters. All doubts about His deity should end in this moving introduction to the third Person of the Trinity.

At the command of God, the great adventure of creation began. Light was created and divided from the darkness. Order came to the heavens and the earth. Trees and plants reached heavenward, thrusting green hands out of the virgin soil. The seas were filled with life and birds made solo flights through cloudless skies. Animals moved about the earth. And man walked and talked with his Maker.

The Holy Spirit still moves in the darkness. He specializes in bringing life and purpose where everything seems to be without form and void. Many who have thought life was not worth living have been rescued by the creative work of the Spirit of God. Chaos has been replaced by order and usefulness. There is no explanation for such a miraculous change apart from the new birth. Jesus described this creative act to Nicodemus, saying: *Except a man be born of water and of the Spirit, he cannot enter into the kingdom of God* (John 3:5).

Respond to the work of the Holy Spirit. Though His convicting voice may make you uncomfortable, that pain is but the prelude to blessing. Face your sins and trust the Saviour. Light and life will be yours. This is the unchanging purpose of the Holy Spirit.

THE PERSON WITHIN

MEMORY VERSE: *But God hath revealed them unto us by his Spirit: for the Spirit searcheth all things, yea, the deep things of God* (1 Corinthians 2:10).

Some reject the personality of the Holy Spirit. To them, He is only a force. But the Bible makes it clear that He is the third PERSON of the TRINITY.

We know that the Holy Spirit is a Person because He has the characteristics of a personality: emotion, intellect, and will.

The Holy Spirit has emotion: *And grieve not the holy Spirit of God, whereby ye are sealed unto the day of redemption* (Ephesians 4:30).

The Holy Spirit has intellect: *For what man knoweth the things of a man, save the spirit of man which is in him? even so the things of God knoweth no man, but the Spirit of God* (1 Corinthians 2:11).

The Holy Spirit has a will: *But all these worketh that one and the selfsame Spirit, dividing to every man severally as he will* (1 Corinthians 12:11).

An example from life, showing that the Holy Spirit is a Person, is found in the experience of Ananias who sold a field and tired to deceive the apostles concerning the price he had received for it. Peter rebuked him, saying: *Ananias, why hath Satan filled thine heart to lie to the Holy Ghost, and to keep back part of the price of the land?* (Acts 5:3). One can lie only to a person—never to a force.

The Holy Spirit is the Person who convicts us when we sin, who comforts us when we are sorrowing, and who lives within us after we are born again.

Once a person is saved, he will never be lonely again. The DIVINE PERSON will always be with him.

NO PLACE TO HIDE

MEMORY VERSE: *Whither shall I go from thy spirit? or whither shall I flee from thy presence?* (Psalm 139:7).

I once heard a preacher say that since God couldn't be everywhere, He made fathers. His statement seemed to please the audience but it was completely false. God is omnipresent—everywhere at the same time. Since the Holy Spirit is God, He is everywhere.

There is no place to hide from the Holy Spirit when He is convicting of sin. We may immerse ourselves in work or pleasure and find temporary relief, but when we emerge from our labor for laughter, He will be there. We may flee to the country or some beautiful vacation spot to find refuge in remoteness, but He will be there. We may try to divert our thoughts through entertainment, but even above the roar of applause, His still small voice can be heard.

When we need comfort, the Holy Spirit is there. (And think how many millions of Christians need comfort daily!) He can dry the tears of the grieving saint and at the same time be lifting a discouraged heart on another continent. Distance presents no difficulty to the Spirit of God.

All Christians need direction and every child of God is promised the leading of the Holy Spirit: *For as many as are led by the Spirit of God, they are the sons of God* (Romans 8:14). Imagine the immenseness of the task of charting the course of everyone born into the family of God. Yet, that is well within the scope of His power and wisdom.

There is no place to hide from the Holy Spirit. This is a blessed truth for it guarantees that we are never beyond the range of His care.

GREAT DAY

MEMORY VERSE: *And I will put my spirit within you, and cause you to walk in my statutes, and ye shall keep my judgments, and do them* (Ezekiel 36:27).

Queen Victoria asked her Jewish prime minister, Benjamin Disraeli, "Can you give me one verse in the Bible that will prove its truth?" He replied: "Your Majesty, I will give you one word—Jew! If there were nothing else to prove the truth of the Bible, the history of the Jews is sufficient!"

Someone asked Daniel Webster to give one reason for believing the Bible to be the inspired Word of God. Instantly he replied, "The Jew."

Though an ocean apart, the two statesmen could not have been closer in their views concerning the Bible. They saw the evidence of God at work in history through His dealings with Israel.

God is not through with His chosen earthly people. They have a wonderful future. While they have endured untold suffering during their years of unbelief, there is a day coming when they will come in faith to Christ. After the Rapture of the Church, 144,000 Jews will be converted and will become missionaries of the cross, carrying the Word of God to every corner of the world. Following that there will be a great turning to the Saviour in the nation of Israel. The Lord's promise to Ezekiel will be fulfilled: *I will put my spirit within you.*

Meanwhile, this same promise is made to all Jews and Gentiles who come to the Saviour now: *For there is no difference between the Jew and the Greek: for the same Lord over all is rich unto all that call upon him. For whosoever shall call upon the name of the Lord shall be saved* (Romans 10:12,13).

November 5   Zechariah 4:1-10

GOD'S WAY

MEMORY VERSE: *Not by might, nor by power, but by my spirit, saith the LORD of hosts* (Zechariah 4:6).

This is the day of gimmicks and promotions. Products are palmed off on the public through slick advertising methods. Candidates buy their way into office with expensive election campaigns. The American dream of going from a log cabin to the White House is in danger. Because of the fallen nature of man, these things are not surprising but it is sad when Christians adopt this faithless way in doing God's work.

Recently someone estimated that 90 percent of present day Christian work would continue as is even if the Holy Spirit did not exist. One hopes that guess is wrong, but it is safe to say that a lot of religious machinery runs on the energy of the flesh. And this is not altogether in apostate or unbelieving circles. The time has come to return to spiritual methods of doing spiritual work.

The Holy Spirit works in answer to prayer. Dr. D. L. Moody said: "Every great work of God can be traced to a kneeling figure." I wonder what would happen in America if church boards began spending as much time in prayer during their meetings as they do in tossing around promotional ideas. Can you imagine the spiritual impact of multitudes in prayer for pastors and all aspects of the ministry of the church?

Two men arrived early at Spurgeon's church on Sunday morning and were given a tour of the building. Opening one door, they saw fifteen hundred people on their knees. "That is the heating plant," said their guide.

Start heating up your church through prayer. You'll end the spiritual energy crisis!

THE SEARCH

MEMORY VERSE: *And Pharaoh said unto his servants, Can we find such a one as this is, a man in whom the Spirit of God is?* (Genesis 41:38).

Year after year America has abundant harvests. Our farmers are the most efficient in the world. We are one of the few nations in which surpluses are a continual problem. Under these conditions it is easy to forget how fragile our food supply really is.

What if God should withhold rain for one season? What if some strange insect plague should devour one year's crop? What if the energy shortage should become so serious that tractors would stand idle in the fields? We are the breadbasket of planet earth. Where would we turn for food?

Egypt had known years of plenty. That mighty empire seemed invincible. But trouble was on the way. Years of famine were just around the corner. God gave a preview of that terrible time to Pharaoh. His peek into the future came, however, in a dream and he didn't know how to interpret it. Fortunately, there was a man of God in Egypt who explained the dream and offered a plan to prevent starvation in the land. The man of God was Joseph.

Faced with the need of finding a national administrator who could lead the people in a program of conservation during the seven remaining good years, Pharaoh chose Joseph. The king clearly saw that Joseph was led of the Spirit of God. He was glad to have that kind of a man available for the coming emergency.

Men and women of God may seem odd to the world under normal circumstances, but nearly everyone knows they are good to have around in crises. Walk close with God so that troubled people will value your presence and prayers.

SOURCE OF VICTORY

MEMORY VERSE: *When the enemy shall come in like a flood, the Spirit of the LORD shall lift up a standard against him* (Isaiah 59:19).

America is in trouble. Her spiritual temperature is low. Scandals rock her leaders. Morality is out of date. Crime marches on. But there have been other periods of spiritual decline and moral confusion. America's greatest revival came as the result of one man's concern at such a time.

A. C. Lanphier was working as a lay missionary in one of the crowded areas of New York City. He let it be known that he was starting a series of weekly noon-hour prayer meetings, the first of which was held September 23, 1857.

For the first half hour Mr. Lanphier prayed alone. Then, one by one, others came until a total of six were praying. The next week twenty appeared, and the third week brought forty. By spring more than twenty daily noon prayer meetings were occurring in New York City. Some of the largest churches were crowded to capacity. The police and fire departments opened their buildings for prayer services. Revival had begun. It spread across the land.

In a Boston meeting, a man said: "I am from Omaha, Nebraska. On my journey here I found a continuous chain of prayer all the way." Mr. Lanphier's prayer meeting had set his nation afire for God.

The revival caused churches to spread across the frontier and made them flourish in the cities. The moral fiber of the nation was strengthened. Old debts were paid. Honesty increased. Missionary work expanded—all because one man listened to the Holy Spirit and started to pray.

The Holy Spirit is still able to bring revival to our land. You may be the one through whom He will work to move His people to prayer.

NEW BIRTH

MEMORY VERSE: *Not by works of righteousness which we have done, but according to his mercy he saved us, by the washing of regeneration, and renewing of the Holy Ghost* (Titus 3:5).

"Your religionists came to visit me," the man stormed. He was angry about what he considered an invasion of his privacy. I listened calmly and thought about his words. If he had been right about the visitors being but religionists, he would have had a legitimate complaint. The world does not need any more religion.

A missionary once said: "You have the same problem here in America as on the mission field—religion." He was right. Religion can be a serious barrier that keeps people from salvation. Trusting in their ceremonies and rituals, they often miss the wonderful simplicity of faith in Christ.

Nicodemus was a religious man, a ruler of the Jews. No one would have guessed the emptiness of his heart. Yet, when he came to Jesus, the Lord saw through his religious exterior and informed him that he needed to be born again. Poor confused Nicodemus asked a logical question: *How can a man be born when he is old? can he enter the second time into his mother's womb, and be born?* (John 3:4). Jesus then explained that this needed new birth was a birth of the Spirit.

The new birth is a mystery. Jesus said: *The wind bloweth where it listeth, and thou hearest the sound thereof, but canst not tell whence it cometh, and whither it goeth: so is every one that is born of the Spirit* (John 3:8). Still, we know how the new birth can be ours: *For God so loved the world, that he gave his only begotten Son, that whosoever believeth in him should not perish, but have everlasting life* (John 3:16).

PENTECOST

MEMORY VERSE: *And it shall come to pass, that whosoever shall call on the name of the Lord shall be saved* (Acts 2:21).

There is a great deal of confusion about the word "Pentecost." To some it signals power for soulwinning (see Acts 1:8). To others it may mean only the name of a denomination or a type of doctrine.

Dr. H. A. Ironside wrote: "Pentecost did not come because they were of a single unity and in one place; they were there expecting Pentecost, in obedience to the words of the Lord Jesus Christ. Pentecost was a predetermined epoch in the mind of God and the Word of God. It had been settled from all past ages just when the Holy Spirit was to descend and take up His abode with the people of God on earth."

Pentecost means "the fiftieth day" and was to come fifty days after Passover. It was the day upon which the Holy Spirit came in fulfillment of the promise of Jesus. Preparing His disciples for the occasion He said: *For John truly baptized with water; but ye shall be baptized with the Holy Ghost no many days hence* (Acts 1:5).

On that wonderful day, believers began to be baptized into the body of Christ. Previous to that time, the Holy Spirit had come upon people for specific purposes, but now He would live within each one who was born again. Jesus had said of the Holy Spirit: *He dwelleth with you, and shall be in you* (John 14:17). Since Pentecost, each believer's body has been the temple of the Holy Spirit (see 1 Corinthians 3:16).

All the power of Pentecost is available to every Christian every moment of every day.

THE BAPTISM

MEMORY VERSE: *For by one Spirit are we all baptized into one body, whether we be Jews or Gentiles, whether we be bond or free; and have been all made to drink into one Spirit* (1 Corinthians 12:13).

Many good things happen when one is born again. At that moment he receives eternal life (see 1 John 5:11-13). His destination after this earthly journey becomes heaven (see 2 Corinthians 5:8). His body becomes the temple of the Holy Spirit (see 1 Corinthians 6:19,20). He becomes a child of God (see John 1:12). All condemnation is past (see Romans 8:1). He becomes a member of the body of Christ through the baptism of the Holy Spirit (see 1 Corinthians 12:13).

It is important to know that the baptism of the Holy Spirit takes place at the moment of salvation. Many seek the baptism of the Spirit after conversion. This is unnecessary. Why? Because the baptism of the Holy Spirit is a one-time experience that takes place at the time of being born again.

Having been placed into the body of Christ through the baptism of the Holy Spirit, the child of God has a very important work to do. He is needed. Not one Christian has the right to feel more important than another. We are each prepared to perform exactly what God wants us to do: *But now hath God set the members every one of them in the body, as it hath pleased him. And if they were all one member, where were the body? But now are they many members, yet but one body. And the eye cannot say unto the hand, I have no need of thee: nor again the head to the feet, I have no need of you. Nay, much more those members of the body, which seem to be more feeble, are necessary* (1 Corinthians 12:18-22).

Aren't you glad you're important to Jesus?

HIS TEMPLE

MEMORY VERSE: *What? know ye not that your body is the temple of the Holy Ghost which is in you, which ye have of God, and ye are not your own? For ye are bought with a price: therefore glorify God in your body, and in your spirit, which are God's* (1 Corinthians 6:19-20).

Your body is important.

Consider the creation.

Everything in the universe, except the human frame, was simply spoken into existence. *And God said, Let the earth bring forth the living creature after his kind, cattle, and creeping thing, and the beast of the earth after his kind: and it was so* (Genesis 1:24).

Not so the body of man. *And God said, Let us make man in our image, after our likeness; and let them have dominion over the fish of the sea, and over the fowl of the air, and over the cattle, and over all the earth, and over every creeping thing that creepeth upon the earth* (Genesis 1:26). *And the LORD God formed man of the dust of the ground, and breathed into his nostrils the breath of life; and man became a living soul* (Genesis 2:7).

When Christ came to earth, He was made in the likeness of men and referred to His body as His temple. He said the resurrection of His body would be the proof of His deity (see John 2:18-22).

The coming resurrection reveals divine regard for our bodies. Christ was resurrected bodily from the grave, just as we shall be at His coming.

The most exciting fact about the Christian's body is that it is the temple of God. This amazing truth should temper every thought and activity. Are you careful about your conduct inside the church building? You should be equally careful at all times. Your body is the dwelling place of God.

BE FILLED

MEMORY VERSE: *And be not drunk with wine, wherein is excess; but be filled with the Spirit* (Ephesians 5:18).

In God's Holy Word we are commanded to be filled with the Spirit. To be filled with the Spirit is to be controlled by the Spirit. Let the famous evangelist, J. Wilbur Chapman share his testimony about the filling of the Spirit.

"I had been struggling for five years. At last I reached the place where I was willing to make a surrender. I simply said, 'I am now willing.' Then He made the way easy. He brought before me my ambition, then my personal ease, then my home, then other things came to me, and I simply said, 'I will give them up.' At last all my will was surrendered about everything. Then without any emotion I said, 'My Father, I now claim from Thee the infilling of the Holy Spirit.'"

There is but one baptism of the Holy Spirit, and that at the moment of new birth. However, there may be many fillings. We are filled with the Holy Spirit when we stop grieving the Spirit; stop quenching the Spirit; and take His filling by faith.

What is keeping you from being controlled by the Holy Spirit? What area of your life remains unsurrendered? How long do you intend to keep struggling on in defeat? As a Spirit-filled person, your life will demonstrate the fruit of the Spirit; love, joy, peace, longsuffering, gentleness, goodness, faith, meekness, self control (see Galatians 5:22,23).

Do you long for that kind of blessing? Tell Him of your total surrender right now and face the day in the confidence of His filling. You will not be disappointed.

November 13

Ephesians 4:25-32

STOP GRIEVING THE SPIRIT

MEMORY VERSE: *And grieve not the holy Spirit of God, whereby ye are sealed unto the day of redemption* (Ephesians 4:30).

You may be surprised to learn that God can experience grief. Yet, there are a number of Bible texts that reveal this.

Moses wrote that God was grieved over the wickedness that was on the earth before the flood. David declared that God had been grieved with the Children of Israel because of their complaining in the wilderness; after their escape from Egypt. Isaiah prophesied that Jesus would be a "man of sorrows" and said that He would be acquainted with grief.

What grieves the Holy Spirit?

The context of today's verse reveals a number of things that grieve Him: *Let all bitterness, and wrath, and anger, and clamour, and evil speaking, be put away from you, with all malice* (Ephesians 4:31).

Notice that all these sins have to do with your attitude toward others. You cannot be bitter toward others without grieving the Holy Spirit. You cannot gossip about others without grieving the Holy Spirit. You cannot carry malice in your heart without grieving the Holy Spirit.

To keep from grieving the Holy Spirit, we must be demonstrating the fruit of the Spirit as shown in Ephesians 4:32: *And be ye kind one to another, tenderhearted, forgiving one another, even as God for Christ's sake hath forgiven you.* Examine your life for attitudes and actions that grieve the Holy Spirit. As they come to mind, confess them to Christ immediately and accept His forgiveness. Enjoy the sweet release that comes from being sure that all is right between you and your Lord.

Grieve not the Spirit.

November 14   1 Thessalonians 5:12-24

STOP QUENCHING THE SPIRIT

MEMORY VERSE: *Quench not the Spirit* (1 Thessalonians 5:19).

If we quench a fire, we stop it in its path. If we quench the Holy Spirit, we halt His work in us. We stifle or suppress Him. When you quench the Holy Spirit, you exalt your will above the will of God. To quench the Holy Spirit is to resist Him. It is going your own way when His leading is clear.

Quenching the Holy Spirit is like changing channels on your television set. It is like turning off the radio to avoid its message. It is turning your mind away from the things you know the Lord wants you to do or say.

When you stop quenching the Holy Spirit, you will find some wonderful things happening. Your day will unfold as a part of His plan. You will see opportunities that you would otherwise have missed. His calming voice will comfort you when everything seems to be falling apart. Life's irritations will be recognized as experiences that enable you to be patient and longsuffering. The needs of others will be brought to your attention and you will be refreshed in ministering to them. Having your own way will become less important. Allowing Christ to have His way in your life will receive priority.

So, stop tuning out that still small voice that always gives the right direction. Lend an obedient ear to the Lord. Be quick to do His bidding. Look for opportunities to follow His leading this very day. Don't be afraid to be an obedient child.

Remember, the Lord always gives His best to those who follow Him completely.

START WALKING

MEMORY VERSE: *This I say then, Walk in the Spirit, and ye shall not fulfil the lust of the flesh* (Galatians 5:16).

Walking demonstrates faith.

Jesus told the man who had been sick of the palsy that he was to take up his bed and walk. That demanded faith. He had not been able to walk. The fact that he did get up and walk gave living evidence of his confidence in the power of Christ (see Matthew 9:2-7).

Peter walked on the water to go to Jesus. That was a walk of faith. When Peter's faith faltered he began to sink (see Matthew 14:28-31). Faith made the miracle possible.

The person who walks in the Spirit has taken the filling of the Spirit by faith. As he moves through the day, he expects the Holy Spirit to control him. And control is what the Spirit-filled life is all about. Does the Holy Spirit control your life? If not, you are controlled by your sinful nature...the old nature...the old man.

It is time to discover who sits on the throne of your life. Who is King? Lord? Master? The Bible teaches that either God rules over that kingdom called your life, or you live under sin's dominion. It's as simple as that. See how Paul explained this struggle to the Christians at Rome: *Let not sin therefore reign in your mortal body, that ye should obey it in the lusts thereof. Neither yield ye your members as instruments of unrighteousness unto sin: but yield yourselves unto God, as those that are alive from the dead, and your members as instruments of righteousness unto God. For sin shall not have dominion over you: for ye are not under the law, but under grace* (Romans 6:12-14).

Walk in the Spirit!

THE GREAT MISTAKE

MEMORY VERSE: *Ye stiffnecked and uncircumcised in heart and ears, ye do always resist the Holy Ghost: as your fathers did, so do ye* (Acts 7:51).

Mendelssohn, the famous composer, once visited a cathedral containing one of the most expensive organs in Europe. He listened to the organist, then asked permission to play. "I don't know you," was the reply, "and we don't allow any strangers to play upon this organ."

At last the great musician persuaded the organist to let him play. As Mendelssohn played, the great cathedral was filled with such music as the organist had never heard. With tears in his eyes he laid his hand upon Mendelssohn's shoulder. "Who are you?" he asked. "Mendelssohn," came the reply. The old organist was dumbfounded. "To think that an old fool like me nearly forbade Mendelssohn to play upon my organ!" he said.

If we only knew what wonderful harmonies the Holy Spirit can draw out of our lives, we would not be content until we have given Him complete control so that He can work in and through us to do His will.

The great mistake of mankind is resisting the work and will of God. Generation after generation blunders along largely rejecting the will of God and therefore forfeiting His blessings. We choose poverty instead of riches; temporary gratification instead of eternal delight; earthly security instead of adventures in faith. But here and there an occasional soul dares to be different. Like Stephen, they surrender all to Jesus. They are the winners in life and even death cannot defeat them.

MONOPOLY

MEMORY VERSE: *Likewise reckon ye also yourselves to be dead indeed unto sin, but alive unto God through Jesus Christ our Lord* (Romans 6:11).

A group of ministers were discussing whether or not they ought to invite Dwight L. Moody to their city. The success of the famed evangelist was brought to the attention of the men as a reason for inviting him.

One unimpressed minister commented, "Does Mr. Moody have a monopoly on the Holy Ghost?"

Another quietly replied, "No, but the Holy Ghost seems to have a monopoly on Mr. Moody."

Search for the spiritual secret of all great servants of God and you will find it to be total surrender. To Moody, life was the great adventure of finding out what God would do with one who was totally and completely yielded to Him. William Booth saw as his reason for success the fact that God had all there was of him. F. B. Meyer looked back to a time when he gave the keys to every room in his heart to Christ. Paul urged the Christians at Rome to yield their members as instruments of righteousness. In other words, he was calling for the yielding of every hand and heart to the service of Christ and the glory of God. He summed it up with this moving challenge: *I beseech you therefore, brethren, by the mercies of God, that ye present your bodies a living sacrifice, holy, acceptable unto God, which is your reasonable service* (Romans 12:1).

We have been furnished with some wonderful examples of all-out dedication in both the Scriptures and in history. What about your personal surrender to the will of God? Are you really willing to do what He wants you to do this very day?

November 18   2 Timothy 2:19-26

A NEEDLE IN A HAYSTACK

MEMORY VERSE: *Nevertheless the foundation of God standeth sure, having this seal, The Lord knoweth them that are his. And, Let every one that nameth the name of Christ depart from iniquity* (2 Timothy 2:19).

Many years ago, when Samuel Levermore of London made his decision to go to France as a missionary, his sister said: "Sammy, you will be wasting your time: to find a troubled soul in France will be like looking for a needle in a haystack." "Yes," he answered, "that is quite true, but you must remember that the Holy Spirit knows where the needle is, and He will direct me to it."

Isn't it interesting that you are reading this message? Another time you might have ignored it. Today, you feel a need within.

Circumstances have made you think more deeply than ever before. World conditions trouble you. Things are not well in your home. You wonder about the future. You have fears about your health. Your job is uncertain. Spiritual truth taught in your youth has been returning to mind. All of these life factors are known to the Holy Spirit. This moment is no accident.

What does God want to do in your life? Are you His child? Have you been born again? Is your devotional life all that it ought to be? Are you right with others? Have you been compromising your testimony? Are you resisting His will?

Recognize the work of God in your life and thank Him for it. See His hand in the moving of circumstances. Respond to the voice of the Holy Spirit. Let God have His way.

THE COMFORTER

MEMORY VERSE: *And I will pray the Father, and he shall give you another Comforter, that he may abide with you for ever* (John 14:16).

There are times when nothing is needed quite so much as comfort. The world has come crashing down. Castles have tumbled. Dreams have become nightmares. You reach for help but grasp only the air. Friends lack understanding of your problems and are much like Job's comforters—miserable. These are the times you need the ministry of the Comforter, the Holy Spirit.

Jesus told His disciples about the coming of the Comforter when preparing them for His death. These men who had left all to follow Him were about to go through the most difficult trial of their lives. Their Lord would soon be taken away and crucified. Their confidence would be shaken. The One they had hoped would free Israel from the yoke of Roman bondage would be nailed to a Roman cross and placed in a tomb sealed by the authority of that hated empire. Roman soldiers would stand guard at His grave.

Knowing their impending dilemma, Christ provided two-way relief. He first gave them a glimpse of glory. *I go to prepare a place for you*, He said (John 14:2). Then He promised them the presence of the Comforter.

Though assured of the blessings of heaven at the close of this life, we need the companionship and comfort of the Lord while here on planet earth. The Holy Spirit provides that for the child of God. Allow Him to lift your load and bring you comfort in your present need.

He is the God of all comfort (see 2 Corinthians 1:3).

CONVICTION

MEMORY VERSE: *And when he is come, he will reprove the world of sin, and of righteousness, and of judgment* (John 16:8).

An evangelist is preaching in a large crusade. Next to the aisle in the fourth row from the front sits a man who appears to be the classic picture of boredom. His wife coaxed him to come to the meeting and he finally yielded to please her. His mind moves from business deals to the golf course. He keeps glancing at his watch, anticipating the final prayer so that he can get on with more important things.

Suddenly a statement from the speaker strikes home. The man who seemed so distant and untouchable fixes his attention on the evangelist and hangs on every word. Though still captured by the message, he becomes uneasy, shifting his weight a number of times and folding and unfolding his arms. Occasionally he wipes his brow.

When the evangelist gives the public invitation, the man who had come to the service so reluctantly steps out into the aisle and makes his way toward the preacher. He wants to be born again.

What happened to change his attitude and melt his heart?

The conviction of the Holy Spirit.

The work of the Holy Spirit is to bring conviction of sin to the world. The human conscience cannot be trusted to recognize the seriousness of sin. Influenced by falling standards, people are able to rationalize immorality and borderline honesty. When under conviction, however, true standards of holiness and sin are brought into focus.

No wonder you have been uncomfortable in your sin!

THE SPIRIT OF TRUTH

MEMORY VERSE: *Howbeit when he, the Spirit of truth is come, he will guide you into all truth: for he shall not speak of himself; but whatsoever he shall hear, that shall he speak: and he will shew you things to come* (John 16:13).

The writing of the New Testament is a miracle. There is no other way to explain the writers' perfect recall of Jesus' very words, and their wonderful insights into spiritual truth. Another strong evidence of inspiration is the amount of recorded prophecy that has since been fulfilled to the letter!

The Holy Spirit guided the writers of the New Testament in their work. It is correct to say that the entire Bible is God-breathed. The result is word-for-word inspiration—the Bible is the Word of God.

Not only did the Holy Spirit give us the Bible but He is its best interpreter. If all Bible study were carried out under the direction of the Holy Spirit there would be no cults in the world. It is not surprising, then, to find many cults denying the very existence of the Holy Spirit—claiming Him to be but a force or an influence.

Serious students of the Scriptures should always seek the leading of the Holy Spirit when reading the Bible. When this done, deep spiritual truths will open to individual understanding. Lessons will be learned in secret that cannot be found in the most expensive commentaries. Verses yield their milk and meat when the student is in tune with the Author of the Bible, the Holy Spirit.

No one ever went astray following the direction of the Holy Spirit.

WHAT TIME IS IT?

MEMORY VERSE: *When they therefore were come together, they asked of him, saying, Lord, wilt thou at this time restore again the kingdom to Israel?* (Acts 1:6).

Currently there is great interest in studying the signs of the times. It is exciting to see God at work fulfilling His prophetic promises. Knowledgeable students of the Bible agree that we are living in the last days. Signs of His coming multiply.

The disciples also lived in a time when the moving of God was clear. Events prophesied for centuries had suddenly come to pass. Christ was born. Miracles were performed. Redemption was wrought. The resurrection of the Saviour had taken place. The miraculous momentum was such that it appeared the kingdom would be set up at any time. It was not surprising then that the question was asked, *Lord, wilt thou at this time restore again the kingdom to Israel?* That was something like present day Christians saying, "Lord, are You going to return today?"

The Lord's response to the disciples' question is noteworthy. First, he informed them that they could not know the exact timing of God in carrying out His prophetic plan. Then he reminded them of their responsibility to serve Him while time remained: *But ye shall receive power, after the Holy Ghost is come upon you: and ye shall be witnesses unto me both in Jerusalem, and in all Judaea, and in Samaria, and unto the uttermost part of the earth* (Acts 1:8).

What time is it? It's time to witness—across the street and across the seas. And time is running out.

THE POWERFUL CHURCH

MEMORY VERSE: *And with great power gave the apostles witness of the resurrection of the Lord Jesus: and great grace was upon them all* (Acts 4:33).

What happens when the members of a church are controlled by the Holy Spirit?

The Church becomes mighty in prayer: *And when they had prayed, the place was shaken* (Acts 4:31). The Church today needs to be bathed in prayer. Pastors need to be upheld in prayer. The New Testament Church was a praying church and it gained the reputation of having turned the world upside down. It is tragic that the spiritual descendants of those world upsetters have become but connoisseurs of sermons. It's time to pray!

The Church becomes united in love: *And the multitude of them that believed were of one heart and of one soul* (Acts 4:32). All preaching is powerless without love and all churches are spiritually weak without love. Genuine revival is impossible without the laying aside of petty differences and old grudges. *We know we have passed from death unto life, because we love the brethren* (1 John 3:14).

The Church becomes power conscious and produces powerful witnesses: *And with great power gave the apostles witness of the resurrection of the Lord Jesus* (Acts 4:33). Christians focus on their problems too much. They spend too much time thinking about what the devil is doing among them. This is a violation of Philippians 4:7. The Church must shift its attention to what God is doing. When this happens, Christians stop quibbling and start winning souls!

Do you want your church to be controlled by the Spirit? Where do you think it ought to start?

THE PERMANENT RESIDENT

MEMORY VERSE: *But ye are not in the flesh, but in the Spirit, if so be that the Spirit of God dwell in you. Now if any man have not the Spirit of Christ, he is none of his* (Romans 8:9).

At the age of twelve, I heard my pastor explain that Jesus was knocking at the door of my heart and that if I would open the door He would come in: *Behold, I stand at the door, and knock: if any man hear my voice, and open the door, I will come in to him, and will sup with him, and he with me* (Revelation 3:20). I believed that promise and received the Saviour that night. The Holy Spirit came into my life and lives within His temple (my body) to this hour.

I am no exception. At the moment of new birth, the Holy Spirit takes up permanent residence within the child of God.

Life is never the same after the Holy Spirit enters. Sin is never really enjoyable again. There may be moments of pleasure in carnal pursuits, but they are short lived. The voice of the One who resides within reminds the citizen of heaven that he is out of character—a poor ambassador of his King.

Sin is never safe again. Though before conversion he may have lived with reckless abandon, the Christian must now expect chastening. He learns that he cannot sin and win (see Hebrews 5:11).

Power is available for victory over temptation. The Resident has resources. All power in heaven and earth is at the disposal of the believer for conquering sin in daily life. He does not have to live in defeat. What good news for those in whom the Lord himself resides!

THE SPIRIT'S WITNESS

MEMORY VERSE: *The Spirit itself beareth witness with our spirit, that we are the children of God* (Romans 8:16).

Since the Holy Spirit lives within each child of God, it is not surprising that He lets us know He is there. When you are at home the lights are on and there is activity. The same is true when the Holy Spirit is in His temple (your body).

The witness of the Spirit is more than just an emotional feeling. God does not do His deepest work in our shallowest part. At the same time, it is a mistake to try to divorce all emotion from spiritual experience. God created us with emotions and our feelings have a rightful part in our relationship with Him.

When our hearts are right with God there is a sense of peace, joy, and well-being. In His explanation of the coming of the Holy Spirit, Jesus said: *Peace I leave with you, my peace I give unto you: not as the world giveth, give I unto you. Let not your heart be troubled, neither let it be afraid* (John 14:27). A. W. Tozer wrote, "The fact is that faith engenders feelings as certainly as life engenders motion."

How then do we recognize the witness of the Spirit? Is there a guide to guard us from illusion?

The witness of the Spirit is assurance deep within as a result of confidence in the Word of God. The Spirit witnesses through the Word. Feelings in themselves are not dependable, but peace produced by a promise from God need not be doubted. That inner rest is the witness of the Spirit of the Lord. (See Psalm 119:105.)

INTERCESSION

MEMORY VERSE: *Likewise the Spirit also helpeth our infirmities: for we know not what we should pray for as we ought: but the Spirit itself maketh intercession for us with groanings which cannot be uttered* (Romans 8:26).

Charles Finney was a great preacher and revivalist in the early days of our country. Before his conversion he seemed unreachable. Christians in his town witnessed to him but without success. He was an attorney and started studying the Bible in order to quote it in court. As a result of his Bible study he was born again.

Finney became a great believer in prayer. While some preachers travel with a musician, he was accompanied by a man of prayer who interceded for Finney during his preaching. God used him to bring a far-reaching revival to the land.

The praying of the people in Finney's town seemed poor to him. He thought they prayed for the same things over and over without results. One thing appears to have eluded Finney, however, and that was the part those poor prayers must have played in his own conversion. It seems sure that some of those believers must have been praying for Finney's salvation and in gaining that they earned a part in moving the whole nation toward God.

Many of us are not eloquent in prayer. We wouldn't want our prayers printed or broadcast to the world. Sometimes, we hardly know how to pray. Our weakness here should not trouble us at all. The Holy Spirit voices our prayers to the Father for us. Though we never hear the words, prayers ascend from believing hearts and blessings come. Those prayers are perfect when they reach the throne.

GIFTS

MEMORY VERSE: *But all these worketh that one and the selfsame Spirit, dividing to every man severally as he will* (1 Corinthians 12:11).

Not all Christians have the same gifts. Much harm has been done by some members of the body of Christ trying to copy the ministry of others rather than using their own gifts. The consequence is often frustration and fruitlessness.

When I was a boy, I lived on a grain and dairy farm. The soil was heavy and usually produced fine crops. A few miles west of our farm, nearer Lake Michigan, the soil was light and sandy. There the farming was very poor, especially during a dry season.

Today, however, this area is a prosperous farming community which ships its produce to many distant places. It is one of the most productive blueberry areas in the United States.

The secret of this agricultural success story is simply planting a crop for which the soil and climate are well suited. This is also a good lesson for life.

If you want to be effective as a member of the body of Christ, serve with the gifts that God has given to you. Stop trying to be someone else. Diversity is part of God's wonderful plan.

Often we discover our gifts by trying different areas of service.

"How would you like to preach tonight?" I once asked a layman, somewhat facetiously. His answer surprised me. "I'll be glad to. I have promised the Lord that I will accept every opportunity He sends my way." He is now a missionary in South America.

Discover your gifts and thank God for them. Use them for His glory. Ask the Holy Spirit to guide you in the use of your gifts today.

FRUIT BEARING

MEMORY VERSE: *But the fruit of the Spirit is love, joy, peace, longsuffering, gentleness, goodness, faith, meekness, temperance: against such there is no law* (Galatians 5:22,23).

What is the evidence of the indwelling Holy Spirit? The fruit of the Spirit.

We have a flowering peach tree in our yard that has produced beautiful blossoms in the spring and tiny peaches in summer. Our last winter was the most severe in recorded history and the tree died. A few leaves appeared this spring but now they have withered. There is no life within. The tree will have to be cut down.

Being born again is entirely different from getting religion. At salvation the Holy Spirit comes into the child of God, bringing new life. Paul told the Ephesian Christians that they had been dead but were now made alive. The fruit of the Spirit was evident in their lives.

The fruit of the Spirit is not produced by human effort. A fruit tree does not try to produce fruit. It brings forth fruit because it is a fruit tree. The same is true in Christian experience. If we set ourselves to work at loving, being joyful, or demonstrating longsuffering, we will fail. Instead, we must simply surrender to the Holy Spirit so that He can produce those qualities in and through us. That is what Paul meant when he wrote of the love of God being *shed abroad in our hearts by the Holy Ghost which is given unto us* (Romans 5:5).

It is important to be yielded to the Holy Spirit so that our lives are fruitful. This is how we glorify God. *Herein is my Father glorified, that ye bear much fruit; so shall ye be my disciples* (John 15:8).

THE RESTRAINER

MEMORY VERSE: *For the mystery of iniquity doth already work: only he who now letteth will let, until he be taken out of the way* (2 Thessalonians 2:7).

The word *let* means "to hinder or hold back." Though the mystery of iniquity is already working, as is evidenced by sinful conditions on every side, the Holy Spirit works through Christians to hold back the flood of evil. This restraining influence is all that keeps the world from total destruction.

Jesus spoke of those who belong to Him as being the "salt of the earth" and the "light of the world." Salt preserves and light penetrates the darkness. To whatever degree this planet is preserved at this hour it is because of the influence of those in whom the Holy Spirit dwells. Whatever light exists in this dark world is here because of the light of Christ that shines through His people.

When Jesus returns to rapture the Church and raise the Christian dead, the restraining work of the Holy Spirit will be complete. Soon after that the Antichrist will come to power and the world will experience its most difficult time. Jesus said there will never have been a time like it in the past, nor will there be any period as terrible in the future. It will end in earth's bloodiest war and be followed by a thousand years of peace and blessing.

Many Christians do little in opposing evil. They have been saved and have settled back to coast to heaven. Others feel that the Christian message is only one of love and consider it a waste of time to battle wrong. They forget that the Bible says, *Ye that love the LORD, hate evil* (Psalm 97:10).

Let the Holy Spirit do His restraining work through you.

THE LAST INVITATION

MEMORY VERSE: *And the Spirit and the bride say, Come. And let him that heareth say, Come. And let him that is athirst come. And whosoever will, let him take the water of life freely* (Revelation 22:17).

The Holy Spirit is the Lord of the harvest. He convicts of sin and works the miracle of new birth. Sinners are called to Jesus by the Holy Spirit. He is the great inviter. No one has ever been saved apart from the work of the Holy Spirit. If you feel your need of salvation, it is because the Spirit of God is speaking to you.

At the end of the Bible, the Holy Spirit gives one more call for sinners to come to the Saviour: *And the Spirit and the bride say, Come.* Notice that the Spirit extends His call in connection with the Bride. The Church is the bride of Christ. The Holy Spirit speaks through Christians, who make up the bride of Christ, in extending His call to lost people. Often He uses those who are newly converted to reach others: *And let him that heareth say, Come.*

Anyone can come to Jesus. The only requirements are recognition of need and the desire to be saved: *And let him that is athirst come. And whosoever will, let him take of the water of life freely.*

The water of life (salvation) is freely offered to those who are thirsty. Many have tried to quench their thirst at the cisterns of this world. Perhaps you are one of them. You have tasted all the world has to offer and are thirsty still. Jesus met a thirsty woman one day and said: *But whosoever drinketh of the water that I shall give him shall never thirst* (John 4:14).

Heed the Spirit's last call. Take the water of life.

December

THIS MONTH'S STUDY

The Birth of Christ

Days 2,8,16,21,23,25, and 29 are from "Let's Communicate" by Roger F. Campbell, Christian Literature Crusade, Ft. Washington, Pa. Days 10,18,22, and 28 contain quotes or information from "Three Thousand Illustrations for Christian Service" by Walter B. Knight, Wm. B. Eerdmans Publishing Company, Grand Rapids, Mich., used by permission. Days 12 and 14 from "John the Baptist" by F. B. Meyer, Zondervan Publishing House, Grand Rapids, Mich. Day 3 contains a quote from "Addresses on Luke" by H. A. Ironside, Loizeaux Brothers, Neptune, N.J. Day 13 from "Great Words of the Gospel," by H. A. Ironside, Moody Press, Chicago, Ill. Day 31 contains a quote from "The King of the Jews" by Dr. John R. Rice, Sword of the Lord Publishers, Murfreesboro, Tenn.; various quotes from "A Complete Bible Commentary" by Matthew Henry, Moody Press, Chicago, Ill.

WONDERFUL

MEMORY VERSE: *For unto us a child is born, unto us a son is given: and the government shall be upon his shoulder: and his name shall be called Wonderful, Counsellor, The mighty God, The everlasting Father, The Prince of Peace* (Isaiah 9:6).

Jesus is wonderful.

He was wonderful in His birth, in His life, in His death, in His resurrection. He is wonderful in His power to change lives today. He will be wonderful in His return for His own, when He resurrects the Christian dead and catches all the saints up to meet Him in the air. He will be wonderful in His kingdom on earth, when all wrongs are made right and all the earth is filled with peace and blessing.

Songwriters have picked up the wonderful theme and have given us:

"Wonderful Grace of Jesus!"

"Wonderful, Wonderful Jesus!"

"His Name Is Wonderful"

"God Is So Wonderful!"

But what does Jesus mean to you?

Does He have first place in your heart?

If your experience with Christ is limited to singing hymns or carols and going through religious ceremonies, you probably find it difficult to understand the feelings of those who truly find Jesus wonderful. You think them over-zealous.

Evangelist Gypsy Smith was once asked how he maintained a constant state of revival…continual joy. He answered: "I have never lost the wonder of it all." Jesus was wonderful to him.

His name is Wonderful.

Is He wonderful to you?

BETHLEHEM

MEMORY VERSE: *But thou, Bethlehem Ephratah, though thou be little among the thousands of Judah, yet out of thee shall he come forth unto me that is to be ruler in Israel; whose goings forth have been from of old, from everlasting* (Micah 5:2).

OH BETHLEHEM, you seem so small
To be the chosen earthly place
Where should be born the Lord of all
Who came to show the world His grace.
Is it not strange that on that night
When strangers filled each home and inn,
Your humblest stable gained the right
To shelter Christ, who saves from sin?

OH BETHLEHEM, you favored town.
Both earth and heaven know your name,
For in your stable God came down
To lift the sinner from his shame.
God chooses still the lowest place;
Not many noble trust His Son.
'Tis in the meek of Adam's race
The greatest work of God is done.

OH BETHLEHEM, let me like thee
Be small enough for God to bless,
That all I meet may see in me
The Saviour whom my lips confess.
...Roger F. Campbell

December 3   Luke 1:1-4

PERFECT UNDERSTANDING

MEMORY VERSE: *That thou mightest know the certainty of those things, wherein thou hast been instructed* (Luke 1:4).

There was no doctor present when Christ was born, but a physician was chosen to write the most complete account of his birth given in the Bible. Dr. Luke had a perfect understanding of all the details of the incarnation. We can depend on the accuracy of his record. Matthew Henry says: "The doctrine of Christ is what the wisest and best of men have ventured their souls upon with confidence and satisfaction. And the great events whereon our hopes depend, have been recorded by those who were from the beginning eyewitnesses and ministers of the word, and who were perfected in their understanding of them through Divine inspiration."

Peter said it well: *For we have not followed cunningly devised fables, when we made known unto you the power and coming of our Lord Jesus Christ, but were eyewitnesses of his majesty* (2 Peter 1:16).

Dr. H. A. Ironside has written: "Luke was an educated man. He was a 'beloved physician,' and yet a very humble man. He never mentions himself, either here or in the Book of Acts...He was a widely traveled man, highly-educated, and was of a scientific mind and temperament.

"Luke gives us a great deal of information that is not found in the other Gospels. It is he alone who relates the stories of the visits of the angel Gabriel to Zacharias and to Mary. No one else tells us the song of Mary, and the prophecy of Zacharias. The birth of Christ in a stable is recorded only here, as also the angel's announcement to the shepherds."

Dr. Luke was able and available for God's use. Are you?

ANGELIC ACTIVITY

MEMORY VERSE: *And there appeared unto him an angel of the Lord standing on the right side of the altar of incense* (Luke 1:11).

There are periods in history when God's plan seems to be unfolding at a snail's pace. Few significant events happen and time drags on as if sameness would be the rule forever. Peter says that some are so convinced of this unchanging character of the ages that they refuse to believe that Christ will come again. "Scoffers," he calls them and of them has written: *Knowing this first, that there shall come in the last days scoffers, walking after their own lusts, and saying, Where is the promise of his coming? for since the fathers fell asleep, all things continue as they were from the beginning of the creation* (2 Peter 3:3,4).

Four hundred years of silence had preceded the angelic announcement to Zacharias. No wonder he was afraid. But now prophetic events would occur with rapidity. And angels would play a major role in these long awaited developments. Mary would be visited. Joseph would be comforted and instructed. Shepherds would be given the good news of the birth of the Saviour.

Now we are living in another period of prophetic activity. When Christ ascended, angels announced that He would return in like manner as He had gone away. The promise of those heavenly messengers seems close to fulfillment. Signs multiply. The stage is set for the endtime drama. It is an exciting time to be alive.

Along with his word about the answer to the prayers of Zacharias and Elisabeth, the angel told the trembling priest not to be afraid. What a good word that is for this troubled time.

God is at work...be not afraid.

SPIRIT FILLED

MEMORY VERSE: *For he shall be great in the sight of the Lord, and shall drink neither wine nor strong drink; and he shall be filled with the Holy Ghost, even from his mother's womb* (Luke 1:15).

Every parent wonders about the future of a newborn child. Zacharias and Elisabeth were given some guarantees about their coming son.

He would be great in the sight of the Lord. Many long for fame for their children, hoping for the presidency or some other high place in the world. But the plaudits of planet earth are temporary; passing. Yesterday's heroes may be today's outcasts. This child would be great in the sight of the Lord. Jesus confirmed this prophecy, saying of John: *For I say unto you, Among those that are born of women there is not a greater prophet than John the Baptist* (Luke 7:28).

He would never use strong drink. What a blessing! Beverage alcohol is an enemy of men: *Wine is a mocker, strong drink is raging: and whosoever is deceived thereby is not wise* (Proverbs 20:1).

He would be FILLED with the Spirit. To be filled with the Spirit is to be controlled by the Spirit. All Christians have the Holy Spirit dwelling within. When fully surrendered, they are filled with the Spirit. The evidence of the filling of the Holy Spirit is the presence of the fruit of the Spirit: *But the fruit of the Spirit is love, joy, peace, longsuffering, gentleness, goodness, faith, meekness, temperance* (Galatians 5:22,23). John was filled with the Spirit from birth. We can be filled with the Spirit upon being born again.

Let us pray that every family member will choose to live John's way: great in the sight of the Lord...free from strong drink...filled with the Holy Spirit. How would this change your lifestyle?

FAITH QUESTIONING

MEMORY VERSE: *And Zacharias said unto the angel, Whereby shall I know this? for I am an old man, and my wife well stricken in years* (Luke 1:18).

Man often staggers at God's promises. Like the apostles, we need to pray, *Lord, Increase our faith* (Luke 17:5). Even godly Zacharias questioned the angelic message, asking for a sign. And a sign he received: he was unable to speak until after the birth of John.

Matthew Henry observes: "Zacharias heard all that the Angel said; but his unbelief spake. In striking him dumb, God dealt justly with him, because he had objected against God's word. We may admire the patience of God towards us. God dealt kindly with him, for thus he prevented his speaking any more distrustful, unbelieving words. Thus also God confirmed his faith. If by the rebukes we are under for our sin, we are brought to give the more credit to the word of God, we have no reason to complain. Even real believers are apt to dishonor God by unbelief; and their mouths are stopped in silence and confusion, when otherwise they would have been praising God with joy and gratitude."

After completing his two weeks of ministering, the old and happy priest hurried home, thrilled but apprehensive. Would Elisabeth believe his story? How would she react to his inability to speak? Would he be able to find the right words when writing out his experience?

Developments erased all doubt. Elisabeth conceived. These two righteous and godly people who had prayed so long now knew they were part of a miracle. And Elisabeth rejoiced.

The weak faith of Zacharias did not prevent God from keeping His Word. But when Zacharias saw that Elisabeth had conceived, he must have regretted his question. If he had seen the answer, he would have avoided the infirmity.

December 7   Luke 1:26-33

FAVOR WITH GOD

MEMORY VERSE: *And the angel said unto her, Fear not, Mary: for thou hast found favour with God* (Luke 1:30).

Understandably, Mary was troubled by the presence of the angel Gabriel. She had not been expecting this unusual encounter. Angelic visits are not everyday occurrences.

Gabriel's word to Mary was one of comfort. Her fears must be put away before she can hear what he has to say. Fear often blocks the voice of God and keeps us from His best.

But Mary was told that she could put away her fear because she had found favor with God. One who is in God's favor can rest in His care: *If God be for us, who can be against us?* (Romans 8:31).

The expression "favor with God" is unique to this portion and one other in the New Testament, Ephesians 1:6. There it is translated "accepted in the beloved." The entire verse reads as follows: *To the praise of the glory of his grace, wherein he hath made us accepted in the beloved.*

Here then is a great truth: sinners saved by grace have come into God's favor. And how is this favor available? Through His sacrifice on the cross: *In whom we have redemption through his blood, the forgiveness of sins, according to the riches of his grace* (Ephesians 1:7).

Now the Christmas account takes on new meaning. The miracle that took place when Christ was born of the virgin was all part of God's plan for bringing lost sinners into His favor. The traditions that have developed around Christmas must never obscure the true message: Christ came into the world to save sinners...to bring them into favor with God...the place of safety. And that could only be accomplished THROUGH HIS DEATH for us all.

Aren't you glad you're "accepted"?

December 8   Luke 1:34-38

MISSION IMPOSSIBLE

MEMORY VERSE: *For with God nothing shall be impossible* (Luke 1:37).

The birth of Jesus Christ was a miracle. Attempts to understand it apart from that perspective are doomed to failure.

Some have tried to come up with a medical explanation of the virgin birth of Christ. These sincere people have searched the centuries for another example of a virgin with child, hoping to make the record more palatable to doubters. It is an impossible dream. Like the Resurrection, the virgin birth of Christ required a miracle.

Others have focused on some bright star that might have been the one that guided the wise men to Bethlehem. But that route disregards the Bible account. Try to get any known star to meet the requirements of Matthew 2:9: *And, lo, the star, which they saw in the east, went before them, till it came and stood over where the young child was.* That was a miracle.

We should not be surprised that the incarnation boggles the mind of man. Even Mary struggled with the angelic announcement that she would bear the Christ child. She asked: *How shall this be, seeing I know not a man?* (vs.34). Gabriel gave her the only answer that makes sense: *For with God nothing shall be impossible.*

So, it is a miracle that we celebrate at Christmas—the incarnation of the Son of God. Let that thought capture your mind and warm your heart. It is the greatest love story ever told, the story of God's love for you and me. Those are not just "catchy" lyrics that announce: "Joy to the world, the Lord is come."

He has come!

For with God nothing is impossible.

Let that truth lift every load you bear.

BLESSED BELIEVERS

MEMORY VERSE: *And blessed is she that believed: for there shall be a performance of those things which were told her from the Lord* (Luke 1:45).

Elisabeth, filled with the Holy Spirit, acknowledged Christ as her Lord before He was born. Mary had gone to the hill country of Judah to spend some time with Elisabeth who was there awaiting the birth of John. At Mary's greeting, the babe leaped in Elisabeth's womb and she began to magnify the Lord for what He was doing in Mary and for the coming Saviour. As she concluded her statement of praise she exclaimed: "Blessed is she that believed."

God always sends His blessings to believers. Some doubt their beliefs and others believe their doubts, but the blessings of God are for those who believe His Word. This truth was again made clear immediately following the resurrection of Christ. Thomas doubted that the Lord was risen since he had missed the Lord's meeting with the disciples. At the next meeting, Thomas was present and Jesus invited him to place his fingers in the nail prints in His hands and to thrust his hand into the wound in His side. Ashamed of his unbelief and sure of the Saviour, Thomas cried, "My Lord and my God." Jesus responded, *Thomas, because thou hast seen me, thou hast believed: blessed are they that have not seen, and yet have believed* (John 20:29).

Believers have the promise of answered prayers. Jesus said, *If thou canst believe, all things are possible to him that believeth* (Mark 9:23).

The final words of Elisabeth's Spirit-directed declaration have to do with receiving blessings. As a believer, Mary became a receiver. Those who dare to believe God for the impossible still receive His blessings in reward of their faith in Him.

GREAT THINGS

MEMORY VERSE: *For he that is mighty hath done to me great things; and holy is his name* (Luke 1:49).

In the days of Joseph Parker, an infidel lecturer in a mining town in the north of England gave an address in which he thought he had demolished all the arguments for the Bible, Christ, and Christianity. He concluded by saying: "Now I hope I have succeeded in explaining to you that the existence of Jesus Christ is a myth."

As he finished speaking, a miner, who had entered in his grimy clothes, stood up and said, "Sir, I'm only a working man, and I don't know what you mean by the word 'myth.' But can you explain me? Three years ago I had a miserable home; I neglected my wife and children; I cursed and swore; I drank up all my wages. Then someone came along and showed me the love of God and of His Son Jesus Christ. And now all is different. We have a happy home; I love my wife and children; I feel better in every way; and I have given up drink. A new power has taken possession of me since Christ came into my life. Sir, can you explain this to me?"

The lecturer had no explanation to give, but that miner sent people home feeling that the Bible was still the Word of God and that Jesus was anything but a myth, and that the gospel was the *power of God unto salvation to everyone that believeth* (Romans 1:16).

Mary acknowledged the miracle power of God in her statement that God had done great things to her. His power is not diminished. He still does great things in the lives of those who trust Him and live for Him.

Trust Him today.

He will do great things for you.

A TIME TO REJOICE

MEMORY VERSE: *And her neighbours and her cousins heard how the Lord had shewed great mercy upon her; and they rejoiced with her* (Luke 1:58).

John the Baptist had been born. It was a time to rejoice.

Isaiah had prophecied of his coming: *The voice of him that crieth in the wilderness, Prepare ye the way of the LORD, make straight in the desert a highway for our God. Every valley shall be exalted, and every mountain and hill shall be made low: and the crooked shall be made straight, and the rough places plain: And the glory of the LORD shall be revealed, and all flesh shall see it together: for the mouth of the LORD hath spoken it* (Isaiah 40:3-5).

This child would become the forerunner of the Lord. He would prepare hearts for the coming Saviour. His preaching would be bold and he would demand repentance. Some would see little in which to rejoice under this man's ministry. The king would finally imprison and execute him. But as a result of his preaching many would turn to the Saviour. And that is cause to rejoice.

When sinners turn from sin to Christ...heaven rejoices.

Does it matter to you?

Sadly, much of the work called Christian service is built around everything but calling sinners to Jesus. The twentieth century church doesn't lack organization, it lacks a passion for souls...a heart that breaks over sinners and over their sins.

It is time to get serious over sin and its consequences. Tears are in order. The Jeremiah type: *Oh that my head were waters, and mine eyes a fountain of tears, that I might weep day and night for the slain of the daughter of my people!* (Jeremiah 9:1).

When people get concerned over sin...it will be time to rejoice.

LOOSENED TONGUES

MEMORY VERSE: *And his mouth was opened immediately, and his tongue loosed, and he spake, and praised God* (Luke 1:64).

Zacharias had been unable to speak from the time of his doubting of the angel's word. Of this experience, F. B. Meyer wrote:

"During the whole period that the stricken but expectant priest spent in his living tomb, shut off from communication with the outer world, his spirit was becoming charged with holy emotion that waited for the first opportunity of expression. Such an opportunity came at length. His lowly dwelling was one day crowded with an eager and enthusiastic throng of relatives and friends. They had gathered to congratulate the aged pair, to perform the initial rite of Judaism, and to name the infant boy that lay in his mother's arms. Ah, what joy was hers when they came to 'magnify the Lord's mercy towards her, and to rejoice with her!' As the people passed in and out, there was a new glow in the brilliant eastern sunlight, a new glory on the familiar hills.

"In their perplexity at the mother's insistence that the babe's name should be John—none of his kindred being known by that name—they appealed to the father, who with trembling hand inscribed on the wax writing tablet the verdict, 'His name is John.' So soon as he had broken the iron fetter of unbelief in thus acknowledging the fulfillment of the angel's words, 'his mouth was opened immediately, and his tongue loosed, and he spake blessing God.'"

What a great day of victory for Zacharias!

What is the iron fetter of doubt that ties your tongue?

Break it. And your loosened tongue will praise the Lord!

THE REDEEMER

MEMORY VERSE: *Blessed be the Lord God of Israel; for he hath visited and redeemed his people* (Luke 1:68).

Zacharias knew that John would announce the coming Redeemer.

But what does a redeemer do?

He buys back something that has been temporarily forfeited.

Dr. H. A. Ironside has written: "The word 'redemption' is one that runs all through the Bible; in fact, we can say without an suggestion of hyperbole that it is the great outstanding theme of Holy Scripture. This important truth runs through the Book like the proverbial red strand that, we are told, runs through the cordage of the British navy. Everywhere, from Genesis right on to Revelation, you find God in one way or another presenting to us the truth of redemption—redemption in promise and in type in the Old Testament; redemption in glorious fulfillment in the New Testament."

He concludes: "Already we have the redemption of the soul; we have been redeemed from judgment. We are experiencing day by day, as we walk in obedience to the Lord, practical redemption, redemption from the power of sin. When our blessed Saviour returns, our redemption will be complete—spirit and soul and body will be fully conformed to the image of our Lord Jesus Christ."

Peter wrote: *Forasmuch as we know that ye were not redeemed with corruptible things, as silver and gold, from your vain conversation received by tradition from your fathers; But with the precious blood of Christ, as of a lamb without blemish and without spot* (1 Peter 1:18,19).

So Christ, born in that humble stable, is the promised Redeemer. And His redemption is all encompassing...complete. Don't forget to thank Him for redemption full and free.

PROPHET OF THE HIGHEST

MEMORY VERSE: *And thou, child, shalt be called the prophet of the Highest: for thou shalt go before the face of the Lord to prepare his ways* (Luke 1:76).

The infant John lay in the midst of the relatives and friends gathered for this special occasion and his father spoke of his future. In other circumstances, one might have taken this as just the spoken dream of a proud father concerning his son, but Zacharias had met with an angel who had revealed the life mission of this child. And the doubts of Zacharias had been permanently put away. He believed.

John would be a prophet sent to prepare the way of the Lord. Jesus confirmed this prophecy by calling John a prophet: *But what went ye out for to see? A prophet? yea, I say unto you, and more than a prophet. For this is he, of whom it is written, Behold, I send my messenger before thy face, which shall prepare thy way before thee* (Matthew 11:9,10).

How encouraging these words must have been to those listening. There had been no prophet in Israel for four hundred years. Now one would speak and break the silence that had surrounded prophetic utterance.

F. B. Meyer says of Zachariah's statement: "What a thrill of ecstasy quivered in the words! A long period computed at four hundred years had passed since the last great Hebrew prophet had uttered the words of the Highest. Reaching back from him to the days of Moses had been a long line of prophets, who had passed down the lighted torch from hand to hand. And the fourteen generations, during which the prophetic office had been discontinued, had gone wearily. But now hope revived, as the angel-voice proclaimed the advent of a prophet."

John had a special work to do for Jesus.

And so do you.

December 15

Matthew 1:18-21

JOSEPH'S FEAR

MEMORY VERSE: *But while he thought on these things, behold, the angel of the Lord appeared unto him in a dream, saying, Joseph, thou son of David, fear not to take unto thee Mary thy wife: for that which is conceived in her is of the Holy Ghost* (Matthew 1:20).

Only one verse in the Bible is taken to tell about Joseph's discovery that his bride-to-be was with child, but the emotional trauma for this good man must have been devastating. His engagement to lovely Mary had undoubtedly set him to building dreams about their life together.

Though a poor man, Joseph was a carpenter and would be able to provide Mary many beautiful items made with his own hands. His heart was filled with anticipation.

Then, all the world came crashing down.

Mary was with child.

There was no simple solution, but Joseph was a just and merciful man and so he decided to break the engagement as quietly as possible.

God often meets us in our times of trouble. An angel appeared to Joseph, calling him by name and getting immediately to the heart of his problem. "Fear not," the heavenly messenger said. Those good words seem always to be in the vocabulary of angels. Explaining the miracle that was happening in Mary, the angel advised Joseph to go ahead with the marriage and assured him that the child conceived in her was of the Holy Ghost.

What good news for Joseph! Beyond his expectations.

The opposite of all his fears was true. What he had thought was the end of his dreams as a husband turned out to be the answer to all his needs as a man. Joseph laid aside his fears and obeyed the Lord. And that is a good course for each of us to follow, the way to live today.

IMMANUEL

MEMORY VERSE: *Behold, a virgin shall be with child, and shall bring forth a son, and they shall call him Emmanuel, which being interpreted is, God with us* (Matthew 1:23).

The prophet was the first to tell
Of our dear Saviour's wondrous birth;
He said the great Immanuel
Would come to dwell with men on earth.

When Joseph's heart was filled with dread,
The angel told him all was well—
That God would do just as He'd said,
Through Mary's son, Immanuel.

Immanuel, means God is here;
No wonder Jesus bore that name,
For in that manger God came down
To save from sin, and guilt, and shame.

The sinner understands that name
The day he takes Christ as his own;
He finds his life is not the same,
And that he never walks alone.

Yes, God is here with us today,
He is not dead as some men tell;
He's just the same in every way.
Our mighty God, "Immanuel."

…Roger F. Campbell

December 17　　　　　John 1:1-5

THE GREAT CREATOR

MEMORY VERSE: *All things were made by him; and without him was not any thing made that was made* (John 1:3).

God's power to create transcends our ability to comprehend. In his Systematic Theology, Lewis Sperry Chafer has written: "In itself, the act of creating is an incomparable undertaking. In His creation of material things, God called them into existence out of nothing. Such a declaration is far removed from the notion that nothing has produced something. It is obvious that out of nothing, nothing of itself could arise. The Biblical declaration is rather that out of infinite resources of God everything has come into existence. He is the Source of all that is. The self-determining will of God has caused the material universe. As stated in Romans 11:36: *For of him, and through him, and to him, are all things: to whom be glory for ever.*"

And the great Creator has become our Saviour.

A mail-boat was returning from the West Indies. Among the passengers was a man who had with him a dog of which he was very fond. One day a small child was playing with the dog. After throwing a stick on deck for the dog to catch, he suddenly turned and threw the stick into the sea. At once the dog jumped over after it. In great distress the owner ran to the captain and begged him to stop the boat and rescue the dog. "Stop the mails for a dog? I can't do it," said the captain. "Then you shall stop the ship for a man!" exclaimed the owner as he flung himself overboard. The ship was then stopped and both man and dog were rescued.

The Word was made flesh and dwelt among us (John 1:14). The great Creator identified himself with us in our danger, that we might be rescued.

Have you thanked Him for such love?

Are you eager to be identified with Him?

THE SONS OF GOD

MEMORY VERSE: *But as many as received him, to them gave he power to become the sons of God, even to them that believe on his name* (John 1:12).

Some stumble at the simplicity of salvation. They imagine it necessary to perform some good work or religious act to become a child of God. But salvation is offered to those who receive Christ by an act of faith...belief.

The good news of this salvation needs to be told to all. George Whitefield, standing in his tabernacle in London, and with multitudes gathered to hear, cried out: "The Lord Jesus will take the devil's castaways!" Two discouraged women standing in the street heard him. Looking at each other, they said: "That means you and me." They wept and rejoiced and gained courage enough to draw near the church door where they saw the face of the earnest preacher drenched with tears as he pleaded with the people to give their hearts to Christ. One of them wrote a note and sent it to him.

Later that day, as he sat at a meal with Lady Huntington, who was his special friend, someone present said: "Mr. Whitefield, did you not go too far today when you said the Lord would take the devil's castaways?"

Taking the note from his pocket, he gave it to the lady and said: "Will you read the note aloud?"

She read: "Mr. Whitefield, two poor lost women stood outside your tabernacle today and heard you say that the Lord would take the devil's castaways. We seized upon this as our last hope, and we write you this to tell you that we rejoice now in believing in Him and from this good hour we shall endeavor to serve Him who has done so much for us."

Receiving Christ, they had become children of God.

December 19   John 1:14-18

HIS GLORY

MEMORY VERSE: *And the Word was made flesh, and dwelt among us, (and we beheld his glory, the glory as of the only begotten of the Father,) full of grace and truth* (John 1:14).

His glory shone in days of old
From clouded hill and starlit sky;
But these had not His passion told—
So Jesus came for men to die.

Jehovah, long the angel's joy
In heaven where they need no sun,
Would now become a baby boy
That God and man might be as one.

"His glory in the highest!" heard
By shepherds on Judean hills,
Announced the coming of "The Word"
To save men's souls and cure their ills.

Who thought the Christ Child born that night
Would someday die on Calvary's tree?
Not one who then beheld the sight
And worshipped Him on bended knee.

His glory now shines from a cross;
The Father knew, but still he gave
His Son, and suffered untold loss,
That He might lift, and bless, and save.

...Roger F. Campbell

THE LAMB OF GOD

MEMORY VERSE: *The next day John seeth Jesus coming unto him, and saith, Behold the Lamb of God, which taketh away the sin of the world* (John 1:29).

Bethlehem's manger was a fitting place to lay the Lamb of God. Later, John the Baptist would point Him out as the Lamb who had come to take away the sin of the world.

As the Lamb of God, Jesus is approachable. Blind men would call to Him. Children would follow Him. Lepers would plead with Him. Grieving people would pour out their hearts to Him. And He would have time for them all.

As the Lamb of God, Jesus paid for our sins. John's listeners would have known immediately the significance of his words. For centuries their forefathers had been bringing lambs to sacrifice speaking of the atonement for sins. With the sacrifice of Jesus, all animal sacrifices were to cease: *And every priest standeth daily ministering and offering oftentimes the same sacrifices, which can never take away sins: But this man, after he had offered one sacrifice for sins for ever, sat down on the right hand of God; From henceforth expecting till his enemies be made his footstool. For by one offering he hath perfected for ever them that are sanctified* (Hebrews 10:11-14).

Rembrandt, the famous Dutch artist saw Jesus as the Lamb of God who died for him. In his painting, depicting the Saviour's death, he included himself among the crowd watching the Crucifixion. This was Rembrandt's way of saying, "I was there too! I helped to crucify Jesus!"

As the Lamb of God, Jesus atoned for all sin: *The blood of Jesus Christ his Son cleanseth us from all sin* (1 John 1:7). Old sins need not haunt us when they have been given to Jesus. His forgiveness is complete. He is the Lamb of God. His sacrifice was sufficient. Even for your sins.

MADE RICH

MEMORY VERSE: *For ye know the grace of our Lord Jesus Christ, that, though he was rich, yet for your sakes he became poor, that ye through his poverty might be rich* (2 Corinthians 8:9).

He left his untold wealth above,
And laid aside His glory
That He might demonstrate His love—
Oh what a wondrous story!

By all the saints and angels known,
He came to earth a stranger;
He stepped down from the highest throne.
And made His bed a manger.

No wonder angels sang His praise
On that first Christmas night!
No wonder shepherds left their flocks
To see this holy sight!

He who was rich had become poor,
To save a sinful race;
He opened wide salvation's door—
This was the work of grace.

We who were poor are rich instead;
Our inner struggles cease.
He conquers over fear and dread;
We're rich in joy and peace.

...Roger F. Campbell

And here you are downhearted. Look up! He has made you rich.

HE HUMBLED HIMSELF

MEMORY VERSE: *And being found in fashion as a man, he humbled himself, and became obedient unto death, even the death of the cross* (Philippians 2:8).

Jesus humbled himself.

If we are to be like Him we will have to forsake the way of pride and choose humility.

He chose a stable instead of a palace.

He chose swaddling clothes instead of costly garments.

He chose a poor family instead of royalty.

He chose shepherds as His first visitors instead of princes.

He chose humble men to be his disciples instead of an honor guard.

He washed the feet of His disciples when they were arguing over who should be the greatest in the kingdom.

He chose the cross in order to purchase salvation for all who believe.

D. L. Moody said: "A man can counterfeit love, he can counterfeit faith, he can counterfeit hope and all the other graces, but it is very difficult to counterfeit humility. You soon detect mock humility. There is an old saying that as the tares and the wheat grow they show which God has blessed. The ears that God has blessed bow their heads and acknowledge every grain, and the more fruitful they are the lower their heads are bowed. The tares lift up their heads erect, high above the wheat, but they are only fruitful of evil. If we can get down low enough, God will use us to His glory."

Andrew Murray wrote: "Just as water seeks to fill the lowest places, so God fills you with His glory and power when He finds you empty and abased."

Let us get low enough for God to bless.

WAITING

MEMORY VERSE: *But when the fulness of the time was come, God sent forth his Son, made of a woman, made under the law* (Galatians 4:4).

How long they had seemed!
Those centuries of waiting;
Some doubted,
Despaired!
While others waited, hoping each new morn
That they might hear the news "The Child is born!"

The promises were there,
There was no doubt about it;
The woman's Seed,
Virgin-born!
The prophet said that Bethlehem was able;
He didn't know the room would be a stable.

Then, right on time,
God sent forth His Son;
Christ was born—
God Man!
The taxing had required them come so far;
As shepherds worshipped, wise men watched a star.

And now we wait again!
His promise just as sure!

Some doubt it—
Scoffers!
But even they are part of prophecy today,
And Christ will come to catch His own away.

...Roger F. Campbell

December 24

Luke 2:1-7

THE MANGER

MEMORY VERSE: *And she brought forth her firstborn son, and wrapped him in swaddling clothes, and laid him in a manger; because there was no room for them in the inn* (Luke 2:7).

The manger was a lowly place,
To lay the Lord of earth and space.
But don't despise that bed of hay,
For God had planned it all that way.

The crowded inn of Bethlehem,
Without a room or bed for them,
Symbolic stands, even today,
Of those who turn the Lord away.

The Christ who came to take our woes
Was wrapped in humble swaddling clothes;
Then Mary took the babe so fair,
And laid Him in a manger there.

The manger: What a place to find
The Lord and Saviour of mankind.
Yet there in Bethlehem's humble stall
Was born the one to save us all.

The manger speaks of God's great love
That reaches down from heav'n above;
It reaches to the lowest place
To give the gift of life through grace.

...Roger F. Campbell

December 25   Luke 2:8-14

ON EARTH PEACE

MEMORY VERSE: *Glory to God in the highest, and on earth peace, good will toward men* (Luke 2:14).

> The angel praises were of peace
> The night of Jesus' lowly birth;
> Yet trouble here still does not cease,
> And wars and wrongs remain on earth.
>
> Where is this "peace on earth" for men
> That rang so sweet on Bethlehem's hills,
> That sent the shepherds seeking then
> The Saviour who would cure their ills?
>
> I've found this peace is at the cross
> Where all our sins on Christ were laid;
> For while He suffered untold loss,
> The sinner's peace with God was made.
>
> I've found it also at His throne;
> For Christ who died, now also lives;
> And as I've met Him there alone,
> I've known the peace the Saviour gives.
>
> Someday the world will know real peace,
> For Christ will come as King to reign;
> Creation then will find release,
> And "on earth peace" will ring again.

...Roger F. Campbell

Thou wilt keep him in perfect peace, whose mind is stayed on thee: because he trusteth in thee (Isaiah 26:3).

THE SACRIFICE

MEMORY VERSE: *And when the days of her purification according to the law of Moses were accomplished, they brought him to Jerusalem, to present him to the Lord* (Luke 2:22).

According to the Law, after a certain period of time had elapsed following the birth of a child, the parents were to bring an offering in recognition of the goodness of the Lord in giving this life, and also in recognition that we are all part of a sinful race and in need of a Saviour. Note the requirements of that sacrifice as given in Leviticus 12:6: *And when the days of her purifying are fulfilled, for a son, or for a daughter, she shall bring a lamb of the first year for a burnt offering, and a young pigeon, or a turtledove, for a sin offering, unto the door of the tabernacle of the congregation, unto the priest.* Joseph and Mary were fulfilling this obligation when they came to present Jesus at the Temple in Jerusalem.

Now see this important fact: Joseph and Mary did not bring a lamb as prescribed in the above verse.

Why?

Because they were too poor to do so and had to take advantage of the exception given in the Law for those who could not afford to bring a lamb: *And if she be not able to bring a lamb, then she shall bring two turtles* [turtledoves], *or two young pigeons; the one for the burnt offering, and the other for a sin offering: and the priest shall make an atonement for her, and she shall be clean* (Leviticus 12:8).

Have you financial difficulties? Jesus understands.

Do you have less than your neighbors? Jesus understands.

He will meet you where you are. He understands and cares.

THE SWORD

MEMORY VERSE: *And Simeon blessed them, and said unto Mary his mother, Behold, this child is set for the fall and rising again of many in Israel; and for a sign which shall be spoken against* (Luke 2:34).

Simeon had been expecting the Saviour. The Holy Spirit had revealed to him that the Lord's Christ would come before his death. When Joseph and Mary brought Jesus to the Temple, Simeon recognized Him as the Promised One. Taking Jesus up in his arms he prophecied and gave thanks to God. Then he gave a difficult word to Mary. Many would speak against Christ. She must prepare for grief: *(Yea, a sword shall pierce through thy own soul also,) that the thoughts of many hearts may be revealed* (Luke 2:35).

Simeon saw the cross in advance.

Standing at the cross, Mary must have remembered Simeon's warning. As the cruel crucifiers did their work and the angry mob mocked Jesus, Mary's heart must have been broken. Nevertheless, she surely remembered also that Jesus had come to do His Father's will and that meant paying the price required to justify the ungodly...death on the cross.

You may have already discovered that the message of Christ is not always popular. Some may speak against you because you are a Christian. Perhaps you have endured hardships that have broken your heart.

Remember that persecution has been the lot of dedicated Christians through the centuries. Identification with Jesus can be costly. He warned: *If ye were of the world, the world would love his own: but because ye are not of the world, but I have chosen you out of the world, therefore the world hateth you* (John 15:19).

Are you willing to suffer for Jesus?

He gave himself for you.

ANTICIPATION

MEMORY VERSE: *And she coming in that instant gave thanks likewise unto the Lord, and spake of him to all them that looked for redemption in Jerusalem* (Luke 2:38).

Anna was eighty-four years old but her faith hadn't weakened. She expected the Redeemer. And He came in her lifetime.

George Muller, the man of faith, said: "Let it be our unceasing prayer that as we grow older we may not grow colder."

Some do.

Muller lived up into his late nineties and was always bright, full of interest, hopeful, joyful. In his last years he would often stop in the midst of his conversation to exclaim, "Oh, I am so happy!" And it was not a mannerism nor was it feigned. "As we advance in years," he had written long before, "let us not decline in spiritual power; but let us see to it that an increase of spiritual vigor and energy be found in us, that our last days may be our best days...Let the remaining days of our earthly pilgrimage be spent in an ever-increasing, earnest consecration to God."

Aged Anna became one of the first missionaries, giving the good news of the Redeemer to all that had anticipated the coming redemption of Jerusalem.

One of the most beautiful times of the year is Indian summer, when the earth seems to reach out and enjoy a season of warmth and sunshine in the late fall. Happy is the older person who insists on a season of Indian summer in life...another period of spreading warmth and sunshine...a final burst of speed before the end of the race, coming down to the winner's tape with full energy.

For Anna, every day had been one of anticipation...hope. And that is the secret of successful living in old age.

WISE MEN

MEMORY VERSE: *Now when Jesus was born in Bethlehem of Judaea in the days of Herod the King, behold, there came wise men from the east to Jerusalem* (Matthew 2:1).

The wise men who came from the East to worship Jesus are the most mysterious of all the characters connected with the Christmas account. Questions rise about them: "How many were there? When did they begin their journey? Where did they come from?" The poem, "Wise Men" probes for answers:

Tell me, Wise Men,
How did you know
That newcomer to the heavens
Announced the news
That Christ was born
King of the Jews?
What was there about that star
That spoke of:
The fullness of time,
The hour of the ages,
The fulfillment of a promise?

Searching for answers, the poem concludes with a sure observation:

Let me tell you, Wise Men,
You traveled not alone:
Following the light,
Carrying your treasures,
Ready to worship;
The wisest men that I have known
Have journeyed too,
Leaving all to get to Jesus,
Just as we've seen you do.

...Roger F. Campbell

December 30   Matthew 2:9-11

GIFTS FOR THE KING

MEMORY VERSE: *And when they were come into the house, they saw the young child with Mary his mother, and fell down, and worshipped him: and when they had opened their treasures, they presented unto him gifts; gold, and frankincense, and myrrh* (Matthew 2:11).

The wise men did not arrive at the manger. They may have come to the house in Bethlehem where Joseph and Mary were staying with their young child as much as two years after the miraculous birth (see Matthew 2:16). The two year span mentioned by the wise men to Herod could refer to the time they had begun their long journey. No one knows.

When the wise men did arrive, they worshipped Jesus and presented gifts to him of gold, frankincense, and myrrh. The gifts are symbolic: standing for His royalty (gold), His coming ministry as our great high priest (frankincense), and His suffering on the cross (myrrh). These gifts were not merely tips...they were treasures...the best that they had to give. They were given as a part of worship. Wise men still worship Jesus and give to His cause.

Matthew Henry sees another dimension to this giving and has written: "The gifts the wise men presented were gold, frankincense, and myrrh. Providence sent these as a seasonable relief to Joseph and Mary in their present poor condition. Thus our Heavenly Father, who knows what His children need, uses some as stewards, to supply the wants of others, and can provide for them, even from the ends of the earth."

Remember that Joseph and Mary were so poor that they could not afford a lamb for sacrifice at the Temple. Now before them lay a trip into Egypt to escape Herod's effort to destroy Jesus. And God sent wise men with gifts to pay the expenses.

December 31   Matthew 2:12-15

FULFILLING THE SCRIPTURES

MEMORY VERSE: *And was there until the death of Herod: that it might be fulfilled which was spoken of the Lord by the prophet, saying, Out of Egypt have I called my son* (Matthew 2:15).

Joseph was warned by the angel of the Lord to take Mary and Jesus and flee into Egypt. This journey would move Jesus out of the reach of King Herod. Interestingly, it would also fulfill the Scriptures.

On this text, Dr. John R. Rice comments: "How careful the Holy Spirit is always to remind us of the infallible inspiration of the scripture! Verse 15 says that the baby Jesus was taken into Egypt, *that it might be fulfilled which was spoken of the Lord by the prophet, saying, Out of Egypt have I called my son.* The scripture is quoted from Hosea 11:1. The meaning was originally twofold. First, God called the nation Israel out of Egypt under Moses, and Israel is called 'My son.' But the more important meaning is prophetic. God would call this baby Son, Jesus, out of Egypt; so Joseph took Him there, by divine instructions.

"Let us learn, then, that the Word of God is God's own writing; that it has richer meanings than the casual eye sees; and most important, let us learn that all the Bible is about Jesus Christ. Old Testament and New have Him in their subject. We should expect to find reference to Christ therefore, in every type and sacrifice, in all historical narratives, and in all prophetic portions as well, of the Word of God."

The Bible then is given to present Christ to you and me. What have you done about it? Have you responded to His call?

Receive Him by faith as your personal Saviour today: *Believe on the Lord Jesus Christ, and thou shalt be saved* (Acts 16:31).